HENRY JAMES AND THE QUEERNESS OF STYLE

Henry James and the Queerness of Style

. . . .

Kevin Ohi

University of Minnesota Press
Minneapolis
London

A version of the Introduction has appeared previously as "'The novel is older, and so are the young': On the Queerness of Style," *Henry James Review* 27, no. 2 (Spring 2006): 140–55; copyright The Johns Hopkins University Press. A version of chapter 4 has appeared previously as "Belatedness and Style," in Peter Rawlings, ed., *Palgrave Advances in Henry James Studies* (Basingstoke, UK: Palgrave Macmillan, 2007), 126–46; reproduced with permission of Palgrave Macmillan.

Published by the University of Minnesota Press
111 Third Avenue South, Suite 290
Minneapolis, MN 55401-2520
http://www.upress.umn.edu

Library of Congress Cataloging-in-Publication Data
Kevin Ohi.
Henry James and the queerness of style / Kevin Ohi.
p. cm.
Includes bibliographical references and index.
ISBN 978-0-8166-5493-2 (acid-free paper)—ISBN 978-0-8166-6511-2 (pbk. : acid-free paper)
1. James, Henry, 1843–1916—Criticism and interpretation.   2. Homosexuality and literature—United States.   3. James, Henry, 1843–1916—Literary style.
4. Male homosexuality, in literature.   I. Title.
PS2127.H63O37   2011
813'.4—dc22
2010032607

Printed in the United States of America on acid-free paper

The University of Minnesota is an equal-opportunity educator and employer.

18 17 16 15 14 13 12 11   10 9 8 7 6 5 4 3 2 1

For my mother

Contents

On the Erotics of Literary Style

A great writer is always like a foreigner in the language in which he expresses himself, even if this is his native tongue. At the limit, he draws his strength from a mute and unknown minority that belongs only to him. He is a foreigner in his own language: he does not mix another language with his own language, he carves out a nonpreexistent foreign language within his own language. He makes the language itself scream, stutter, stammer, or murmur.

—Gilles Deleuze, "He Stuttered"

Henry James and the Queerness of Style seeks to trace such a "nonpreexistent foreign language" in the writings of Henry James and thereby to find in James's style a queerness that, not circumscribed by whatever sexualities or identities might be represented by the texts, makes for what is most challenging about recent queer accounts of culture: a radical antisociality that seeks to unyoke sexuality from the communities and identities—gay or straight—that would tame it, a disruption that thwarts efforts to determine political goals according to a model of representation, the corrosive effect of queerness, in short, on received forms of meaning, representation, and identity. To perceive such a potential, it suffices to engage in that most old-fashioned and, by now, almost marginalized activity: close reading—in the very disgrace to which it has been consigned now that, no longer synonymous with literary study *tout court*, it seems almost an antique curiosity (at best irrelevant, and at worst a pernicious, or somehow complicitous, indulgence), in, as D. A. Miller writes, "its humbled, futile, 'minoritized' state."[1] Through such a marginal, wasteful form of attention to James's texts, and to the foreign language murmuring audible there, this book seeks to delineate what it calls the queerness of style.

Henry James's writing continually throws the reader off balance with disorienting mixings of register and sudden shifts of tone, with unexpected syntactical inversions and equivocal reifications that hover at indeterminate levels of abstraction, with pronouns that divide their allegiances between any number of more or less distant antecedents, with symbolic and figural language that spurns subservience, determining plots and becoming visible on depicted landscapes, and with coercively authoritative voices that unexpectedly cede their perspective or suddenly give way to ironical deflation. Such effects inevitably lead acute critics to confront the consequences for the novel form of a style that presents a surface of such redoubtable complexity, to examine, in consequence, ways that this eminently "psychological" writer imagines consciousness in curiously nonpsychological terms and formulates a "realism" that does something other than represent reality. Meanwhile, other acute critics, influenced by Eve Kosofsky Sedgwick and by queer theory more generally, have at last made the question of sexuality, and particularly homosexuality, unavoidable for any serious consideration of James's works. The intensity of relations between men and between women, the thematization of homophobic panic in his writing, the erotic energies that escape containment in marriage or heterosexual romance, the authorial and narrative investments across or within genders that resist assimilation to heterosexual models—these are just a few of the elements that a criticism of James attuned to questions of sexuality has made it impossible to ignore.[2] It suffices to attend to what is explicitly there in the work of this legendarily reticent writer to perceive that it hardly shies from sexual detail and that (among the many diverse incarnations of human sexuality that preoccupy it) so-called normative heterosexuality is perhaps the sole form in which it can hardly muster even a glancing interest.

Implicit in Sedgwick's work—and that of one or two other recent critics—is the intuition that these two strands are connected; otherwise, unfortunately, these parallel preoccupations with style and sexuality have remained separate—and have even seemed inimical—in critical readings of James.[3] This book seeks to bring out the common ground of these two critical preoccupations, suggesting that each is incomplete to the extent that it does not consider the other. The daunting complexity of James's writing *is* its queerness: the erotic in his work can be most fully understood when it is considered in linguistic rather than representational terms. The queerness of Henry James's writing resides less in its representation of marginal sexualities—however startlingly explicit those may be—than in its elusive and multivalent effects of syntax, figure, voice, and tone, in its systematic challenging of the presumption that desire can be, or ought to be, represented. Conversely, the full significance of James's formal and stylistic innovations is best grasped by considering their sexual resonance. The intuitions that have emerged from critics' detailed attention to James's language—about its antimimetic, antipsychological strands, for instance—are foundational to a queer reading of his writing. "Queerness" thus offers, to my mind, one way to conceptualize the effects of James's late style and to illuminate some of the stakes of the interruptions of intelligibility that style presents.[4] The effects that come to fruition (in very different ways) in the novels and tales of the turn of the century, the late autobiographical and critical texts, the New York Edition prefaces, and *The American Scene*—the shifting and variegated elasticities of syntax and challenges to intelligibility that make even the late letters and occasional texts elusive and fascinating—are legible, I would argue, in James's framing of his novelistic project much earlier in his career. To explore this possibility, I turn to "The Art of Fiction" of 1884 and "The Future of the Novel" of 1899.

In "The Art of Fiction," James argues against Walter Besant's effort, in his lecture of the same name, to dignify the novel as a fine art by providing guidelines for writing one, to ground the genre's prestige in teachable, formalizable rules. James frames his central disagreement with Besant as a question of temporal perspective: "As I shall take the liberty of making but a single criticism of Mr. Besant, whose tone is so full of the love of his art, I may as well have done with it at once. He seems to me to mistake in attempting to say so definitely beforehand what sort of affair the good novel will be."[5] The novel's form can be deciphered only after the fact, James repeatedly insists; it cannot be given in advance. The critic must therefore concede the novelist's choice of form; the critic's duty, throughout this essay, is one of retrospective appreciation and judgment.[6] The critic's categories look back, not forward, and are useless for generating a new novel: however a critic might classify what he reads, "It is as difficult to suppose a person intending to write a modern English as to suppose him writing an ancient English novel: that is a label which begs the question" (56). Such labels presuppose what they purport to define— in part because they short-circuit a temporal unfolding crucial to their coherence. "Modern" makes sense only after the fact, or as a way of anticipating a future retrospection: one can write as an ancient writer no more than anyone could ever have conceived of writing in a contemporary language called "Middle English." Writing and its formalization cannot coincide in time, and James thus brings out the distance separating a critical classification of the novel from a proscriptive or prescriptive account of how to write one. Knowing what a novel is—even being able to recognize a good one—will not suffice to generate one.

This shift in temporal perspective corresponds to James's central disagreement with Besant over the possibility of giving formalizable rules for novel writing. Thus, against Besant, who defends the prestige of the novel by asserting that it is *teachable*, James suggests that the novelist's "manner is his secret, not necessarily a jealous one. He cannot disclose it as a general thing if he would; he would be at a loss to teach it to others" (50). The writer's manner is, like the painter's, James asserts, "best known to himself," but this knowledge cannot be disclosed—suggesting a knowledge that may be a secret even from the person who "has" it, an uncanny dispropriation that follows from James's argument against formalization. To say that writing and its formalization cannot coincide in time suggests that the novel cannot know itself—or that the "knowledge" of its form that one might communicate is separate from the knowledge that would allow one to write. To see why this insistence on undisclosable knowledge is not simply a belletristic defense of art's mystique, it is necessary to dwell on what is at stake in James's argument against formalization. A form that cannot "know" itself; a resistance to reification, to models that might generate a form (or, likewise, a "content," mimetically understood)—this suspicion of formalization can be seen even in the framing of James's essay, which he calls "these few remarks, necessarily wanting in any completeness" (44).

The argument against formalization initially seems to assert, conventionally enough, that the novel must be taken seriously as a "direct representation of life" (50). Like Besant, he argues for the seriousness of the genre, and he opens his essay invoking the old "superstition" about fiction's wickedness that "lingers in a certain oblique regard directed toward any story which does not more or less admit that it is only a joke" (49). Trollope's parenthetical admissions that his stories are "really make-believe" mark a "betrayal of a sacred office," a "terrible crime" that shocks him as much in Trollope as it would in Gibbon or Macaulay (46).[7] He thus seems to assert the referential validity of the novel, to see in it a mode of reference equivalent to the writing of historians. The only reason for the novel's existence, he writes, is that it "does represent life" (46); it is a "direct representation of life" (50). Directness and immediacy link, he suggests, the novel as a fine art to painting, and the pairing initially seems to privilege mimetic reproduction. His formulation of the novel's mode of reference, however, turns on a complicated analogy: "as the picture is reality, so the novel is history" (46). The *as*—to make the obvious point—leads one to wonder what relation is named by *is*: the novel's relation to history depends on the (potentially multiple) ways the picture can be said to *be* reality. The form of the analogy sets up a series of equivalences: the painting to reality, the novel to history, the painting's relation to reality to the novel's relation to history, and so on, where each asserted equivalence redoubles but does not resolve the central question, which is whether the equivalence signaled by *is* asserts identity or a relation (metaphorical or representational) that merely simulates identity. The fact that the modes of identity can be made equivalent (that is, the painting "is" reality in a way that can be compared to the way that the novel "is" history) disrupts the claim of identity made on behalf of each term. The novel is history, in this sense, insofar as it is a representation that refers to reality; James's analogy seems to stress less the transparent relation between painting and reality or between novel and history than the mediating representation that links all the terms. "Reference" here—as the immediate, direct representation of "life"—marks a relation to reality that can be grasped only through another form of representation.[8]

James's strategy throughout is to concede Besant's claims while redefining their terms. Perhaps the central category reshaped in this way is "experience"; the writer, he suggests, should, as Besant argues, write "from his experience" (51):

> What kind of experience is intended, and where does it begin and end? Experience is never limited, and it is never complete; it is an immense sensibility, a kind of huge spider-web of the finest silken threads suspended in the chamber of consciousness, and catching every air-borne particle in its tissue. It is the very atmosphere of the mind; and when the mind is imaginative—much more when it happens to be that of a man of genius—it takes to itself the faintest hints of life, it converts the very pulses of the air into revelations. (52)

Thus, there is no necessary presumption in a provincial damsel's daring to write about barracks life: experience is not "direct" or naïvely empirical in this literal sense.[9] "Experience" is not the simple registration, within, of what the mind perceives without. Thus, James's definition insists, on the one hand, that experience is not a thing: it is never limited, and it is never complete. On the other, by making experience "the very atmosphere of the mind," he interrupts the model of registration that would make writing from experience a mimetic process. Experience is the atmosphere of the mind, not the events that that atmosphere might lead the mind to register. Experience thus resists objectification; it is not an object because the mind cannot objectify its own atmosphere. Neither the mind itself nor an object in the world, experience transgresses the dichotomy between inside and out that would ground an analogy linking cognition and representation as simple mimetic processes. In the terms of yet another of James's analogies, "impressions *are* experience . . . , just as they are the very air we breathe" (53).[10] If experience consists of "impressions" made on the mind, the ostensible "object" of representation is neither inside the mind nor outside it: the mind can neither identify itself with nor distinguish itself from the "objects" it represents.

One implication, then, is that if James suggests that the novel is a "direct" representation of life, the directness does not consist in the conveying of content. In James's theorization of the novel, it is thus "style" that matters—as opposed to any "object" of representation. The privileging of style is bound up with his insistence that the novel cannot be given formalizable rules in advance, and his rewriting of "experience" thus intimates a logic that also governs his parodic rendering of judgments of novels based on their content.[11] Insisting that the novelist be conceded his starting point, his subject, James writes that the reader is free simply to ignore subjects he doesn't like: "I needn't remind you that there are all sorts of tastes: who can't know it better? Some people, for excellent reasons, don't like to read about carpenters; others, for reasons even better, don't like to read about courtesans. Many object to Americans. Others (I believe they are mainly editors and publishers) won't look at Italians" (57–58).[12] The motive of selection behind this liking, James writes, "is experience" (58).

James's argument links the dignity of the novel to the existence of a theory of the novel as opposed to a formalization locating it as an artifact with definable attributes—a formalization that, in James's wry version of Besant, "demands not only that [the novel] shall be reputed artistic, but that it shall be reputed very artistic indeed" (47). Against such for-malizable rules, which turn the artistic into a quantifiable thing, James's proposed theory, which makes the novel, in the essay's French term, "dis-cussable" (*discutable* [44])—that is, disputable or doubtful as opposed to unquestionable or incontestable—disrupts the possibility of reifying the novel. The English novel, he begins his essay by suggesting, has been naïve, has lacked a theory of itself:

> During the period I have alluded to there was a comfortable, good-humored theory abroad that a novel is a novel, as a pudding is a pudding, and that our only business with it could be to swallow it. But within a year or two, for some reason or other, there have been signs of returning animation—the era of discussion would appear to have been to a certain extent opened." (44)

The "era of discussion" thus arrives with the disruption of a comfortable model of reading as consumption—of the assumption that "a novel is a novel, as a pudding is a pudding." The novel becomes open to discussion, James's formulation suggests, when it ceases to be identical to itself.[13]

The possibility of "discussion" frames James's exploration of the novel's "morality." At the opening of the essay, the question of the novel's imposed diffidence (its need to treat itself as a joke) leads James to the mistrust of art in "Protestant communities," which perceive a "vaguely injurious effect" on those who "make it an important consideration" (47); the spe-cial mistrust of the novel, he suggests, has to do with its mode of represen-tation. Unlike painting, which "stands before you, in the honesty of pink and green and a gilt frame" and in which "you can see the worst of it at a glance," literature is more insidious: "there is danger of its hurting you before you know it" (48). "When it is embodied in the work of the painter . . . you know what it is" (47): literature, in James's formulation, seems to be constituted by one's not knowing what it is, and its "vaguely injurious effect" is thus linked to its curious mode of representation.[14] And, again, James shifts his understanding of "morality" away from terms of repre-sented content; he dissents from Besant's view that what James calls "a cautious silence on certain subjects" is evidence of the novel's morality. "In the English novel . . . , more than in any other, there is a traditional difference between that which people know and that which they agree to admit that they know, that which they see and that which they speak of, that which they feel to be part of life and that which they allow to enter into literature" (63). It is not, James writes, "that the English novel has a purpose but that it has a diffidence." That diffidence is guided by a desire to protect the young: "There are certain things which it is generally agreed not to discuss, not even to mention before young people. That is very well, but the absence of discussion is not a symptom of the moral passion" (63). The reappearance of the term *discussion* encourages us to read the suppression of sexual reference in relation to the naïve view of the novel that preceded "the era of discussion." To enjoin upon the novel a moralized reticence about certain topics is also to understand the form in terms of the "subjects" it "contains," a reifying logic where, implicitly, a "novel is a novel, as a pudding is a pudding."

The moralism of Victorian preoccupations with representations that might corrupt the young (or impressionable women) has, of course, scarcely abated today, and queerness is one name for the threat corrupting representations are seen to pose to young people[15] (or, indeed, the threat posed by representation as such insofar as initiation and corruption make manifest a generalizable permeability to other minds). The thematic link between James's argument about the morality of fiction and the specific worry about youthful encounters with representations of sex spells out a more important link—makes explicit, that is, the ways that James's disruption of mimetic models of representation might entail an infraction interpretable, from certain quarters, in sexual terms. The queerness of his style, in other words, overlaps with a queer power of representation to corrupt or seduce. Such a conclusion seems almost unavoidable in "The Future of the Novel," where this argument about the morality of fiction—and, specifically, the question of the representation of sex and the protection of the young—is continued. This essay performs a complex series of interrelated de-reifications: of the novel as "book" or artifact or thing, of "youth" as an essential category for representation or address, and of the "subject" a novel might be said to represent. As in the earlier essay, the question of the novel's mode of representation is put in temporal terms—here, of the relation between "beginnings" and "continuations":

> Beginnings, as we all know, are usually small things, but continua-
> tions are not always strikingly great ones, and the place occupied
> in the world by the prolonged prose fable has become, in our time,
> among the incidents of literature, the most surprising example to

be named of swift and extravagant growth, a development beyond the measure of every early appearance. It is a form that has had a fortune so little to have been foretold at its cradle. The germ of the comprehensive epic was more recognisable in the first barbaric chant than that of the novel as we know it to-day in the first anecdote related to amuse.[16] (100)

Viewing the novel, as the essay's title suggests, from the perspective of its future brings out the contingency of a "development beyond the measure of every early appearance." With a "fortune so little to have been foretold at its cradle," the novel is a form that thwarts the possibility of "recognition"—of seeing in its "germ" what it will become.[17] If "continuations" are neither visible nor inevitable in beginnings, James paradoxically makes this principle of temporal unfolding a generalized formal principle of the novel itself: the essay opens up the possibility that the novel is this resistance to being foretold.

In parallel to the claims of "The Art of Fiction," the essay dissociates the novel from the book as a locatable—and representable—object whose "penetration," James writes, has been "directly aided by mere mass and bulk" (100). The adulteration of the novel that leads one to be uneasy about its future comes from its being confounded with the book, whose material proliferation is made possible by a public that treats it as a (merely) material thing, a public that, in James's words, "subscribes, borrows, lends, that picks up in one way and another, sometimes even by purchase" (100). The ease of the book's manufacture, he later writes, has made it "a thing of small ceremony" (103). The proliferation of the book as object is part of the essay's preoccupation with the novel's referential status and with the changing context out of which it emerges. Along with the possibility of mass production in publishing, the dissemination of functional literacy and the consequent formation of new audiences, the changing social status and education of women, the emergence of children's fiction, and the question of censorship are some of the contextual questions raised by the essay's exploration of the novel's future.[18]

These questions ask to be read in terms of the relation between the essay's de-reifying strands and its understanding of reference—and hence in terms of the queerness of James's style. Midway through the essay, James formulates the relation of the novel to its context in typically elusive terms, and collocates, again, the question of reference with the question of a critical relation to the novel. Turning to the future for fiction promised by the "English novel of commerce," he suggests that this "future" is, in a sense, a social problem: "There is nothing to prevent our taking for granted all sorts of happy symptoms and splendid promises—so long, of course, I mean, as we keep before us the general truth that the future of fiction is intimately bound up with the future of the society that produces and consumes it" (106). The relation, as James elaborates it, links the development of critical acuity and a "literary sense" to the successful fostering of fiction. Revisiting the question pursued in "The Art of Fiction" of the possibility of constraining the content of the novel's representations, James turns to a particular critical proscription. The general question of reference—of what, for instance, the novel might be said to represent, and of what its effect might be on the society it (in some more or less refracted way) "mirrors"—then becomes, for the essay, the specific question of representing sex. The problem of representing sex for an audience that includes the young makes the novel, James writes, "exactly a reflection of our social changes and chances":

> Nothing, I may say, for instance, strikes me more as meeting this description [of the present situation of the novel as "exactly a reflection" of social changes and chances] than the predicament finally arrived at, for the fictive energy, in consequence of our long and most respectable tradition of making it defer supremely, say, of a delicate case, to the inexperience of the young. (107)

The rendering of youthful innocence as "inexperience" is striking in light of "The Art of Fiction," where *experience* names a mode of registering *impressions* that James contrasts with mimetic representation—where, as we have seen, it names an "atmosphere" that the mind can neither identify with nor objectify, the "motive" of selection in reading that might "almost name" the "cluster of gifts" underlying the artist's power of perception (58, 53). "Experience" seems crucial for the essay at hand, too, which initially casts the appeal of the novel in terms of human beings' "eternal desire for more experience" (103). The framing of the propositions that mark the essay's turn to the inexperience of the young presents considerable complications—not least, as I will suggest, the difficulty of deciphering how the predicament arrived at in consequence of this tradition meets the description of the novel as "exactly a reflection of our social changes and chances." Perhaps most important, the essay makes the question of the novel's deference to the young the question of the future of the novel itself: "By what it shall decide to do in respect to the 'young' the great prose fable will, from any serious point of view, practically see itself stand or fall" (107).

The question of queerness thus emerges in the essay in relation to the representation of sex, and in relation to the power of representation to corrupt or influence the young. Again, there can be no question of sexuality as a "theme" or as the "content" of a representation; the question of queerness in the essay in fact moves us away from such themes toward a more general consideration of the essay's understanding of reflection and of the novel's relation to its social context. Here, in its entirety, is James's assertion that the novel is "exactly a reflection":

> As the novel is at any moment the most immediate and, as it were, admirably *treacherous* picture of actual manners—indirectly as well as directly, and by what it does not touch as well as by what it does—so its present situation, where we are most concerned with it, is exactly a reflection of our social changes and chances, of the signs and portents that lay most traps for most observers, and make up in general what is most "amusing" in the spectacle we offer. Nothing, I may say, for instance, strikes me more as meeting this description than the predicament finally arrived at, for the fictive energy, in consequence of our long and most respectable tradition of making it defer supremely, in the treatment, say of a delicate case, to the inexperience of the young. (107)

The suggestion that the novel offers "exactly a reflection of our social changes and chances" locates it as fully embedded in its social context, and yet that contextualizing "reflection" is not straightforward. It is not, first of all, the novel itself but the predicament (the "situation") in which it finds itself (as a practice of representation) that is "exactly a reflection of our social changes and chances" (107). The sentence's subordinate clause, moreover, makes things even trickier: "As the novel is at any moment the most immediate and, as it were, admirably *treacherous* picture of actual manners . . . , so its present situation . . . is exactly a reflection" (107).[19] Evoking the claim in "The Art of Fiction" that "as the picture is reality, so the novel is history," James's ostensible claim for exact reflection not

only has that exact reflection capture not a content but a mode of representing ("the situation" of the novel), but also couches its assertion in a
form—analogy—that might be said to represent a relation of reflection
but whose links seem to be made by the disruption of asserted equivalences. The present situation is "exactly a reflection of our social changes"
in the same way that the novel is (at any moment) the most immediate
and (as it were) "admirably treacherous picture of actual manners." The
relation of the picture to the actual, the treacherous to the immediate, the
novel to the picture (or to manners), the immediate in the sense of "at
any moment" to the immediate in the sense of the actual or the exact, the
actual in the sense of the exact and the actual in the sense of the contemporary: the multivalent conceptual allegiances figure the fact of analogy
itself and disrupt the particular analogy's coherence. Immediacy, in this
sense, is synonymous with, or results in, treachery. This "treachery," the
interruption of direct reflection, seems, paradoxically, to be what offers an
"exact reflection" of "social changes." The novel reflects the social directly
or immediately insofar as it does so treacherously.

The two readings that might initially occur to one as parsings of the
sentence's "as"—the novel's situation is exactly a reflection either in the
same way that the novel is (at any moment) the most immediate and (as
it were) admirably treacherous picture or *because* it is so—turn out to be
themselves synonymous. The analogy becomes a relation of consequence
as the sentence disrupts the coherence of its analogy. The two disjunct
conceptual registers—synonymity and consequence—are made treacherously to mirror one another, a relation that then disorients our sense of the
"exact" reflection claimed by the passage, which in fact continues to pile
up such treacherous analogies—and at every syntactic level, starting with
the (merely) phonetic proximity, and therefore treacherous reflection, of
changes and *chances*. The "present situation" of the novel is "exactly a reflection of our social changes and chances," which, the sentence's structure
of apposition implies, reflects yet another (treacherous) reflection, "the
signs and portents that lay most traps for most observers"—all of which is
returned to social reality as a form of representation: "what is most amusing in the spectacle we offer."

The predicament facing the novel because of its deference to the
impressionable young "meets this description" in part because it makes
visible the novel's embeddedness in the mores of the society that produces
it; censorship of supposedly objectionable material, for instance, leaves a

"reflection" of social changes through the marked absence of such material. Once again, however, the framing of this relation introduces significant complications:

> While society was frank, was free about the incidents and accidents of the human constitution, the novel took the same robust ease as society. The young then were so very young that they were not table-high. But they began to grow, and from the moment their little chins rested on the mahogany, Richardson and Fielding began to go under it. (107)

"The young" can be "so very young then" because they inhabit a traditional figure that imagines cultural progress through an analogy to individual development, moving from, in this case, the naïve (or "natural") openness of "robust ease" to a more refined sophistication about what is not to be mentioned. The young, in this figure, seem destined to miss the novel: when they grow enough to see above the table, Richardson and Fielding begin to go under it. The further difficulty is that "the young" not only names a typical person or anthropomorphic embodiment of a given *Weltanschauung*—a figure simply synonymous with cultural attitudes at different historical moments—it also names a demographic or empirical category: persons of evolving educations to whose inexperience the novel must defer. "The young," in this sense, marks the impinging of the sociohistorical on the world of the novel—a consideration for the demands of an audience that alters what can be represented there. Thus, "the young" offers two conflicting, mutually interfering articulations of the novel's relation to its context. A literary history of the novel—from Fielding and Richardson to Dickens and Trollope to the "present day" of the turn of the century—figuratively rendered as individual development (thus rendering, as allegory, the novel's embeddedness in a social context) is articulated with "youth" as an empirical category, as an imagined novelistic audience that constrains the novel's possibilities of reference (thus literalizing the impinging of sociohistorical forces on the genre). These various intertwinings of literary history with a quasi-empirical scenario of address disorient one's sense of what James means by his assertion that the novel's situation provides "exactly a reflection" of "our social changes and chances."

The allegory of development is further vexed because, as we have seen, James views the novel form as all but defined by its thwarting of such developmental narratives. The future of the novel—that is, its development if the form is to stay true to itself—will be to make manifest its difference from what would have been foretold. For this reason, then, he argues against those who suggest the subject of sex should be avoided because Dickens and Trollope avoided it; one does not wish their novels different from what they are, he suggests, but that does not mean that novels should be modeled on their example. Again, literary language, for James, eschews the possibility of understanding the novel as a model to be imitated; this antimimetic understanding of the form is rooted—and in yet another slippery formulation—in social changes. The novel cannot be generated from a model because it is "exactly a reflection" of those changes: in the contemporary situation, James writes, "the difficulty lies in the fact that two of the great conditions have changed. The novel is older, and so are the young" (108). Suggesting that "youth" is not an essential category but a relative one—youth can be older or younger depending on the era in which it finds itself—James's formulation stages the confrontation between "youth" filling a slot in an allegory of aesthetic development and "youth" as the sometime (and historically shifting) addressee of art. "Youth" indexes historicity insofar as it does not coincide with itself. In James's wry rewriting of the truisms that the novel form has evolved and that youngsters are (at any given moment) more experienced, more sophisticated, and more corrupt creatures than they once were, what initially seems to be a moralizing proposition—that the representation of sex is a question of the novel's effect on young people and that how the novel comes to address the young will determine its future—renders, instead, the complicated and finally nonrepresentational relation of fiction to its culture. *Youth* and *the novel* become parallel terms (the novel, we remember, having a "fortune so little to have been foretold at its cradle" [100]) not insofar as they are reified things subject to representation but insofar as they disrupt the possibility of understanding representation in mimetic terms. The essay's series of de-reifications—separating the book as thing from the novel, dissociating the novel from a subject it might be said to represent, and transforming "youth" into a relative category—suggests that the disruption of a moralizing argument about the representation of sex is, at the same time, an argument against the reification of the novel and against an understanding of its mode of representation in mimetic terms. The essay's insistence on viewing the novel as "mirroring" its social context disrupts the possibility of thinking of that mirroring as a direct

representation. Yet again, the queerness of this essay lies less in the particular argument against strictures placed on (sexual) representation than
in the de-reifications from which this argument follows as a consequence.

The relation to a social context is abstracted in the closing paragraph
of the essay as the relation between "life" as the "subject" and "the novel"
as the "treatment." "Man," James writes, will give up the novel only when
life ceases to appeal to him, and, even then, "may fiction not find a second
wind, or a fiftieth, in the very portrayal of that collapse? Till the world is
an unpeopled void there will be an image in the mirror" (110). The novel,
James suggests, will never lack a subject to represent, and yet he also seems
to suggest that it will continue to prosper only if it maintains its distance
from "life." "It is certain," James writes in the previous paragraph, "that
there is no real health for any art—I am not speaking, of course, of any
mere industry—that does not move a step in advance of its farthest fol-
lower" (109). The novel will prosper, this reformulation of the argument
against critical prescription suggests, as long as it *is* the future to which
life aspires but with which it does not coincide; hence, "the future of the
novel" signals a lag between the present and the novel that "represents" it
and therefore a lag between the novel as form and its formalization. The *of*
in "the future of the novel" seems at this moment to be appositional, like
"the city of Paris" or "the art of fiction," as opposed to partitive, that part
of the novel named by its future, the novel's future as it might be distinguished from its past.[20]

The future of the novel, as an argument against formalization and
mimeticism, names a (queer) potential of literary language to disrupt
what Lee Edelman calls "futurism"—the reduplication of the social order
in the name of an ever-deferred future (and thus James's "future" is close
to the opposite of Edelman's "futurism").[21] "Futurism" names a fantasy of
form—of a totalizable image that could overcome the constitutive division of subjects as subjects of the signifier, a form that could bring into
self-presence a subject that is constituted by a deferral of presence and a
division from itself. Queerness punctures this fantasy of a future where
the subject would be identical to itself, figures the eruption of the Real
in the Symbolic, makes manifest that what Edelman calls "the structure
of the political"—"the governing fantasy of achieving Symbolic closure
through the marriage of identity to futurity in order to realize the social
subject" (13–14)—is constituted by its impossibility. The emblem of this
fantasized recovery is the child, in whose name the social is held in trust.

The inevitable corruption of the child makes manifest the self-subversion of the subject, and so provokes the demonization of the queer to cover over the internal impossibility structuring the subject's emergence—and to cover it over by locating blame for that rupture elsewhere than in its own constitution. Naming the figure for the way this fantasy of politics punctures itself, queerness becomes linked, according to Edelman, to the death drive, and to the dissolution of the social order as such. Rather than resisting the particular assignment of that figural place—asserting one's good citizenship, and thus, implicitly, by shifting the burden of that figuration to some other demonized group, affirming the underlying structure of "politics" as the reduplication of the social order—Edelman suggests that the "ethical" choice for queerness is to "accede" to the figural place of the death drive (30). Acceding to figurations of queerness in this sense thus holds out the possibility of making manifest the fantasy of "futurism" and its own disruption of itself.

If, like James, Edelman frames his argument, in part, by way of the felt urgency of protecting the child—from corrupting representations and the depredations of deviant sexualities—his argument also offers one way to conceptualize the queerness of James's understanding of the novel, and thus to bring into view some of the stakes of these essays and their understanding of the novel as an antimimetic form. This potential, I think, is part of what "The Future of the Novel" aims to protect when it returns, at the very end of the essay, to the register of health, this time specifically in terms of the novel's potential to survive: "So long as there is a subject to be treated, so long will it depend wholly on the treatment to rekindle the fire. Only the ministrant must really approach the altar; for if the novel *is* the treatment, it is the treatment that is essentially what I have called the anodyne" (110). Even more striking, to my mind, than the (seemingly both ironized and invested) sacralized tones with which the novel's future is treated is the curious proliferation of conflicting figural contexts this peroration presents. "Ministrant" links nursemaid and priest; writing as a sacred office, even, perhaps, a form of sacrifice, overlaps with a ministration to a future made equivocal by shaky health. Similarly, "treatment" seems both to name the novel as form (treatment as opposed to "life" or subject matter)—the mirror in which the image finds itself—and to offer a synonym for "anodyne." In yet another treacherous reflection, if life or the novel be in need of an anodyne, the "treatment" would seem to be the novel as the "treatment" of life, or its rendering. Ministering to a sacred fire or to a patient in pain, alleviating suffering or representing, the multivalent figure with which the essay ends resists concretization in a single image and condenses the antimimetic effects I have sought to trace in these essays—and the resistance to formalization that, like "The Art of Fiction," "The Future of the Novel" names "freedom." The purpose of his argument against a priori rules for the novel is, he says in "The Art of Fiction," to suggest "that the good health of an art which undertakes so immediately to reproduce life must demand that it be perfectly free" (49). Freedom, in both essays, marks a liberation from mimetic models, from constraints on form imposed in advance. "The form of the novel that is stupid on the general question of its freedom," James writes in "The Future of the Novel," "is the single form that may, *a priori*, be unhesitatingly pronounced wrong" (106–7). And the disorientations of the novel as an "exact reflection" of "social changes and chances" take shape as James's unfolding of "a sense of that freedom cultivated and bearing fruit"—and the inevitable interest of that unfolding (107). James's antimimetic theorization of the novel form marks a queer practice of representation that offers a way to frame the emergence of sexuality in his late writing not as a topic or content for a representation but as a "treatment" or style—and to differentiate that practice from the omission of sexual reference that would call itself evidence of the moral passion. In this sense, "The Art of Fiction" and "The Future of the Novel" frame the queer erotics of James's late style.

A novelistic form divided from itself in time and a curiously unlocatable "experience" that is captured by the novel to the extent that treacherous reflection distances it from any immediacy—with a shift in focus, the theorization of the novel in these two essays could be retold as one of the dominant preoccupations of James criticism: the sexual life he may or may not have had, the attributed (and disputed) celibacy that was (allegedly) a symptom (or cause) of a passionate life that realized its desires too late for their actualization. Here, for one such retelling, is "Henry" with Hendrik Andersen, in a celebrated moment from Colm Tóibín's *The Master*:

> To the left of the entrance there was a wall of books, and when
> Andersen had studied the view and marveled at the light, he
> walked over to inspect the books, not appearing to realize at first
> that all of them bore his host's name. He took down one or two
> and then gradually it seemed to dawn on him that this large high

bookcase contained the novels and stories of Henry James in all their editions from both sides of the Atlantic. He became agitated and excited as he took volumes down and looked at the spines and the title pages. . . .

"Did you always know that you would write all these books?"

"I know the next sentence," Henry said, "and often the next story and I take notes for novels."

"But did you not once plan at all? Did you not say this is what I will do with my life?"

By the time he asked the second question, Henry had turned away from him and was facing towards the window with no idea why his eyes had filled with tears.[22]

However perceptive this moment seems in its assessment of Andersen's erotic excitement (and ambition), the suggestion that one might pity the author of *The Golden Bowl*—whether or not he ever had sex, and whatever feelings he might privately have sheltered looking back on his life of writing—is, to say the least, startling. My ambivalence about Tóibín's sometimes very affecting novel comes from my not being sure whether the many reconstructions of scenes from the fiction as (in retrospect, germinal) moments in the author's life are meant to be read as self-conscious reconstructions—second-order novelizations of a life—or whether they are in fact imagined to be originary, a more subtle, infinitely more erudite version of depictions of writers and scholars in Hollywood film—whose ideas and intellectual passions appear there primarily as more or less expensive wallpaper for the ostensibly more pressing concerns of "life," and who, when more active participants, appear in the films only to denounce, in the two or three possible narrative modes available to them, the manifest boredom and contemptible corruption of such "unreal" interests and passions. Here, perhaps, too, one cannot be absolutely sure that we, as readers of Tóibín's novel, are not supposed to imagine that, unlike the eminent author, we do definitely know why his eyes fill with tears; beyond that presumption, to have had an artistic future so little to have been foretold at the authorial cradle risks becoming, through the pathos of these tears, a matter of merely psychological interest.

Whatever their intent (achieved or not), recent novelizations of James's life, Tóibín's among them, pose—if not explicitly, then in the mere fact of their existence and their vogue—the question of art's relation to "life," and the question of what relation, if any, the affects of art bear to those of one's psychological existence. The moment in Tóibín does not simply retell the traditional account of James's life; it also invokes a recurrent topos in James's writing: the "missing" of experience by those temporizing characters for whom life seems not to coincide with their experience of it. To Lambert Strether, Milly Theale, John Marcher, Spencer Brydon, Hyacinth Robinson, the telegraphist of "In the Cage," the lovers in "The Bench of Desolation," Maria Rimmle in "'Europe,'" among many obvious others, and to James himself in the autobiography, perpetually belated in relation to William, we could add those characters for whom experience comes too soon: Maisie, Miles, Flora, Dolcino Ambient, Daisy Miller, Nanda Brookenham. To these, moreover, could be added figures who preoccupy James's nonfictional writing: Rupert Brooke, with his wasted promise; Shakespeare, with his unaccountable, premature renunciation of a superhuman gift; Hawthorne, wandering Salem, alone, too early for his posthumous fame. (From this perspective, "Is there life after death?" poses a similar question: does the asynchronicity of conscious life mean that consciousness reaches beyond the boundaries of organic life?) As Leo Bersani writes of the story that provides perhaps the most condensed formulation of this temporality, "*The Beast in the Jungle* thematizes the Jamesian tendency to extract all events, as well as all perspectives on them, from any specified time, and to transfer them to a before or an after in which they are de-realized in the form of anticipations or retrospections."[23] For Bersani, what he sees as the characteristic flatness of late style—"writers, painters, filmmakers frequently move in their late work not toward a greater density of meaning and texture, but rather toward a kind of concentrated monotony that designates a certain negativizing effect inherent in the aesthetic" (25)—points to the "virtuality" of art: "represented happening in art, however meticulously detailed, is inherently unspecifiable happening" (26). In this sense, art has the power to return potentiality to actualized existence (to make manifest the potentiality inherent in actualization).[24] The withdrawal from experience, from this perspective, looks less like one's personal—regrettable, sad, or, on the contrary, liberating—fate than like art's reflection on its own redoubtable capacities for what James calls "freedom." The becoming-impersonal that is one characteristic of this freedom might have something to do with the withdrawal of "late style," which, writes Edward Said, "is what happens if art does not abdicate its rights in favor of reality."[25] Insisting on an "increasing sense of apartness and exile and anachronism" (17), late style, for Said, is "*in*, but oddly *apart* from the present" (24), "beyond its own time" (135), "strange and out of season" (142), "an unlikely jamming together of youth and age" (136).

I will have more to say about the derealized time of James's late writing; Said and Bersani suggest, though, that the "time" the works represent is the time of art. James's late fiction—like *The Tempest* or Pater's *Marius* or, for that matter, the *Art of the Fugue* or Beethoven's late quartets—lead one to the intuition that the time of the work of art is not that of human life.[26] For this reason, however sympathetic I am to her desire for a theory of novelistic form that could account for the duration that marks the experience of reading novels, it seems to me that Catherine Gallagher's objection to style-focused analyses—that they habitually find form in "the detached, and often atypical, stylistic details of a literary composition rather than in its structure conceived as an ordered series of differentiated parts"—may too readily assimilate the time of the novel to the temporality of history and experience.[27] The extraction of atypical moments—moments that, in the particular rhythm with which they puncture inattention or equanimity or readerly assurance, probably do constitute an experience of style—could describe (for all I know) a typical experience of novel reading (insofar as I think it describes mine), but, more crucially, could be better posed to generate "analytic insights into the temporal nature of narrative" (251).

It is therefore partly because it names a principle of temporal extraction that my readings here are structured by what Frances Ferguson calls "the unanalyzable notion of style."[28] *Style* is in fact a diffuse concept, and different writers use it in vastly different ways. In its colloquial acceptation, *style* often means what is most personal and, in a sense, unanalyzable, about the texture of a writer's corpus—the unspecifiable something that makes a writer recognizable, the idiosyncratic stamp he puts on a language that makes it his own. If that meaning of *style* is unavoidable here, it applies only insofar as that highly personal something shades into a more impersonal force—like the gestures that, for Deleuze, form the basis of an affiliation much more aesthetic than erotic (an affiliation that has nothing to do, he persuasively suggests, with a community of ideas—one shares a language, not an opinion) and that lead us to find someone charming, characteristic phrases and inflections and movements that at once attract us to one person in particular and constitute something beyond the person.[29] For many of the most compelling considerations of style, the term marks a tension between particularity and abstraction, personality and impersonality. "Style," writes Roland Barthes, "always has something crude about it: it is a form with no clear destination, the product of a thrust, not an intention, and, as it were, a vertical and lonely dimension of thought."[30] The "decorative voice of hidden, secret flesh" (11), plunging into "the closed recollection of the person," "style is always a secret. . . . Its secret is recollection locked within the body of the writer" (12). Style is at once what is most intimate about a writer and most inaccessible to him; if, for the Barthes of *Writing Degree Zero*, style names what is idiosyncratic about a particular person's writing—at times, too, the biological basis that writing can work on but not choose, almost like the timbre of a voice that is the given for any subsequent modulation—as a secret, it does not coincide with any psychological particularity. For D. A. Miller—whose account of style in Jane Austen I take up in detail in chapter 2—style names just such an alternation, a magisterial remove from the particularities of a psyche yearned for and all but unachievable, or achieved only once (and by Jane Austen), and, as a consequence of the yearning, the lining of the distance itself with a falling back toward a secret embodiment.

Style is also a recurrent concern in the writings of Gilles Deleuze, beginning as early as *Proust and Signs*, which uses three terms in (shifting) proximity: *essence, viewpoint,* and *style*. The apprenticeship in signs that, for Deleuze, constitutes the movement of the *Recherche*, moves toward essence, the "unity of an immaterial sign and of an entirely spiritual meaning . . . as it is revealed in the work of art,"[31] by overcoming the objective and subjective fallacies—which search for essence either in a particular object (madeleine or desired person) or, on the contrary, in a particular train of subjective associations. (Among other reasons, this is why Deleuze can make the bracing claim that the *Recherche* is not primarily about memory.) The unity thus formed, however, is not preexisting; it is made in the encounter with art. Constituted by the movement of the Search, "essence" is not objectifiable; it is pure difference, one that is "not an empirical difference between two things or two objects, always extrinsic" (41), and it is defined by a viewpoint: "the essences are veritable monads, each defined by the viewpoint to which it expresses the world, each viewpoint itself referring to an ultimate quality at the heart of the monad" (41). "The difference itself" (42), viewpoint serves to move beyond the subjective associations to which the apprentice turns in default of discovering truth in the object. What initially looks like an individual imprint on the world (a particular way of seeing, a particular chain of associations) is not defined by an individual but, on the contrary, defines him:

> Each subject therefore expresses an absolutely different world. And doubtless the world so expressed does not exist outside the subject expressing it. . . . But the world expressed is not identified with the subject; it is distinguished from the subject precisely as an essence is distinguished from existence, even from the subject's own existence. . . . It is not reducible to a psychological state, nor to a psychological subjectivity, nor even to some form of a higher subjectivity. . . . [I]t is essence that constitutes subjectivity. It is not the individuals who constitute the world, but the worlds enveloped, the essences that constitute the individuals. (42–43)

As he later writes, viewpoint "is not individual, but on the contrary a principle of individuation" (110).

It seems possible to think of style in *Proust and Signs* as a viewpoint of viewpoints—the desubjectifying, dematerializing principle that unites the essences in the work to which it gives its only unity: "It is in the meanders and rings of an anti-Logos style that it makes the requisite detours in order to gather up the ultimate fragments, to sweep along at different speeds all the pieces, each one of which refers to a different whole, to no whole at all, or to no other whole than that of style" (115). In any event, Proustian style is a force of transmutation through which art surpasses both objective and subjective fallacies: "Art is a veritable transmutation of substance. By it, substance is spiritualized and physical surroundings dematerialized in order to refract essence, that is, the quality of an original world. This treatment of substance is indissociable from 'style'" (47). Style "spiritualize[s] substance and render[s] it adequate to essence" (48); "an essence is always a birth of the world, but style is that continuous and refracted birth, that birth regained in substances adequate to essences, that birth which has become the metamorphosis of objects. Style is not the man, style is essence itself" (48).

As, perhaps, the viewpoint uniting the multiple viewpoints contained in each sentence, style is a principle of transversality (the concept to which Deleuze ultimately turns in the chapter of the book about style):

> The new linguistic convention, the formal structure of the work, is therefore transversality, which passes through the entire sentence,

which proceeds from one sentence to another in the entire book, and which even unites Proust's book to those he preferred, by Nerval, Chateaubriand, Balzac. For if a work of art communicates with a public and even gives rise to that public, if it communicates with the other works of the same artist and gives rise to them, and if it communicates with other works of other artists and gives rise to works to come, it is always within this dimension of transversality, in which unity and totality are established for themselves, without unifying or totalizing objects or subjects. (168–69)

"Objectivity," Deleuze writes of the shift from a Greek world to a modern one, "can no longer exist except in the work of art; it no longer exists in significant content as states of the world, nor in ideal signification as stable essence, but solely in the signifying formal structure of the work, in its style" (111). Likewise, style names the subtraction of the individual: to create "is *to reach that point where the associative chain breaks, leaps over the constituted individual, is transferred to the birth of an individuating world*" (111, emphasis in original).

> To remember is to create, not to create memory, but to create the spiritual equivalent of the still too material memory, to create the viewpoint valid for all associations, the style valid for all images. *It is style that substitutes for experience the manner in which we speak about it or the formula that expresses it, which substitutes for the individual in the world the viewpoint toward a world, and which transforms reminiscence into a realized creation.* (111, emphasis added)

Style thus marks something like the *virtuality* of art that Bersani sees in James's temporalities of retrospection and anticipation. Recovered by the Search is not the past as it was, or even as it was experienced, but rather the past as it never was and as it was never experienced. The Search moves toward the signs of art in their extraction from any experience, the past recovered, but *as* past:

> Combray rises up in a form that is absolutely new. Combray does not rise up as it was once present; Combray rises up as past, but this past is no longer relative to the present that it has been, it is no longer relative to the present in relation to which it is now past.

This is no longer the Combray of perception nor of involuntary memory. Combray appears as it could not be experienced: not in reality, but in its truth; not in its external and contingent relations, but in its internalized difference, in its essence. Combray rises up in a pure past. (60–61)[32]

The noncommunicating cells and sealed vessels of the work are traversed by style, which recovers objects no more than it constitutes a self to total-ize the movement of the Search. Considered in the terms of James's aes-thetics, style thus names something very close to the relays among time, "experience," and novelistic representation condensed by the term *belated-ness*.[33] The paradoxical recovery of a pure past—Combray as it was never experienced—resonates with the fundamental asynchronicity of con-sciousness and experience in James. The out of season and the out of sync—this temporal misalignment, central to the queerness of style, surfaces in the question of art's relation to "life," which is also a question posed, for Deleuze's later work, by "style." Style, in the formula Deleuze takes from Proust, is "the foreign language within language"; great writers "invent a *minor use* of the major language within which they express them-selves entirely."[34] The "state of disequilibrium" resulting from this *use* of language "exceeds the possibilities of speech." This is the sense in which "a great writer . . . carves out a nonpreexistent foreign language *within* his own language. He makes the language itself scream, stutter, stammer, or mur-mur" ("He Stuttered," 109–10, emphasis in original). The "minorization of this major language, a delirium that carries it off" Deleuze links to becom-ing: "syntactic creation or style—this is the becoming of language."[35]

Style is thus fundamental to the impersonality of writing. "To write," begins "Literature and Life," is

certainly not to impose a form (of expression) on the matter of lived experience. Literature rather moves in the direction of the ill-formed or the incomplete. . . . Writing is a question of becoming, always incomplete, always in the midst of being formed, and goes beyond the matter of any livable or lived experience. It is a process, that is, a passage of Life that traverses both the livable and the lived. Writing is inseparable from becoming: in writing, one becomes-woman, becomes-animal or vegetable, becomes-molecule to the point of becoming-imperceptible. (1)

Deleuze is unequivocal: "To become is not to attain a form (identification, imitation, Mimesis) but to find the zone of proximity, indiscernibil-
ity, or indifferentiation where one can no longer be distinguished from
a woman, *an* animal, or *a* molecule—neither imprecise nor general,
but unforeseen and nonpreexistent, singularized out of a population
rather than determined in a form" (1, emphasis in original). Style, as "the
becoming of language" (5), is thus linked to what Deleuze's enigmatic
late essay calls "immanence: a life."[36] Throughout his work, Deleuze is
(justly) disdainful of the notion of writing as personal recollection, as
the writer's "own" life transcribed.[37] (This is, in part, his complaint about
psychoanalysis, which transforms "*an* animal . . . *a* horse, *a* chicken . . .
a stomach, *some* eyes . . . *a* father, *some* people" into "*my* father, *me, my*
body": "It has a mania for the possessive and the personal, and interpretation consists in recovering persons and possessions. 'A child is being
beaten' must signify 'I am being beaten by my father,'. . . and 'a horse falls
down and kicks about with its legs' means that my father makes love
with my mother."[38]) Literature, in contrast, recovers "a childhood that
is not my own" ("He Stuttered," 114); the task of literature, he asserts in
the *Abécédaire,* may be to recover a childhood, but not the writer's *own*
childhood.[39] Art, he writes,

> attains this celestial state that no longer retains anything of the
> personal or rational. In its own way, art says what children say. . . .
> Art is defined, then, as an impersonal process in which the work is
> composed somewhat like a *cairn,* with stones carried in by different
> voyagers and beings in becoming (rather than ghosts) [*devenants*
> *plutôt que revenants*] that may or may not depend on a single author.
> Only a conception such as this can tear art away from the personal
> process of memory and the collective ideal of commemoration.
> ("What Children Say," 65–66)

Such a tearing away is not the same thing as the sacrifice of a life or a personality to art—terms that would, after all, remain determined by (even if
they renounced) personal possession and psychological experience. "The
only biography," we read at the beginning of *Roland Barthes by Roland Barthes,* "is of an unproductive life."[40] One way of understanding this assertion
would be comparatively banal: the writer, scribbling away, is too busy to
do anything interesting. Art arrives, in this view—the view that dominates

many understandings of James's life—through sacrifice of life, renuncia-tion of "living." In its resistance to biography, however, the productive life intimates a more paradoxical exchange. ("This book," Barthes later writes, "consists of what I do not know" [152].) To write is to submit oneself to a subtraction or purification thematized, among other places, by Barthes's description of listening to recordings of himself:

> I record myself playing the piano; initially, out of curiosity to
> *hear myself*; but very soon I no longer hear myself; what I hear
> is, however pretentious it may seem to say so, the *Dasein* of Bach
> and of Schumann, the pure materiality of their music; because it
> is my utterance, the predicate loses all pertinence; on the other
> hand, paradoxically, if I listen to Horowitz or Richter, a thousand
> adjectives come to mind: I hear *them* and not Bach or Schumann.
> —What is it that happens? When I listen to myself *having played*—
> after an initial moment of lucidity in which I perceive one by one
> the mistakes I have made—there occurs a kind of rare coincidence:
> the past of my playing coincides with the present of my listening,
> and in this coincidence, commentary is abolished: there remains
> nothing but the music (of course what remains is not at all the
> "truth" of the text, as if I had rediscovered the "true" Schumann or
> the "true" Bach). (*Roland Barthes by Roland Barthes*, 55–56)

What initially looks like self-regard in fact turns out to work somewhat like noise-canceling headphones: superimposed on itself, coinciding with itself across a gulf of time, the shadow of the self disappears. What is revealed is not the "truth" of the music but Barthes's playing with his self subtracted from it, his playing rendered impersonal—which he terms "the pure materiality of . . . music." Although in a very different register this discovery, in a sense, of an impersonal "sameness" linking Barthes to Schumann and Bach evokes Leo Bersani's notion of a narcissism that could constitute a form of impersonality.[41] To write is to confront—if also, perhaps, to flee—the impersonal entity Giorgio Agamben calls *genius*, "our own life insofar as it does not belong to us."[42] The readings that follow often pursue, in a variety of different ways, this kind of self-subtraction in Henry James's writing—recurrently, through *belatedness* as a way of articulating the relationship between art and life in the queer-ness of style.

Tóibín and other recent biographical novelizers are attracted to James in large part, it seems to me, because they intuit that there is something queer about belatedness. Too often, though, the intuition goes astray because it never questions the assumption that that relation is a consequence of the particularities of the writer's life—born too early for gay liberation (or too late for Greek pederasty) or simply personally out of sync so that any cognitive grasp of homoerotic possibility arrives too late for any experiential use ("But it was too late; he was too old; he was not wanted.").[43] At worst, belatedness is sad (if, therefore, for some, compelling); at best, it designates a predicament for which the writer finds some (more or less satisfying) compensation in art. For the most part, art is seen to fail in this meager compensation because it is conceived (albeit sometimes implicitly) as entirely extraneous to the "life" it would compensate. That there is in fact no need for art to be involved in this scenario at all—presumably, any number of passional lives have been sacrificed to conformity with homophobic imperatives, and, if that is the story, *my* life would do just as well for a novel—suggests not only an effort to "dignify" that sociosexual transaction, but also, and more important, that the interest in James's case has to do with the way the homoerotic "thematics" at issue makes visible something about belatedness and style, about what Deleuze calls "a life."

The mistake is to understand the queerness of the belated life psychologically, and therefore to seek to root one's exploration of it in homoerotic thematics. Foundational to queer theory (and what separates it from "gay studies") is the axiom that its analyses extend beyond (indeed must extend beyond) elements of culture where same-sex desire is explicitly at stake. Eve Kosofsky Sedgwick's *Epistemology of the Closet* asserts, famously, "that an understanding of virtually *any* aspect of modern Western culture must be, not merely incomplete, but damaged in its central substance to the degree that it does not incorporate a critical analysis of modern homo/heterosexual definition"; she argued for "the centrality of this nominally marginal, conceptually intractable set of definitional issues to the important knowledges and understandings of twentieth-century Western culture *as a whole.*"[44] Lee Edelman's concept of homographesis names, among other things, the centrality of this "nominally marginal" question of homosexual definition: the disproportionate anxiety produced (for homophobic culture) by the interpretable (and therefore misinterpretable) signs of homosexuality points to the proximity of homosexuality to problematics of writing and inscription. One implication of Edelman's argument is that the insistence that queer analyses be visibly rooted in thematics of same-sex desire is homophobic: the insistence that gay "difference" be visible and, at any moment, producible serves, he argues (in the broadest strokes) to underpin difference itself, and hence meaning and identity as such.[45] As a critique of homophobia, queer theory cannot limit itself to homosexual thematics. For Sedgwick's, Edelman's, and other foundational works of queer theory, homophobia—in its more or less unstable formulations, in its instability itself—is intractable because it serves to structure "heterosexuality," which is to say the social.

The widely perceived impasse for queer studies—that it must choose between a homosexual specificity that spells its irrelevance to ostensibly "larger" concerns and a generality that, losing that specific reference, all but generalizes queer theory out of existence—replays a central fracture in modern conceptions of homosexuality, what Sedgwick's book calls "minoritizing" and "universalizing" conceptions of homosexuality. *Queer* appeals to me as a term because it does not resolve that tension but keeps it open—retaining its sexual resonance even at the farthest remove from specific sexual thematics and abstracting specific sexual practices so that they, in turn, resonate with linguistic and conceptual categories (ostensibly) far removed from sex. In recent years, queer work has been subject to more pressure to retain an explicit sexual referent—one is often led to imagine a game of Twister, where at least one toe, or the sliver of a pinky, must be kept on the colored circle representing a locatable act of gay sex or a producible instance of gay identity: the resulting contortions are sometimes beautiful but often unnecessary—because it has come to view, for whatever (more or less compelling) pragmatic reasons, the movement of specification and abstraction in the term *queer* as synonymous with the appearance and disappearance of homosexual persons. Politics, in other terms, is understood, albeit most often implicitly, according to a model of representation. Or a queer is a queer as a pudding is a pudding: bon appétit. Not least among the pressures acting on conceptions of queerness is a felt need to define (and defend) a field with a specifiable object of study. The impasse is an impasse only insofar as queer theory is forced to defend its existence in terms inimical to its own theoretical insights (and repeatedly, moreover, forced to defend its existence while being enjoined not to repeat itself). For specific inquiries, the term *queer* remains immensely productive—largely in its unresponsiveness to efforts to resolve its purview: as Sedgwick wrote in *Epistemology of the Closet*, "no one *can* know *in advance* where the limits of a gay-centered inquiry are to be drawn, or where a gay theorizing of and through even the hegemonic high culture of the Euro-American tradition may need or be able to lead" (53). At times, the readings here will no doubt seem to some to abstract *queer* beyond the limits of such an inquiry. A central, even germinal, term for this study, for its exploration of belatedness and style, *queer* animates its readings without always becoming an explicitly thematized term, sometimes allowed to drop out of sight altogether and sometimes invoked without an immediate justification for the connection to sexual concerns. ("In an author's lexicon," writes Barthes, "will there not always be a word-as-mana, a word whose ardent, complex, ineffable, and somehow sacred signification gives the illusion that by this word one might answer for everything? Such a word is neither eccentric nor central; it is motionless and carried, floating, never *pigeonholed*, always atopic (escaping any topic), at once remainder and supplement, a signifier taking up the place of every signified" [*Roland Barthes by Roland Barthes*, 129].)

For this book, *queer* names, among other things, a particular experience of time linked in the late writing to James's style. James begins *The Middle Years* by equivocating on the death of his youth, announced at the end of *Notes of a Son and Brother*:

> We are never old, that is we never cease easily to be young, for all life at the same time: youth is an army, the whole battalion of our faculties and our freshnesses, our passions and our illusions, on a considerably reluctant march into the enemy's country, the country of the general lost freshness; and I think it throws out at least as many stragglers behind as skirmishers ahead—stragglers who often catch up but belatedly with the main body, and even in many a case never catch up at all.[46]

How, in such a view, can anything come "too late," or, rather, how would it be possible for anything to come "on time"? As I discuss in greater detail in chapter 4, there are various reasons gay forms of life force one to confront—to salutary, if not always reassuring, effect—the ways in which one's life is out of sync with itself. Whatever insights are available to or, on the contrary, elude individual persons, against the patterns of transmission, inheritance, and replication that structure heterosexual sociality,

the discontinuities of gay life—histories, to say nothing of whole generations, lost to homophobia or to the more or less violent disregard shown
gay existence and gay culture; or, for the individual, a life narrative made
discontinuous by "coming out," a rupture that replays as a moment of
quasi-decision the imponderable question of gay origination—force an
encounter with the way different cells of our lives, our capacities, our passions, our knowledges, are out of sync with each other, and with themselves, and wax and wane according to no overarching development,
perhaps according to no development at all.[47]

It is the notion of development—a concept that, among many other
things, secures identity against the depredations of its own unknowable
origins, and against the disarray of sexuality—much more than the well-
being or happiness of any actual child that is protected by the image of the
innocent child. Against the child of "reproductive futurism," taming sexuality by submitting it to a "future" that repeats a fantasized past of wholeness and plenitude, we might pose the child of Deleuze's "What Children
Say"—who responds to the imposition of an Oedipal archaeology with a
cartography in which one can trace multiple, unhierarchized trajectories.[48]
Although the child is not the focus here, in many ways it could have been.
What Kathryn Bond Stockton calls the "asynchronous self-relation" of
the gay child—one cannot be a gay child, she suggests, but only have been
one, and this fundamentally belated identification and self-recognition can
occur, paradoxically, only in the past tense—points to some of the reasons that to explore James's career-long interest in queer children is also
to explore the effects of queer style.[49] Likewise, Michael Moon's beautiful
exploration of queer initiation could be said to lay the theoretical foundation for an exploration of queer style, not only in its various phrasings
of what he calls "imitation," as against forms of identification understood
as varieties of mimesis, but also in his focus "on a series of instances of an
adult artist's productive revisitation of a remembered scene of himself as a
proto-queer child 'looking to be' (as the colloquial phrase has it) ravished
by images of his own desire," a scenario to which Moon movingly and illu-
minatingly recurs.[50] Among late-nineteenth- and early-twentieth–century
writers, it is perhaps with Walter Pater, whatever his otherwise wide divergence from him in tone and sensibility, that James, in his erotics of time and
cultural transmission, shares most: "A distinguishing element of the relation of James's writing to male-male erotics," Moon suggests, "is its intense
and strategic anachronism and anatopism" (31). What Pater does for art

history and aesthetic spectatorship, James does for the history of consciousness, and for both writers, belatedness and asynchronicity are erotic
categories. That anachronism and anatopism, I hope it by now goes without saying, are not most interestingly to be understood as a personal failing
or loss.[51] Moon's explorations of the mystery of aesthetic initiation—both
"locally," in his account of James's initiation by "style" in (James's) *A Small
Boy and Others,* and, more generally, in his rich accounts of queer transmission, from classical sources to the Renaissance to the nineteenth century, or
from visual art to literature—are also explorations of queer style.

   "Being well spoken," writes Deleuze, "has never been either the distinctive feature or the concern of great writers" ("He Stuttered," 111); James
may seem to be almost too well spoken a writer for the effects of "style" I
have described here. Yet to attend in detail to the movements of his prose
is to discover the ways it stutters and screams. As Deleuze also writes,
"there are many diverse indications and procedures that the writer can
apply to language in order to create a style. And whenever a language is
submitted to such creative treatments, it is language in its entirety that is
pushed to its limit, to music or silence."[52] The chapters that follow attempt
to pursue some of these diverse indications and procedures, tracing the
queerness of style through a series of texts written between 1900 and 1916:
the major late novels—*The Ambassadors, The Wings of the Dove,* and *The
Golden Bowl*—the autobiography, and several late essays and occasional
texts. The readings recur to a number of interrelated categories—including
belatedness—understood not as thematic terms but as terms shaped in
various ways by a resistance to the reification and formalization of the
novel. That refusal of formalization cannot but have its effects on how one
reads the fiction—how one understands the relation between a novel's
mode of narration or its figurative language, for instance, and its putatively
"larger" thematic questions. Most explicitly in chapter 1, but implicitly
throughout, the readings often privilege such elements over what might
otherwise be assumed to "motivate" them. Thus, for example, marriage
and adultery are, for my reading of *The Golden Bowl,* instances of syllepsis
or zeugma, rather than providing a thematic rationale for the novel's recur-
ring to those tropes. Chief among these thematic questions is perhaps the
representation (or nonrepresentation) of sex; the late fiction (sometimes)
avoids representing sex in various, and variously fascinating, ways. Again,
"The Future of the Novel" suggests that, like belatedness and missed experience, such omission is perhaps not most productively read in terms of

pathos or lack—or in terms of any "thing" (any theme or object of repre-sentation) one somehow missed. My guiding intuition, in fact, has been, as I have suggested, that such nonrepresentation is the marker of queer-ness in the late style. To understand the thematic questions as, in a sense, motivated by the antimimetic theory of the novel is, therefore, to pursue the queerness of style, even, or especially, in the absence of thematic mark-ers of nonnormative sexualities.

Unified by a commitment to the queer erotics of style, these chapters address the different texts in different ways, with sometimes heteroge-neous protocols of reading. Chapter 1, on *The Golden Bowl*, focuses on the blurring of linguistic register—of literal and figurative language, for instance, or of the novel's plot and a metalevel commentary on its mode of writing—that may be conceptualized through the tropes of syllepsis or zeugma (double governance). Chapter 2 examines free indirect narration in *The Wings of the Dove*, suggesting that the alienation visible in scenes of identification be understood as a short-circuit in this mode of narra-tion; tracing various syntactical idiosyncrasies in the novel's prose, it sug-gests that free indirect narration, by positing a perspective inhabited by no one, thematizes a form of (paradoxically) nonpsychological identifica-tion. Chapter 3 focuses on three words—*hover, torment,* and *waste*—that resurface at striking moments in a series of late texts: his introduction to Rupert Brooke's *Letters from America; A Small Boy and Others;* "Is There a Life after Death?", James's letter to Robert S. Rantoul for the 1904 Haw-thorne centennial; and his preface to *The Tempest.* The chapter examines James's description of Rupert Brooke's early death in the context of the theorization, in these late texts, of the relation between art and life, and text and world. Finally, chapter 4 approaches *The Ambassadors* as an alle-gory of life within James's queer style, as a novel that reflects on what it means to "live" according to the principles of the late style. By examining the peculiar experience of belatedness for Lambert Strether, the chapter suggests that, as moving as the novel can be, Strether's predicament is not, finally, a sad one; "belatedness" is less the particular predicament of a man who has wasted his life than the condition of possibility of consciousness itself in late James. That consciousness, and the compensations of readerly absorption it generates, offers, for this book, a final way to think about the particular exactions—and pleasures—of a queer experience of style.

CHAPTER 1

Writing Queerness: Zeugma and Syllepsis in *The Golden Bowl*

Henry James's style is perhaps nowhere more importunate than in his 1905 novel *The Golden Bowl*. The novel's redoubtable linguistic texture—especially the densely metaphorical language of narrator and characters alike—and the formalism of its structure can cause one momentarily to forget its startlingly lurid premise: its plot has a billionaire and his daughter (Adam and Maggie Verver) each marry other people, the better to sustain their own incestuous relationship. Or, from the perspective of the victims, a couple (Prince Amerigo and Charlotte Stant), whose poverty leaves them unable to marry each other, marry instead a billionaire and his daughter—partly for the money but partly to transform their commonplace affair into one bordering on incest: marriage allows the Prince to have sex with his wife's stepmother, and Charlotte, with her husband's son-in-law. (Were gay marriage able to make such things possible, one might be tempted to embrace it.) The affair, however, soon gives way to—or reveals the story as always having been—a closet drama. The novel's plot often boils down to the striving of variously embattled characters to refrain from speaking of what they know (about, in particular, what others know)—and to the implications of that effort in the registers of desire and power. *Betrayal* refers not principally to the violation of marriage vows but to the "giving away" of knowledge: betrayed spouses are of less interest to the story than betrayed secrets. The text could have been subtitled "Epistemology of the Closet," and its plot—insofar as it has one—is a paranoid one, a "vicious circle" centered on the unspeakable.

The recessive, elliptical quality of James's late style makes it particularly well suited to such a story; however, the relation of plot to style extends beyond any accord between medium and message. In a novel focused largely on the deciphering of secrets and on the consequences—thrills, terrors, pleasures—of their detection or betrayal, the potential for the

characters' predicaments to redound on a reader faced with the novel's linguistic complexity is one of many ways that the novel challenges
boundaries and forms of differentiation upon which meaning—and style's
instrumental relation to plot or sense—rests. Most generally, it is less the
case that the style befits the plot of *The Golden Bowl* than that its style simply *is* its plot. If I argue for the queerness of this overlap, it is, in part, to
counteract a traditional reading of James's style as an evasion of sexuality.[1]
In this view, the complexity of the novel's style compensates for an author
whose sexual inhibition left him no more able to represent sex in general
than to express "his" sexuality in particular. The relation of style to sex in
The Golden Bowl, however, is not that of sublimation.

Reading the novel as evidence of sexual inhibition is dissatisfying
not only because it must proceed by means crudely psychologistic and
reductive, and not only because such a psychologizing reading implicitly
discounts the more or less brutal, more or less state-sponsored sanctions
levied against any expressed desire outside procreative heterosexuality
that greeted James's contemporaries—and, to a slightly lesser extent, still
greet our own—by understanding sexual reticence as a mere (pathologi-
cal) reflex of individual psychology. Such a reading is dissatisfying also
because the novel is not, finally, sexually inhibited. To argue for the novel's "sublimation" of sexuality into style is to perform for oneself much of
the diagnosed sublimation—while knowingly tittering at an author who
could inadvertently name a character Fanny Assingham. The passages
in *The Wings of the Dove* about Densher's all-but-physical pain at finding
himself aroused without sexual release are almost matched here by the
explicitness—the narrator's, Fanny's, and Maggie's—about the affair, for
instance, and by moments such as the discovery, by the guests at Fawns,
of Maggie and Charlotte kissing to "make up," which leads them to separate "as if they had been discovered in some absurdity." "Any spoken or
laughed comment," the text continues, "could be kept from sounding
vulgar only by sounding, beyond any permitted measure, intelligent."[2]
The intelligence threatening to peep out bears, most immediately, on
Maggie's specific grounds for resentment, but the alternative proposed
relies on a formulatable sense not only of the affair but of the particular
absurdity that two women caught together might be suspected of, and
that might, if only by vulgar others, be mentioned. That we remember
The Golden Bowl as reserved suggests not only that its volubility about
the unspeakable has its effects, but also that what we remember about

the novel is not its plot but its style: its reticence is a stylistic effect and not a thematic one. Thus, while, from one angle, the central love affairs culminate in various refinements of renunciation and unrequited longing (the "romance" of Charlotte and the Prince's relationship lies, from the beginning, as Fanny remarks, in nothing happening except "their having to recognize that nothing could" [53]), this transformation is important less for any Jamesian preference for thwarted love it might be seen to announce than as an intimation, in the novel's plot, of a particular structure of representation pursued by the writing. The love affairs are unrequited because the plot is its style: thwarted love is the narrative equivalent for the antimimetic theory of the novel. "The Art of Fiction" and "The Future of the Novel" become the story—or theme or content or plot—of *The Golden Bowl*.

Thus the whole of the New York Edition preface might be read as an extended gloss on its opening:

> Among many matters thrown into relief by a refreshed acquaintance with *The Golden Bowl* is the still marked inveteracy of a certain indirect and oblique view of my presented action, unless I make up my mind to call this mode of treatment, on the contrary, any superficial appearance notwithstanding, the very straightest and closest possible. (xli)

Its emphasis on repetition, marked in its all-but-stuttering invocation of *re* (*re*lief, *re*freshed, even t*re*atment)—"the 'old' matter is there, re-accepted, re-tasted, exquisitely re-assimilated and re-enjoyed" (liii)—and on revision as a mode of rereading appears, in this context, as an insistence on mediation and on a temporal delay in "re-presentation" that spells a recovery always diverging from original intentions. (This gap is marked, too, in the [indirect?] relation between figure and ground in James's language, which may lead one to wonder how an "indirect view" could be "thrown into relief.") The noncoincidence inherent in representation is the value, James suggests, of the Coburn frontispieces for the New York Edition: they avoid the "lawless incident" of being mere secondary illustration that would compete with the author's own because their act of "re-representation" makes manifest another level of mediation. This mediation he calls discretion or shyness: the photographs, he writes, would have been "disqualified" if they had kept,

or pretended to keep, anything like dramatic step with their
suggestive matter. . . . [T]hey were 'all right', in the so analytic modern phrase, through their discreetly disavowing emulation. Nothing
in fact could more have amused the author than the opportunity
of a hunt for a series of reproducible subjects—such moreover as
might best consort with photography—the reference of which
to Novel or Tale should exactly be *not* competitive and obvious,
should on the contrary plead its case with some shyness. (xlvi–xlvii)

The disqualification of images that would have kept—or pretended to
keep—"dramatic step with their suggestive matter" makes the out-of-
step photographs another form of revision, which the preface elsewhere
describes as a tracking of uncontrollable footsteps that, notably, diverge
from the precedent of authorial stride as he rereads his earlier works.[3] The
novel is older, and so is its author; the description of the Coburn frontispieces suggests, however, that the lapse of intention, the deviation over
time is—no matter how much the effect is magnified by the passing of
time—structural to James's understanding of representation. Belatedness is a principle of novelistic representation, not the predicament of an
aging novelist. It is not that a personal condition has been translated into
art, but something more like its opposite: a personification of style. Thus,
the photographs' "shyness" reminds us of his love, particularly in the late
texts, of wry little personifications—diminutive cousins, perhaps, of the
voluble buildings and landscapes of *The American Scene*. That "shyness" is
a quality attributed to representation—as if its obliquity were a function
of its personality—also signals another common crossing in late James,
where a vocabulary of affect moves away from persons and psycholo-
gies and toward modes of representation. (This can be seen, too, in the
personification—and even a distant echo of sexualization—in "subjects"
sought to "consort with photography.") The crossing of these two registers
is often left unresolved; these texts are "psychological" not because they
depict, with redoubtable subtlety, the tribulations of characters' psyches,
but because psyches are, disorientingly, textual. The psychological and the
textual are crossed in ways that confound the possibility of reading the
texts as "renderings" of psychology.[4] In other terms, the late novels create
the impression of depth psychology not because the characters are deep
but because the seemingly infinitely variegated language that has absorbed
them appears as if *it* were.

Likewise, the revision James describes in his New York Edition preface is not merely something that the text of *The Golden Bowl* undergoes; it is in many ways the novel's subject. Amerigo's very name, the text reminds us several times, reappropriates a misnaming and commemorates a belated discovery: Amerigo "was the name, four hundred years ago, or whenever, of the pushing man who followed, across the sea, in the wake of Columbus and succeeded, where Columbus had failed, in becoming god-father, or name-father, to the new Continent." He "discovered America—or got himself honored as if he had" (59, 60). His is an eminently *fictional*, or, in other terms, *virtual*, success: arriving too late for discovery, he leaves a name to commemorate a nonevent. His catachresic name transcribes a characteristic narrative rhythm of the novel, which habitually builds up to events that are then skipped over in an ellipsis to be described, or some-times only referred to, in retrospect. The novel's two weddings are not nar-rated, for instance, and we learn of the birth of the Principino (the son of Maggie and the Prince or, as it more often seems, of Maggie and Adam) in a parenthetical phrase: "It didn't look like much for a whole family to hang about waiting—they being now, since the birth of his grandson, a whole family" (109). The novel over and over recurs to this structure. The description of the effect Maggie and Charlotte's kiss has on its viewers, for instance, appears only after an intervening chapter giving a conversa-tion three days later between Maggie and her father; the explanation of what Maggie learned from the Bloomsbury shopkeeper (who, telling her of Charlotte and Amerigo's visit, thereby gives her "proof") appears only after her long conversation with Fanny detailing the discovery's conse-quences and only after Fanny has shattered the bowl; the narration of the conversation between Maggie and Adam that leads to his marriage with Charlotte is given in full only through their recounting of it to each other much later in the novel (488); and the departure of Charlotte and Adam—perhaps the text's climactic event—is similarly narrated parenthetically as having already occurred:

> They went in to receive the boy, upon whose introduction to the room by Miss Bogle Charlotte and the Prince got up—seemingly with an impressiveness that caused Miss Bogle not to give further effect to her own entrance. She had retired, but the Principino's presence, by itself, sufficiently broke the tension—the subsidence of which in the great room, ten minutes later, gave to the air

something of the quality produced by the cessation of a sustained
rattle. Stillness, when the Prince and Princess returned from
attending the visitors to their carriage, might have been said to be
not so much restored as created. (565)

The novel's "reticence" is, in this sense, specifically an effect of its narrative
structure, its tendency to leave crucial events unnarrated; if such events
are narrated, they are not narrated *by* the novel so much as they are narrated *in* the novel. Events do not occur; occurrences are reflected upon,
which creates an effect of temporal delay, as if happening lagged behind
itself in time.[5] "Reticence" is linked to belatedness, but not because the
latter provides the psychological etiology of the former. Rather, both are
forms of withdrawal or temporal staggering that are principles of representation in this novel.

If the novel skips ahead to events it will narrate in retrospect, the hiatus
that separates an event from its telling also often foregrounds the uncertainty of causality, the gulf that separates a potential cause from its actualization in an event, and an event from any secure deduction of its cause.
Repeatedly returning to severed links between cause and effect, it also
highlights willful or tendentious assertions of causality and events whose
origins—like the art of the golden bowl itself, "a lost art . . . of a lost time"
(85)—have been lost (through "steps and stages conscious computation
had missed" [218], through the shuffling "away [of] every link between
consequence and cause," leaving intention, "like some famous poetic
line in a dead language, subject to varieties of interpretation" [549]). At
moments, the loss of a cause is made to seem, paradoxically, causal. Adam
Verver, whose "kindness, in the oddest way, seemed to have nothing to do
with his experience" (50), is wealthy in such a mode: his wealth is attributed not to the person he was but to the discontinuity between Adam and
the person the novel can only posit he must have been in order to have
made such a fortune (94).

It therefore seems inaccurate to describe shuffled temporality as a narrative effect in the novel; ellipsis and retrospection do not so much render happenings that could have been represented otherwise as share with
these happenings a common temporal structure—and share it, too, with
the "consciousness" of characters in the text. The gap between cause and
effect does not strike one as an effect of narrative ascesis because such a
gap might describe, in fact, the novel's most generalized understanding of

consciousness—as the (perpetually retrospective) discovery of discontinuity. Consciousness is belated, which is to say novelistic: the temporality
of consciousness, in other terms, entails a resistance to formalization analogous to that detailed by the essays on the novel—a form, as James repeatedly asserts, legible only in retrospect. ("Amerigo" offers a condensed
version of this structure by naming a misnaming that arrives after the fact.)
Retrospective construction is the characteristic pattern of cognition in the
text. On one level, it describes a temporality of illumination where knowledge is out of step with the realization that one has it. To put it that way,
however, risks externalizing the temporal lag—as if "realization" could be
separated from the consciousness that "has" it (or an "atmosphere" from
the mind that shelters it). The temporal lag of "realization" introduces a
discontinuity into consciousness—delayed cognition and shuffled narrative ordering rendering a consciousness out of sync with itself. This
temporal structure not only marks the larger rhythms of the novel's narrative unfolding, but also recurs in smaller articulations throughout the
text. Charlotte's "extraordinarily fine eyes," we are told, "as was [Adam's]
present theory that he had always thought them, shone at him the more
darkly" (170). Similarly, a remark from Charlotte leads the Prince to this
awareness: "it was as if he then knew, on the spot, why he had been feeling,
for hours, as he had felt" (217). Maggie's epiphany at the opening of Book
Two likewise takes the form of a temporal lag: "these instinctive post-
ponements of reflection were the fruit, positively, of recognitions and perceptions already active" (299). When the Prince returns from Matcham
to discover Maggie unexpectedly waiting for him, her thought—itself the
tracing of patterns visible in retrospect—redoubles the retrospection: "It
was not until afterwards that she discriminated as to this; felt how the act
had operated with him *instead* of the words he hadn't uttered" (318). By
the end, Maggie anticipates this kind of retrospection: "She was going to
know, she felt, later on—was going to know with compunction, doubtless,
on the very morrow, how thumpingly her heart had beaten at the fore-
taste of their being left alone together: she should judge at leisure the sur-
render she was making to the consciousness of complications about to be
bodily lifted" (547). There is a difference, it seems, between knowing you
are going to know something (even knowing full well what you will know)
and knowing it, which has the effect of alienating consciousness from,
making it a sort of narrator of, itself. Less important, perhaps, than the
anticipation of leisure is the temporal structure of realization. Knowledge

is always too early or too late; moving forward or backward, thoughts, feelings, and illuminations in the novel over and over fail to coincide with themselves in time.

This temporality of realization also marks the text's understanding of character development, which, in a novel that presents little other than developments catalyzed by realizations (more precisely, second-order realizations of others anticipated or remembered), is therefore vexed as a concept—as with it is, potentially, character itself. The narrative of Adam's aesthetic development (like that of his financial ascendancy) continually recurs to such effects, and attributes a kind of causality to a gap in ret-rospection. "To think how servile he might have been was absolutely to respect himself, was in fact, as much as he liked, to admire himself as free" (110). The initiation is curiously groundless—circular, and indistinguish-able from the thinking back on it: what seems to be initiating is the percep-tion of what "might have been" had there been no initiation. No content is given for Adam's awakening; we are, rather, told of "the memory of his freedom as dawning on him," which occurred when he began to appreciate how his patronage might place him above Julius II and Leo X in their treat-ment of Michelangelo. (In his thinking about "the character of the Patron of Art"—with which he does not here identify but into which he is said to have "read a richer meaning than any Pope or prince"—Adam does not distinguish between commissioning art and collecting it. The artwork's own genesis vanishes much as Adam's own awakening does [111].) Another crucial moment narrated after the fact, the epiphany presents a realization not of an identity—the collector, the philanthropist, the patron—or even of a pleasure, but of a difference. Pondering his aesthetic awakening, and wondering whether he would have developed as he did had his wife lived, the question is, strangely, resolved by Adam's recognition of himself as Cortez in Keats's "On First Looking into Chapman's Homer":

> Would she have led him altogether, attached as he was to her, into the wilderness of mere mistakes? Would she have prevented him from ever scaling his vertiginous Peak?—or would she, otherwise, have been able to accompany him to that eminence, where he might have pointed out to her, as Cortez to *his* companions, the revelation vouchsafed? No companion of Cortez had presumably been a real lady. Mr. Verver allowed that historic fact to determine his inference. (105–6)

The strange literalization of Adam's aesthetic mountaineering I will return to later.[6] Another instance of lost origins—Adam repeats Keats's mistake, taking Cortez for Balboa—the causality is reversed; the later recognition (in a reading of a text), itself the product of a figure linking two kinds of exploration, two species of peaks, is made to resolve the necessity of the contingent path that will, in turn, have made possible the comparison to continental conquest in the first place. Adam's epiphany that his marriage to Charlotte could usefully "put his child at peace" is phrased with a similar reversal: "It wasn't only moreover that the word, with a click, so fitted the riddle, but that the riddle, in such perfection, fitted the word. He might have been equally in want and yet not have had his remedy" (154). The narrative sequence from question to answer—riddle to word—is disrupted, made reflexive, which might describe, in the condensed form of a chiasmus, recurrent patterns of discovery in the text. At stake, at one level, is perhaps a generalizable insight about realization (even when it isn't enmeshed in paranoid plots such as those of *The Golden Bowl*): realization might be the ability to formulate the question to which the knowledge one already has supplies the answer. The Keats reference—where "Cortez" seems to answer the riddle of the relation of marriage to adventure —likewise fits its parts together in reverse, and links that inverted causality to the reversals inherent in literary identification. That process—for which Dorian Gray's equivocal commerce with his portrait might stand as an emblem—is of interest insofar as it charts a reciprocal, which is to say groundless, formation of reader and text, and an abyssal temporality: Dorian learns from Lord Henry not what his dreams and passions are, but what they *have been*, and we recognize ourselves in the literary work insofar as it brings into being the self that will have been adequate to the experience of reading it. The riddle made to fit the word, finally, like the transformation of a figural proximity (of two [or three] conquistadors) to a "historic fact" thereby allowed to "determine" an "inference" cannot but evoke the novel's own procedure in fitting plot and theme to its style.

The specific question in the case of Adam here—what disappears into the various recursivities of cause and effect—is, as we noted, character development. The metafictional quality of Adam's citation of Keats links the terving outward and flattening, the curiously perned quality, of character in late James both to these temporal inversions and to a becoming-textual of consciousness (insofar as the "cause" of Adam's development seems to be the retrospective reading of a poem). The severing of causal links and the retrospective discovery of difference are, of course, also the grounds of the paranoid plots in the novel, which opens with the Prince noting an "effect" that was "nowhere in particular," even as he "constantly felt himself at the mercy of the cause" (13): each of the characters is, at various moments, held in thrall by a structure similar to Maggie's sense, as she contemplates the effects of her husband's adultery without yet seeing it, that "her grasp of appearances was thus out of proportion to her view of causes" (336).[7] Conversely, the shuffling away of legible links between cause and effect also describes the exercise of power in *The Golden Bowl*. His particular resistance to being read makes Adam, in this sense, the most powerful character in the text:

> His greatest inconvenience, he would have admitted, had he analysed, was in finding it so taken for granted that, as he had money, he had force. It pressed upon him hard, and all round, assuredly, this attribution of power. Everyone had need of one's power, whereas one's own need, at the best, would have seemed to be but some trick for not communicating it. (96)

The overlap between narrative structure and the wiles of power offers compelling evidence for Mark Seltzer's claim that "the art of the novel is an art of power."[8] Indeed, the novel never lets us assume that this narrative structure is without consequences or stands aloof from such effects of power (as Charlotte's exile to the Midwest must give her cause to realize).

Without asserting that it is neutral in its effects, however, I would dwell on the interrupted causality, which is what James's description returns to:

> His lips, somehow, were closed—and by a spring connected moreover with the action of his eyes themselves. The latter showed him what he *had* done, showed him where he had come out; quite at the top of his hill of difficulty, the tall sharp spiral round which he had begun to wind his ascent at the age of twenty, and the apex of which was a platform looking down, if one would, on the king-doms of the earth and with standing-room for but half a dozen others. (96–97)

His survey of the kingdoms of the earth is troubled a little by the fact that his eyes seem to be closed; the potentially monstrous image of a connected spring linking the (mechanical) action of his eyes and his mouth ties the wish for "some trick for not communicating" his power—admitting to it, it seems, but also having it operate by the force of contact—to his inability to account for it. Also at issue here is the question of voice—of who compares Adam to Christ in the wilderness, and to what effect, and of the extent to which the specific context of the Miltonic reference is audible or, on the contrary, dissipates.[9] There are any number of questions raised by the reference: whether, in the first place, Adam can be said to turn down the proffered kingdoms; whether he thinks he has; and, more generally, whether the secularizing of the reference is supposed to be audible (as Adam's potential misreading, as the text's ironizing of his self-regard, as the text's rendering of the power accorded money, as the transformation—with, again, multivalent parodic effects—of the Miltonic mountain overlook to a sort of corporate boardroom, and so on). However one decides those questions, what initially looks like a figure of magisterial purview linked, implicitly, to a clarity of demystified self-knowledge (or perhaps simply to the infinite potential of infinite wealth) turns out, like the citation of Keats, to contain a highly equivocal literary reference, where the boundary separating the cited text from the text that cites it is not at all clear. A relation of (mis)reading; a collision of different, incompatible figural contexts (Christ, mechanical doll, conquest, mountain tourism, life as a more or less perilous journey, and others); a baffling of causal relations, or of their discovery; and an exploration of a kind of power that is "communicated" by the knowledge of it not being "communicated": a whole series of different registers (character development, causality, figuration, plot) are, as it were, flattened into a single plane.

Among the more striking instances of the communication between divergent registers is the overlapping of the paranoid plots of the novel with its narration, which works to suspend, for a reader, any presumed continuity between narrative order and causality. The emphasis on retrospective construction therefore also links paranoia in the novel to the argument against formalization in the essays on the novel—delineating a form legible only in retrospect, a genre that cannot coincide with its formalization. The lag in consciousness registered by the characters might thus be read as an after-effect of this principle of novelistic antiformalization. Or, at the very least, the psychological determinants (and their representation) cannot be presumed to be primary or motivating. For the characters in the novel, the paranoid plot takes shape through the reaccepted, retasted,

exquisitely reassimilated and reenjoyed old matter; the old matter, moreover, is often there only in its revision, comes into being only in its exquisite reassimilation. Such an emphasis might shift one's sense of the final
separation of the erotic couples—Charlotte and the Prince, and Maggie
and Adam. Charlotte, we are told early on, is "irretrievably contemporane-
ous" with the Prince (35); similarly, for Maggie, the difficulty of her marriage is that in marrying she has "sacrificed a parent, the pearl of parents,
no older than herself: it wouldn't so much have mattered if he had been of
common parental age. That he wasn't, that he was just her extraordinary
equal and contemporary, this was what added to her act the long train of
its effect" (153). Shipping Charlotte off to the Midwest serves, from this
angle, to interrupt these contemporaneities, just as the affair itself disrupts
the "perfect accord," to which the Prince may at the beginning lay claim,
"between conduct and obligation" (38). Both interruptions might be said
to make these moments metanovelistic; at stake, for example, is not the
punishing of adultery but the introduction of the temporal lag necessary
for narration. Paranoia itself—the torment that many of the characters
in the novel experience as they fear betraying what they know, or what
they know that others know—strikes one, in this regard, as an experience
of an antimimetic style from within: the lapse of time that characterizes
consciousness in the novel and makes for its paranoid predicament also
describes the novel form as James theorizes it.[10]

Fanny Assingham's sense that she is "embarrassed by the difference
between what she took in and what she could say, what she felt and what she
could show" (195), not only describes a particular predicament within the
novel's paranoid plots; it also describes a character's becoming cognizant
of an interruption of representation—a gap in the movement from inner
sense to outward expression. (As with the "shyness" of the frontispieces,
"embarrassed" marks a crossing of psychological and narrative registers in
the novel's affective vocabulary; one is therefore unsure about what, finally,
the statement suggests that Fanny is feeling.) The novel's thematization of
knowledge and power can thus be brought into relation with a series of
other narrative effects that likewise disrupt such significatory movement.
As Leo Bersani and Ruth Bernard Yeazell have, in different ways, noted,
metaphor in the late fiction ceases to be subordinated to the representation
of consciousness.[11] Many of the figures—particularly, but not exclusively,
that of the golden bowl itself[12]—migrate to descriptions and even to the
spoken dialogue of characters who can, at these particular moments, have

as yet no inkling of the context ostensibly motivating them.[13] Characters think and talk in elaborate figures they share with each other and with the narrative voice—figures that do not, therefore, serve as vehicles of characterization (either thematically or as a free indirect rendering of habits of cognition).[14] One effect is to turn consciousness inside out; another is to disrupt any understanding of language as a "rendering" of consciousness by giving agency instead to the figures that ostensibly convey it, making consciousness an after-effect of its rendering. Character and psychology seem less to motivate than to be generated by narrative effects and effects of style. By foregrounding the linguistic construction of character— denaturalizing what, arguably, realist fiction naturalizes—these effects also reflect on the taking place of the fiction. In this sense, Fanny's inability to represent herself indexes not only the social predicament in which she finds herself but also the principle of representation in the novel. Such is what it means to be "embarrassed" in *The Golden Bowl*. Hence, with respect to Maggie's surprise after the Prince's return from Matcham— "she hadn't expected the least shade of embarrassment. What had made the embarrassment . . . what had made the particular look was his thus distinguishably wishing to see how he should find her" (308)—the psychological determinants are perhaps secondary to the sense indexed here of an untraceable (*embarrassed* as impeded, obstructed, or encumbered) relation between appearances and their causes. Rather than signaling a particular predicament for a particular character, such moments intimate a troubling of character itself.[15]

There is a similar effect in what Arlene Young calls "hypothetical discourse": "dialogues or monologues which are presented as quoted speech on the page, though not in fact (or fiction) ever verbalized" (382).[16] Hypothetical discourse, she notes, disorients perspective, floating, like free indirect discourse and like the images and figures in *The Golden Bowl* more generally, between character and narrator, unsettling any certain sense of who is speaking and from where. The quotation marks that often accompany these speeches make them even more vexing because they give "a semblance of precision and authenticity to what is actually vague and indeterminate" (Young, 390). Or, in other terms, they look like—and often function as—quoted speech while disarticulating their various effects— diegetic effects of communication, effects of meaning for a reader—from their grounding in (and grounding of) represented happening in the novel. Such hypothetical speech has effects without, however, ever taking place;

mimicking the form of direct speech, these moments shape character, plot, and meaning but are never given utterance by anyone. "Some such words as those," the narrator remarks of a long putative speech by Maggie, "were what *didn't* ring out, yet it was as if even the unuttered sound had been quenched here in its own quaver" (311).[17] "Since she put it so," we are told a few lines later, and it is perhaps unclear whether this latter (ventriloquized) narration of the Prince's thought refers to the particular phrasing of Maggie's unuttered speech or to his summary (also unuttered) of what he understands her to be to "saying." At another moment: "'Yes, look, look,' she seemed to see him hear her say even while her sounded words were other" (436). Characteristically, we are also given a speech representing what "Charlotte might under this pressure have been on the point of replying," after which appears another quoted "point" that "Mrs. Verver might in fact have but just failed to make" (327). Such speeches could be read as representing, for a reader, the characters' predicament, their perpetually having to be attuned to the unspoken: "she had turned away from him with some such unspoken words as that in her ear, and indeed she *had* to represent to herself that she had spiritually heard them, had to listen to them still again, to explain her particular patience in face of his particular failure" (459). However, whereas one possible reading would emphasize a representation of psychic "depth"—"hypothetical discourse" registering, in such a reading, multiple "levels" of consciousness, a character's attending to multiple questions or angles on a question simultaneously—before explaining (and assuming) their psychological function, it is worth attending to their peculiar status "in" the novel as speech that is spoken by no one.[18] Thus, such speeches link the paranoid plots that emerge from the unspoken in the novel to the novel's own disconcerting patterns of narration, to quoted language that both does and does not take place, and that takes place in not taking place ("since she put it so . . .").

The regime of the unspoken thus marks a reflection on the novel's fictional status, an effect that, transcribed from the plot to the mode of narration, intimates perhaps analogously unsettling self-reflexive or metafictional effects. And it is not only speech that both does and does not take place. Also striking is the text's disorienting, habitual use of "as if," which suspends the diegetic "reality" of narrated events:

> He faced her awhile longer in the same way; it was, strangely, as if,
> by this sudden arrest, by their having, in their acceptance of the

unsaid, or at least their reference to it, practically given up pretend-
ing—it was as if they were 'in' for it, for something they had been
ineffably avoiding, but the dread of which was itself, in a manner,
a seduction, just as any confession of the dread was by so much an
allusion. (492)

Or, again, "She had never turned away from him before, and it was quite
positively for her as if she were altogether afraid of him" (201).[19]

Such effects ask to be read, I think, in several different ways. On one
level, they mark the emergence of the novel's paranoid plots on the level of
its narration: for readers and characters alike, the "events" of the novel resist
definitive verification. The novel suspends certainty on nothing less than
what happens in it. On another level, "as if" might be read as a reflection
on the narration's own taking place and thus as a marker, within the text, of
its fictional status. (All novelistic events could be preceded by "as if" to the
extent that they are fictional.) As in the (multivalent) jamming together of
different registers in the citations of Keats and Milton, these moments—
and, more generally, the blurring of different "levels" of narration in the
crossing of psychological and textual vocabularies of motivation and affect,
of characters' views of themselves and the novel's view of them, of "style"
and "plot"—mark instances of one of the favored figures of the novel (and
of James's late writing more generally): zeugma, or "double governance,"
defined in the *Oxford English Dictionary* as "a figure in which a single word
is made to refer to two or more words in a sentence, especially when properly applying to only one—or applying to them in different senses."[20] The
discordance of grammatical construction—of masculine and feminine or
singular and plural forms, for instance—which is more properly designated
syllepsis,[21] can also, in zeugma, apply to a collocation of literal and figurative registers.[22] Pope's nymph staining "her honor or her new brocade," or
Alanis Morissette's crooningly apostrophized lover's holding "your breath
and the door for me" (or "Maggie's sense . . . that though the bowl had
been broken, her reason hadn't" [434]) provides a grammatical analogue
of a more thoroughgoing mixing of literal and figurative registers in *The
Golden Bowl*.[23] Fanny Assingham is "wrapped in her thoughts still more
closely than in the lemon-coloured mantle that protected her bare shoul-
ders" (267). Such mixing offers a way to describe what can be so daunting
about the novel's language, where figurative language takes on a disorienting agency and hovers at an indeterminate remove from (which is also

to say proximity to) depicted events. Dunking the characters in baths of benevolence or dragging them about by silken cords, dropping Palladian churches into town squares and rubbing up against them to test the social polish of a Prince, the novel's prose features abstract and extended figures often presented as if they were literal description.[24]

The blurring that might be conceptualized through syllepsis or zeugma often appears in disrupted relations between vehicle and tenor in the novel's figures—in literalized tenors or vehicles that become part of the text's action. Wrapping Fanny in her thoughts as if in her mantle is one instance; the result is both to dematerialize the mantle and to materialize the thoughts, or, rather, to leave both at an indeterminate level of actuality. At another moment, Italy "serenades" the Prince after his marriage, making enough noise to keep him up at night (146–47). Figures in the text are subject to unexpected literalization: Maggie "might" hear her father say, "Sacrifice me" as they stroll together in the park. "Should she want to, should she insist on it, she might verily hear him bleating it at her, all conscious and all accommodating, like some precious, spotless, exceptionally intelligent lamb" (359). The literalization reminds us how intelligent a lamb would have to be, no matter how spotless, to find itself so articulate. That the simile marks Adam's ovine supplication as hypothetical—unspoken words that "she might verily hear him bleating"—links the wavering between literal and figural registers to the novel's similar suspension of certainty in hypothetical speech and in the novel's repeated use of "as if" (which likewise could be called instances of zeugma insofar as they waver between a diegetic event and a figural rendering of fictionality). Instances of such equivocal mixings of register could be multiplied.[25] Thus, as Mrs. Rance approaches Adam in the Fawns billiard room, "the vast table, draped in brown holland, thrust itself between them as an expanse of desert sand. She couldn't cross the desert, but she could, and did, beautifully get round it" (97). The coming together of vehicle and tenor produces a comical effect. The billiard table retains characteristics of both desert and table: the desert has to be reduced to the size of a billiard table (and dragged into the house) so that Mrs. Rance can walk around it, even as the impossibility of "crossing" it reminds us that she is prevented—by her lack of agility or her sense of social decorum or both—from simply crawling over the table. This figure is echoed in a later description of the Sunday intruder's marital situation: she wanders the "great alkali desert of cheap divorce" (98). The latter instance indicating, on one level, her threat to Adam should she trade in her de facto divorce for a more expensive de jure model, her distance from him in the billiard room (and the ease with which she crosses the desert) thus makes tangible, in retrospect, the threat posed by unmarried women now that Maggie's marriage to the Prince leaves her less able to interpose herself between Adam and would-be suitors. It isn't simply, then, that Mrs. Rance's desert excursion hovers at an indeterminate level of figurality. To follow Adam's (and Maggie's) reading of the ominous potential encrypted in that Sunday invasion of the billiard room invokes that kind of figural reading, a geographical transposition that can read the billiard table as a desert and connect the desert to "the great alkali desert of cheap divorce." (It is less that figures render characters' thoughts than that the thoughts themselves seem to occur in, even to be "caused" by, the movement between [or within] figures.)

Thus, on another level, the reappearance of the desert is perhaps not motivated by psychological or causal logics; the later figure seems to be generated by the earlier one, as if figuration exerted its own, independent agency. Such a claim could be generalized to the figurative language of the text, which seems to have a plot of its own, separate from any "story" told. The golden bowl—and its tendency to appear outside of psychologically motivated contexts (in the thoughts of those who have no knowledge of it, for instance)—is one example. Another is the figure used to describe Maggie's deferral of unanswered questions as a "roomful of confused objects" that she has been "passing and repassing along the corridor of her life," avoiding, whenever possible, "opening the door" (307); the figure returns in a series of more or less related contexts—and in shutting and opening doors, figurative and literal—in the rest of the text (for instance, 329, 402, 441). The reversal in which figurative language seems to motivate or shape what it ostensibly figures replays, in another register, the reversal of literal and figural. Figurative language in *The Golden Bowl* often spurns any subservient role, becomes a visible element in depicted landscapes, and determines elements of character and plot. Hence when the Prince's entry interrupts Maggie's ruminations about the corridor of her life, the effect is potentially disorienting: "It made her in fact, with a vain gasp, turn away, and what had further determined this was the final sharp extinction of the inward scene by the outward. The quite different door had opened and her husband was there" (308). It isn't simply a matter of a crossing of "inward" and "outward," a thought, for example, taking on agency in the world (although it is such a crossing, too). In this extinction of the inward scene by the outward, a crux of the paranoid plot appears, at the same time, in relation to a crossing of linguistic registers. The uncertain status of the inward door disrupts the presumed solidity of the outward one, and it is "as if" the two registers—of thought and action, mind and world—even as they are asserted to be "quite different," come together in a shared indeterminacy. The uncertain boundaries of inside and out that characterize both paranoid thinking (Schreber experiences his thoughts as if they occurred in the outside world; similarly, one of Freud's paranoid lesbians hears, at least in Freud's reading of her delusion, her clitoris "knocking" in the stairwell outside the apartment where she is having an affair)[26] and the markedly powerful effects of thought in the novel, by pointing to the shared ontological status of the two doors (Maggie's imagined door is no less fictional, which is also to say no less real, than the one the Prince opens), also gesture, in yet another blurring of registers, toward the novel's own taking place.

As Fanny speaks to her husband, her "whole ample, ornamented person irradiated" the truth that had "begun to glow" (283); said to have "touched with light for him connections hitherto dim" (284), Fanny becomes "crystalline" (288). The "upshot" of the drama before Fanny and her husband, the passage continues, was that the Colonel had "the most luminous of wives," leaving him to turn off, "in this view of her majestic retreat, the comparatively faint little electric lamp which had presided over their talk" (293). The increasingly predominant figures of light in the passage finally absorb its "dramatic" activity, and luminous Fanny illumines with a disconcertingly literal radiance. Similarly, Adam's view of his proposal to Charlotte as a risky adventure of an explorer or conquistador is rendered in figures that cast his decision as a "burning of his ships" (159)—committing him (figuratively) to a plan of action without possibility of retreat. They walk closer to where he will see his ships burn (159–60), and he applies the torch (160) and asks her the question that "represented the sacrifice of his vessels" (161):

> Just these things in themselves, however, with all the rest, with his fixed purpose now, his committed deed, the fine pink glow, projected forward, of his ships, behind him, definitely blazing and crackling—this quantity was to push him harder than any word of her own could warn him. All that she was herself, moreover, was so lighted, to its advantage, by the pink glow. (163)

This passage annoyed F. R. Leavis, who remarked that it lacked "the concrete immediacy of metaphor."[27] And, indeed, one is unsure whether her reaction to the proposal "illuminates" her character, whether she is blushing, or whether the burning ships literally light Charlotte, as the "fine glow, projected forward, of his ships, behind him" suggests.[28] Like Fanny's equivocal glow, the burning of Adam's ships is at once a figure and an event in the text.

I would therefore also read as instances of zeugma figures that have been arresting for critics in thematic terms: when it is said of Charlotte that "she was thus poor Charlotte again for Maggie" (504), "poor" seems to signify in two registers simultaneously, evoking both the crypto-despotic pity that Mark Seltzer has traced as the text's regime of "care" and, more literally, the poverty that led Charlotte to marriage in the first place. Thus, the connoisseurial gaze of the Ververs is yet another instance of mixed registers—"nothing perhaps might affect us as queerer, had we time to look into it, than this application of the same measure of value to such different pieces of property as old Persian carpets, say, and new human acquisitions" (145)—a mixing that transforms, at the novel's close, Charlotte and Amerigo into "high expressions of the kind of human furniture required, aesthetically, by such a scene" (561). It isn't only Charlotte and the Prince who are described as aesthetic objects. Here is Adam's view of ("shyly mythological and nymph-like") Maggie:

> She had got up with these last words; she stood there before him
> with that particular suggestion in her aspect to which even the long
> habit of their life together had not closed his sense, kept sharp, year
> after year, by the collation of types and signs, the comparison of
> fine object with fine object, of one degree of finish, of one form of
> the exquisite with another—the appearance of some slight, slim
> draped "antique" of Vatican or Capitoline halls, late and refined,
> rare as a note and immortal as a link, set in motion by the miracu-
> lous infusion of a modern impulse and yet, for all the sudden
> freedom of folds and footsteps forsaken after centuries by their
> pedestal, keeping still the quality, the perfect felicity, of the statue,
> the blurred, absent eyes, the smoothed, elegant, nameless head, the
> impersonal flit of a creature lost in an alien age and passing as an
> image in worn relief round and round a precious vase. (138–39)

"Governed," one might say, by zeugma—"it came," the passage explains, "from his caring for special vases only less than for precious daughters" (139)—the passage presents any number of crossings. The crossing of the antique with "a modern impulse" is one; the similes "rare as a note and immortal as a link" present another. The synecdoche "folds and footsteps" for the statue—which elements, as parts, moreover, signify the whole they represent in different ways—is immediately followed by a reversal: the folds and footsteps are not forsaking but are forsaken. The unexpected assignment of agency seems to figure the reversal of the Pygmalion myth as Maggie passes from sentient, flesh-and-blood girl to statue to "an image in worn relief," and her movement, from "she had got up," to "footsteps" forsaken by their pedestal, to an image "passing . . . round and round a precious vase." In that transition, movement turns figural—it is no longer Maggie's but that of a viewer, who lends motion to a static image by following a pattern "round and round" a vase. Maggie's becoming-antique (or becoming-an-antique) is not only a transition between different kinds of movement; it is also a sort of conjugation of them. A girl passing round and round a room and an image passing round and round a vase are identical descriptions differentiated by their differing degrees of remove from a literal "ground," their differing figural "levels." Another way to describe the effect is to note that the "passing" of the "image" at the end of the quoted section makes manifest that the "infusion" of "modern impulse" that sets the "statue . . . in motion" is itself (only) figural. One is then led to realize that "she had got up" is no different: figured here is not only the commodifying aestheticization of the collector but also the animating, vivifying power of a text—and, vice versa, the petrifying, deanimating effect when that power is made explicit as a figural one. Adam's connoisseurial gaze is, notably, described as a kind of figural capacity—the discipline of simile, or, perhaps, of zeugma, depending on one's sense of what it is his sharpened sense compares: his sense has been "kept sharp . . . by the collation of types and signs, the comparison of fine object with fine object, of one degree of finish, of one form of the exquisite with another." Adam's capacity is in a sense the novel's own, and indeed Maggie's transformation here strikes one as a representation of character in the text: human figures fade to "blurred, absent eyes," to "the impersonal flit of a creature lost in an alien age," flatten to images in worn relief—become, that is, effects that stand out, if minimally, from the style of that precious vase called *The Golden Bowl*.

However one might judge the transformation of persons into "human furniture," and the economico-aesthetic terms through the lens of which Adam apprehends the world—Charlotte is repeatedly referred to as a hired hand or purchased object, and the Prince, as a rare museum piece— the use of these terms marks yet another instance of colliding registers and double governance. The "action" in the passage that turns Maggie into a figure on a vase is, in a sense, the working of zeugma. Functioning as both characterization (of Adam's particular mode of commodification, for example) and as a metareflection on the novel's language, the passage perhaps leaves us uncertain about whether Maggie "really" becomes an image on a vase. And—in yet another crossing—instances of zeugma become difficult to distinguish from reflections on that particular trope and on its role in the text's language. The transformation of the adulterers into furniture thus also suggests that the plot of the novel might be read as a narrativization of zeugma, and thus as a reflection on the novel's own taking place. Adultery—like marriage, for that matter—is, for this novel, perhaps first and foremost an instance of zeugma. (One way to phrase the effect of *The Golden Bowl* on the marriage plot is to suggest that it makes explicit how that generic plot may, all along, have been but the working of this rhetorical figure—and the manifold ways it generated sympathy for characters and impetus for narrative, the obscuring of the figural nature of the trope.) The "as if" and "as" with which the novel habitually narrates its events points to the way this figure marks the narration in its entirety, suspending it between diegesis and simile. And, yet again, events within the novel—the movement of its paranoid plot—are inseparable from the novel's own mode of narration. Adultery and the paranoia it arouses represent narrativizations of the blurring of registers that characterizes the novel's style. In other words, the style of *The Golden Bowl* is both its (sole) character and its plot.

In the extraordinary passage about the ivory tower or pagoda that opens Book Second, the novel offers a striking image for this turning back on itself to reflect on its own taking place. That recursive gaze, in the context of the novel's paranoid plot, also stands in for Maggie's growing "knowledge":

> This situation had been occupying, for months and months, the
> very centre of the garden of her life, but it had reared itself there
> like some strange, tall tower of ivory, or perhaps rather some

wonderful, beautiful, but outlandish pagoda, a structure plated
with hard, bright porcelain, coloured and figured and adorned,
at the overhanging eaves, with silver bells that tinkled, ever so
charmingly, when stirred by chance airs. She had walked round
and round it; . . . looking up, all the while, at the fair structure that
spread itself so amply and rose so high, but never quite making out,
as yet, where she might have entered had she wished. She had not
wished till now—such was the odd case; and what was doubtless
equally odd, besides, was that, though her raised eyes seemed to
distinguish places that must serve, from within, and especially far
aloft, as apertures and outlooks, no door appeared to give access
from her convenient garden level. The great decorated surface had
remained consistently impenetrable and inscrutable. . . . She had
knocked, in short—though she could scarce have said whether for
admission or for what; she had applied her hand to a cool, smooth
spot, and had waited to see what would happen. Something *had*
happened; it was as if a sound, at her touch, after a little, had come
back to her from within; a sound sufficiently suggesting that her
approach had been noted. (299–300)

Maggie's walking "round and round" this tower or pagoda recalls her image
"passing . . . round and round a precious vase" (139); if there is perhaps
something almost queasy about the later image, it could have to do with
the telescoping of scale in that transition, and with the quasi-literalization
as the vase, enlarged, seems to rear itself in the garden. The aestheticized
placidity of the earlier image gives way to something more like panic, and
the collation of the two moments leaves one with an uncanny sense of a
confrontation of two incompatible forms of space (like the golden bowl
itself, whose crack gives it two incompatible "insides"); it is as if the figure "on" the surface of a vase suddenly sought to communicate with the
inside of the space it enclosed. That—for lack of a better word—introver-
sion offers a spatial image (or an "image" of an unvisualizable space) of
the novel's "surface" (its language, its figuration) exchanging places with
its "content" (its theme, its plot, its characters). Perhaps recalling this passage, the novel's preface uses an image of a garden to figure the novel's
imaginary landscape and the reader's imaginary realization of it (xlvi);
it is as if Maggie contemplated the novel itself. "The great decorated surface," so oddly impenetrable, thus figures at once Maggie's predicament

and the novel's thick surface of figuration, and thus figures also the coming together of registers that characterizes the text's language. Maggie's coming to knowledge about the affair is at the same time the novel's reflection on its own taking place; paradoxically, the novel's "plot" *is* at this moment, metanarrative. The uncannily undead verb "reared," among other details, points to both the eroticism and the potential disgust of the uncanny materialization of the novel's gaze upon itself, the reflection, as it were, of the novel's own procedures of reflection, a figural effect *en abîme*.

The self-reflexivity of the moment is also marked in that the figure of Maggie's tower resembles nothing so much as James's "house of fiction" seen from the outside. The "house of fiction," he writes in the famous passage from the preface to *The Portrait of a Lady*,

> has in short not one window, but a million—a number of possible windows not to be reckoned, rather; every one of which has been pierced, or is still pierceable, in its vast front, by the need of the individual vision and by the pressure of the individual will. These apertures, of dissimilar shape and size, hang so, all together, over the human scene that we might have expected of them a greater sameness of report than we find. They are but windows at the best, mere holes in a dead wall, disconnected, perched aloft; they are not hinged doors opening straight upon life. But they have this mark of their own that at each of them stands a figure with a pair of eyes, or at least with a field-glass, which forms, again and again, for observation, a unique instrument, insuring to the person making use of it an impression distinct from every other. . . . [T]here is fortunately no saying on what, for the particular pair of eyes, the window may *not* open; "fortunately" by reason, precisely, of this incalculability of range. The spreading field, the human scene, is the "choice of subject"; the pierced aperture, either broad or balconied or slit-like and low-browed, is the "literary form"; but they are, singly or together, as nothing without the posted presence of the watcher—without, in other words, the consciousness of the artist.[29]

Like the pagoda in Maggie's garden, which, though it has "far aloft" "apertures and outlooks," has "no door . . . to give access from her convenient garden level," the house of fiction has "windows at best, mere holes in a dead wall, disconnected, perched aloft; they are not hinged doors opening straight upon life." That the "piercing" gaze leaves mere holes in a dead wall suggests that the shaping of material by form—"the pierced aperture, either broad or balconied or slit-like and low-browed, is the 'literary form'"—is not without its violence. There would be much to say about the ambivalent reversals in this seeming celebration of authorial power, the uncanny consequences, for watcher and watched, of this image of a "figure" perched over the spreading field of life. (One's hesitation as to whether that figure is a *face* or a trope may be one way to gauge the uncanniness.) Among many other details, one might dwell on the "expected . . . sameness of report," where "report" seems not only to mean both a statement and a resounding noise (as of a firecracker or gun), but also, potentially, to invoke Puttenham's use of the term for the trope of *anaphora*—itself a figure of sameness—which transforms the house of fiction into a figure for a rhetorically constructed unity of linked gazes that are like repeated elements in a sentence or series of sentences.[30] It isn't—as one might expect—that the divergence of "reports" comes from the variety of the human scene itself; the surprise seems to be that, given that we are dealing with a rhetorically structured whole, the whole is not *more* unified. Nor is the variety attributable to idiosyncrasy: offered instead is a strange redoubling of figures of prosthesis that gives vision and agency to the "pierced aperture" or to an idiosyncratic "field-glass" serving an uncannily instrumentalized (which is to say, independent from the bearer) "pair of eyes."[31] What initially is attributed to the "individual vision" and the "individual will" becomes the effect of a "unique instrument." And the "figure" standing there becomes a "mark" characterizing the particular *aperture* ("they have this mark of their own"). These objectifying or dehumanizing strands in the description of authorial view bring to mind Deleuze's concept of "viewpoint"—which "is not individual, but on the contrary a principle of individuation."[32] Here, indeed, it seems to be the perspective that determines the watcher "posted" there, and not the other way around. The withdrawal from "life"—"mere holes in a dead wall, disconnected, perched aloft," not "hinged doors opening straight upon life"—by giving us something like Combray as it was never experienced, also describes, in a different register, belatedness and style. And these effects potentially extend to the "consciousness of the artist," which comes to seem the effect as much as the cause of the scene that, without him, is "as nothing." The disappearance of a face into an aperture—or a field-glass—or, on the other hand, an aperture in a dead wall that, pierced, seems to materialize a figure to

give meaning to the spreading scene over which it is perched—what initially looks like an (ostensibly) living author's perspective on "life" turns
into a more unsettling exchange between two equivocally animated forms,
where the vivifying agency is given to a perspective seemingly abstracted
from any human gaze.

The "impenetrable and inscrutable" pagoda in Maggie's garden suggests how unnerving it could be to find oneself outside the house of fiction, and thus subjected to such a penetrating but invisible—and, because
it is multiple and inhuman, unplaceable—gaze. More than that, read in
relation to the house of fiction, the moment in Maggie's garden suggests
the queasy possibility that she might stumble upon the scene of her own
creation. In the figured convergence of this metafictional moment with
the novel's own paranoid plot, it is as if the outside of the vase turned
inward to communicate with its inside, or as if the inside turned out and
flattened into a plane. Maggie's garden seems, when the figures are read
together, to be identified with the "spreading field, the human scene," as
if the whole drama of the form-giving gaze of the artist took place within
the fiction (and as if the plot—of infidelity—were that giving of form, as if
Maggie perceived marriage and infidelity alike to be instances of zeugma).
Maggie's contemplation of her situation—of the adultery that she senses
but doesn't yet "know"—is thus linked to her taking cognizance of her
predicament as a character in a novel.[33] The paranoid plot of the novel, in
other terms, is the plotting of the novel; the effect, to put it most simply, of
the novel's inside-out topographies and mixing of registers is to make the
novel's style indistinguishable from its plot.

"The work has merit," James wrote to Mrs. Humphrey Ward, "but it
is too long and the subject is pumped too dry, even; that is, the pump is
too big for it (it isn't itself so big), and tends thereby to usurp space in
it."[34] That difficult sentence and its confusing profusion of pronouns seems
to distinguish between the "too long" novel and the not-so-big "subject,"
seeming to offer the novel itself as synonymous with the pump that pumps
its subject too dry, even as the one is "too big" and the other "not so big."
The distinctions upon which the assertion would seem to rest—the material of a novel, for example, as opposed to its treatment—are complicated by the difficulty of mapping the relations among the various terms.
Among other questions, one wonders where the "inside" is that might be
pumped or that might find its "space" usurped. "The poor old G.B.," he
calls the novel in a letter to Edith Wharton, putting the novel in the place

of doomed, exiled, and to-be-pitied Charlotte and, in that wry personification, confounding registers in (at least) two ways: by suggesting that
Charlotte might be another such personification and by putting the novel
as a whole at the same figurative level as a character in it. [35] *The Wings of the
Dove*, James wrote to Mrs. Cadwalader Jones, "has too big a head for its
body"; *The Golden Bowl*, he suggested, was an effort to "write one with the
opposite disproportion—the body too big for its head."[36] However else
we might understand this further fond personification of the text, the disproportion of head and body, invoking and parodying an understanding
of aesthetic objects by analogy with organic form, signals a hierarchy of
meaning gone awry—of mind or soul over body, for instance, or meaning
over form. That disproportion thus suggests that the disorientation of register in zeugma be read as a governing principle of the late style. More than
any thematic element—adultery or incest, the objectification and artifac-
tualization of persons, or the thwarting (or transcendence) of consumerist
relations to a world—that stylistic principle accounts for the queerness
of *The Golden Bowl*. From this perspective, zeugma or double governance
might be a way to conceptualize the novel's erotics: nothing might perhaps affect us as queerer than its disorienting mixing of registers, than its
interruptions of presumed representabilities. In these terms, *The Golden
Bowl* presents us with a queer plot because it presents a narrativization of
James's late style.

CHAPTER 2

The Burden of Residuary Comment: Syntactical Idiosyncrasies in *The Wings of the Dove*

For D. A. Miller's *Jane Austen, or The Secret of Style,* free indirect style is of interest in large part because of its power to catalyze effects of shame; the virtuoso shadings of a narration's proximity to and distance from its characters excite a fantasy of imperturbable remove—a total depersonalization that threatens, from the very start, to collapse into personification and abjection. (Shame emerges as one travels that circuit back toward personification.) Discussing Austen's *Emma,* Miller describes the free indirect mode as a dynamic of identification: "For, no less than close reading, the close writing that is free indirect style is also given over to broaching an impossible identification. In the paradoxical form of an impersonal intimacy, it grants us at one and the same time the experience of a character's inner life as she herself lives it, and an experience of the same inner life as she never could."[1] The most "daredevil feats" of this narration occur

> when, in the course of vainly aspiring to narration, a character in
> turn inspires it [the narration] with an equally impossible desire to
> renounce its condition for her own, as a fully representable person;
> in other words, in a case where it seems that if the structural bar of
> antithesis ever slipped away—and it never does—its place would
> be immediately taken by a mirror. (59–60)

The "open secret of an impossible identification between the No One who is narrating and the most fully characterized Person in all Austen" (that is, Emma Woodhouse) sustains, by virtue of the impossibility of that identification, the equilibrium that Miller describes as Style's transcendent impassivity. In *Persuasion,* on the other hand, the narration falls into personification. The movement from *Emma* to *Persuasion* is enacted in Miller's own "daredevil" beginning, which evokes the "siren lure" of Austen's texts: a reader's absorbed self-loss mirrors the magisterial—because absolutely unmarked—Style that therefore excited the fantasy of a like impassivity, a fantasy that in turn threatens the reader with abjection through the particular social identity ("woman," "gay man") legible, for observers, in that very dream of transcendence. Like the power of a cruelly placed mirror to return one, insuperably, to a particular body, a particular gait, at the moment when one's retreat into abstraction has achieved its fondest remove, absorption has the potential to turn into shame when one reflects that one is, in one's very absorption, nevertheless visible.

Miller's terms are strikingly apt for *The Wings of the Dove*—in which the narrative's movements "closer" to and "farther" from the perspectives of the characters dictate what have come to seem its "moral" conundrums, and in which the "personification" of the characters is in question perhaps no less than that of the narrator. In Miller's account of *Persuasion,* the equilibrium of Style is disrupted by a character moving too close to the narrator; Anne's witheringly unforgiving view of herself closes the distance between her and the narration, foreclosing the narrative's margin of ironical comment by comprising a sort of narrative perspective (71–73). In *The Wings of the Dove,* something similar happens, but with different results: the characters seem to view themselves as if in the mode of free indirect narration, to achieve a depersonalizing equipoise of proximity and distance in relation, paradoxically, to themselves. The result is a form of nonpsychological identification, one whose rigors (which depersonalization, or Miller's "impersonal intimacy," might describe) form another facet of the queerness of James's late style.

James's novel might be said to be about, simply, perspective. If the plot of *The Golden Bowl* in some sense "is" the effects of language named by syllepsis or zeugma, *The Wings of the Dove* is perhaps a story of perspective that might be conceptualized through free indirect style: free indirect style as plot. To begin with the simplest, though not the least consequential, level, the shifts among the more or less indirect renderings of particular "centers" bring to the fore identificatory dynamics of reading, demonstrating their power to shape effects of sympathy and "moral" judgment. (It is arguable that the long tradition of moralizing readings of the novel enacts, more or less blindly, the power of these identificatory movements within the narrative to extort judgments.)[2]

Locally, the various virtuosic shifts in the course of a given sentence, the minute calibrations of the narrative's proximity to and distance from the perspectives it inhabits, lead one to suspect that the foregrounded possibility of such calibration, and of such effects of proximity, might in fact be the point.[3] More globally, the novel's largest "moral" questions are shaped by perspective: one thinks, for instance, of the difference it would make for one's understanding of the use Kate Croy and Merton Densher make of Milly Theale were the novel to have remained focalized, as it is at the beginning, through Kate. Kate's particular plight, which is palpable in the first book, weighs less heavily in critical assessments of the end partly because the intervening perspectives of Milly, Susan, and, finally, Densher make us forget, for instance, the implicit demands of the Condrips, and the less implicit ones of Aunt Maud, make us almost forget, even, Kate's poverty. Beyond the sympathies created at specific moments and the readings that might follow from them, this effect seems in itself to be of interest to the text. When Densher's (or, for that matter, Kate's) thoughts about Milly are rendered—"It might be true of her also that if she weren't a bore she'd be a convenience" (193); "It was perhaps pathetic for her [Milly], and for himself was perhaps even ridiculous; but he hadn't even the amount of curiosity that he would have had about an ordinary friend. . . . He was acting for Kate—not, by the deviation of an inch, for her friend. He was accordingly not interested, for had he been interested he would have cared, and had he cared he would have wanted to know" (296)[4]—the seeming callousness is striking less for anything it reveals about the characters than for what it makes visible about narrative perspective's power to shape effects of sympathy. Visible is the difference made by the narrative's having moved "closer" to Milly and having to a certain degree "withdrawn" from Kate.

Other, less thematically freighted moments come to mind, such as the wavering authority of Susan Stringham. This is a perhaps common effect in late James, where seemingly functional, sometimes even parodic, characters suddenly assume a striking acuity, and, with it, an authority, only to recede again a few pages or chapters later. Such transitions leave uncertain whether the authority lent to such characters rewards an acuity we are to imagine operating all the while, even when the narrative is not attending to it, or whether such moments reveal, instead, the narrative's power to shape our sense of reality, unveil, that is, an illusion generated by the focalization's moving into a character's orbit. It never seems absolutely clear whether that authority comes from a disinterested judgment of the perspective or from an inhabiting of it, whether the narrative voice is assessing, or simply taking on, a character's view of him or herself (or the view of a more or less interested or invested or deluded bystander). Not just authority but also its receding might be conceptualized this way: the diminished acuity (of Susan, for instance) sometimes seems to be a function of the narrative's sharing the perspective of characters (for instance, Kate) who aren't interested in it. There are yet other possibilities. The narrative voice in (particularly, late) James has such authority that characters come to be more or less equivocally invested with it simply by being in its vicinity; we "feel with a strange mixed passion," as we are told of Densher's view of Kate, "the mastery of her mere way of putting things" (292). Yet another possibility is that acuity itself is intermittent—that it is determined by certain situations or simply emerges at uneven intervals, so that at very particular moments otherwise imperceptive characters suddenly have unexpected insight. Like sympathy and moral judgment in the novel's larger plot, such effects of intermittent acuity raise—and, in this novel, perhaps thematize—questions of the narrative voice's proximity and distance to characters whose consistency is thereby simultaneously put into doubt.

It is not a matter, in short, of determining whether Susan is "really" acute—or Kate brutal—or of determining what Milly "knows." For the "impersonal intimacy" that Miller charts in free indirect style troubles a topography that would give characters "insides" and "outsides," a topography upon which the ostensible personhood of characters depends. Thus, late James is a particularly fertile place to look at the effect that Ann Banfield traces in free indirect style: the necessity of conceptualizing, in linguistic terms, sentences that are not—that cannot be—uttered by anyone. "Voice" and "perspective" in free indirect style are in this sense not functions of a person.[5] (That is the "germ" of the depersonalizing identification I chart in the novel.) "Essence," writes Gilles Deleuze,

> is not something seen but a kind of superior *viewpoint,* an irreducible viewpoint that signifies at once the birth of the world and the original character of a world. It is in this sense that the work of art always constitutes and reconstitutes the beginning of the world, but also forms a specific world absolutely different from the others and *envelops a landscape or immaterial site quite distinct from the site where we have grasped it.* Doubtless it is this aesthetic of the point

of view that relates Proust to Henry James. But the important thing is that the viewpoint transcends the individual no less than the essence transcends the mood, the state of the soul; the viewpoint remains superior to the person who assumes it or guarantees the identity of all those who attain it. *It is not individual, but on the contrary a principle of individuation.*[6]

In his seminar on Leibniz, Deleuze again mentions James and point of view. James's innovation in the novel, he suggests, is a "perspectivism," a "mobilization of points of view" in which—*"c'est beau et c'est même poétique"*—the subject comes to be that which is determined by inhabiting a certain point of view: for James as for Leibniz, "it is the point of view that explains the subject and not the inverse."[7] Such a conception is perhaps most strikingly true in *The Wings of the Dove*, where the novel's great axes of difference—wealth, illness, acuity, gender, desire, national origin—often strike one as less the attributes of persons than as ways of articulating differentials of perspective. Paired with Banfield's "unspeakable" sentences, Deleuze's remarks condense the effect of free indirect style in late James, and the curiously nonpsychological understanding of point of view that animates these texts.

In *The Wings of the Dove*, such effects of free indirect style and focalization emerge in a striking textual effect before they ever emerge thematically. If the governing trope of *The Golden Bowl* is perhaps zeugma, *The Wings of the Dove* is presided over by a particular syntactical structure, a form of apposition or quasi-"extraposition" (in Otto Jespersen's term for a form of apposition that leaves a "word, or a group of words" stranded "outside the sentence as if it had nothing to do there"):[8]

She waited, Kate Croy, for her father to come in.... (21)[9]

She knew herself now, the sensitive niece, as having been marked from far back. (36)

She painted, patient lady, famous pictures in great museums.... (71)

She knew, the clever lady, what the principle itself represented.... (79)

They found, her eyes, it should be added, other occupation as well. ... (175)

But she *passed*, the poor performer—he could see how she always passed.... (204)

He met, poor Densher, these inquiries as he could.... (205)

She believed she made out besides, wonderful girl, that he had never quite expected.... (272)

She asked, it was true, Aunt Maud, questions that Kate hadn't.... (367)

Typically, a verb intervenes between the pronoun and the noun phrase in apposition, which foregrounds both the reflection in the renaming and the interruption of that reflection. The delayed resolution of syntactical inversions or suspensions often makes such structures of apposition even more conspicuous:

Literally, furthermore, it wouldn't really depend on herself, Sir Luke Strett's friendship, in the least. (143)

They had plenty, on these lines, the two elder women, to give and to take.... (111)

[I]t came, as a subject for indifference, money did, easier to some people than to others.... (125)

Such repetitions also appear within parenthetical phrases ("She saw already—wonderful creature, after all, herself too—that there would be a good deal more of him to come for her . . ." [107]), and they mark sometimes not just the subject of a sentence but also its object or predicative:

To see her alone, the poor girl, he none the less promptly felt, was to see her after all very much on the old basis.... (224)

[T]he only delicate and honorable way of treating a person in such a state was to treat her as *he*, Merton Densher, did.... Lord Mark had, without in the least intending such a service, got it straight out of the way. It was *he*, the brute, who had stumbled into just the wrong inspiration.... (329)

Kate's most constant feeling about her was that she [Marian, "Kate's elder and Kate's own"] would make her, Kate, do things.... (38)

In the most general terms, the novel's syntax is marked by a doubling of the subject ("The sustaining sense of it all moreover as literary material—that quite dropped from her" [111]), a renaming by pronoun or appositive that has the effect of a reflection—or a stutter. Gallicisms, perhaps, of a sort that, if more marked in this novel, are not uncommon in James's writing, these particular structures nevertheless link idiosyncrasies of the novel's style to larger interpretive questions.

On the level of character, these syntactical structures suggest a dynamic of expropriation legible as "alienation," a distancing, for instance, of a proper name ("Kate Croy") or a descriptive noun phrase ("patient lady") from the pronoun and verb that express their action in a given sentence. (Such forms literally remove the subject from the sentence, or, in Jespersen's terms, "extraposition" them.) This is one of the most striking effects of the first sentence of the novel, which leaves Kate Croy in a sense stranded outside the novel she initiates:

> She waited, Kate Croy, for her father to come in, but he kept her unconscionably, and there were moments at which she showed herself, in the glass over the mantle, a face positively pale with the irritation that had brought her to the point of going away without sight of him. (21)

Disarticulating Kate Croy from "she waited," the syntax enacts the gaze into the mirror that the novel depicts.[10] The sentence, moreover, details a strangely expropriated cognition: Kate does not "feel" irritation but rather shows herself "a face positively pale with the irritation that had brought her to the point of going away without sight of him." Making "show" reflexive is more alienating than consolidating in relation to the "self" it "reflects," and feeling is a matter of external signs—signs, moreover, that have to be read. The mirror shows her the appearance that might, in turn, explain the action she had been brought "to the point" of taking. Such a perception is alienating because it erodes any ground for assuming the existence of a cognition or feeling (or self) prior to this externalized perception. To gloss the novel's syntactical inversions as "alienation" therefore potentially domesticates the effect; it is uncertain whether such effects even refer to a self. The mirror doesn't seem to "reflect" a feeling; rather it seems to attest to an externalization, an instrumental mode of sensation. Kate seems to "feel" outside of herself—that is, not to feel alienated (to feel *herself* as alien) but rather to experience feeling in an externalized mode. Kate's redoubtable lucidity—the clear-sightedness that Michael Wood, for instance, emphasizes in the novel—is, partly, an effect of this external-ized perception.[11]

One characteristic difficulty of James's late fiction is its crossing of differ-ent logics—often to indeterminate effect. The overlapping of style and plot in *The Golden Bowl* is one instance, and syllepsis and zeugma offer a way, more generally, to conceptualize such crossings. One thinks, for example, of the parallel preoccupations of *What Maisie Knew*: on the one hand, a particular child's predicament as she is shuttled between parents and step-parents and, on the other, the difficulty posed by narrating a novel from an unrepresentable perspective. Or, in different terms, the novel presents both a narrative of development—of a consciousness coming to be—and a study of linguistic effects that, pointing to the constitution of a system of tropes as a form of exchange, resist being understood developmentally, or indeed, as functions of consciousness.[12] Similarly, *The Spoils of Poynton* presents per-fectly plausible psychological motivations—Mrs. Gereth's and Felda Vetch's paired, but perhaps not complementary, drives to thwart their own desires—and an aesthetic causality—the particular aesthetic logic of Poynton itself as an indivisible aesthetic whole. The former leads both Mrs. Gereth and Fleda to torpedo their ostensible desires on the eve of their realization. The latter dictates that Fleda not possess Owen, and that Poynton incinerate itself to remain, likewise, unpossessed—and, indeed, leads Fleda to desire an Owen whose attractiveness is perhaps otherwise unfathomable in the first place. Both causalities are fully elaborated while being, at the same time, incom-patible, if only because the latter pursues to its limit James's suggestion that the beautiful objects are the novel's central characters—and these objects certainly are the things (or "the Things, the splendid Things") that, in the preface's description of the novel, are most alive and most accorded the faculty of consciousness.[13] James's late novels present exhaustive examina-tions of various (ethical, epistemological, sexual, and so on) modalities of consciousness; such modalities are fully articulated and sometimes even coextensive without thereby proving interdependent, interrelated, or even mutually governed. Linked in ways analogous to the yoking performed by zeugma, such exhaustively charted modalities, because their governing by a single agency seems more grammatical than organic, therefore emerge in nonpsychological terms.

The opening of *The Wings of the Dove* might be read both in thematico-psychological terms and in terms of the "impersonal intimacy" of free indirect style. ("She waited, Kate Croy" might be read both as evidence of psychological "alienation" and as a reflection on the novel's free indirect mode, a moment of reflexivity that is as if a calibrating of the free indirect style.) The thematic and psychological reading is perfectly plausible, and the novel's opening chapter links Kate's externalized perspective to particular thematic elements and psychological determinants—to Lionel Croy's unspecified and possibly sexual shame and to the constraints of economic dependency.[14] In such terms, the novel's opening signals various aspects of Kate's excruciating position of dependence; the externalization might be read as a consequence of that position and of Kate's particular relation to her father. Lionel's peculiarly insinuating apartment is one that reverses polarities of inside and out. The armchair's upholstery "gave at once—she had tried it—the sense of the slippery and the sticky" (21). The distressing tendency of matter to adhere to one renders Lionel's—and his apartment's—power of insinuation.[15] The sticky furniture complements a vulgarity figured as a lack of privacy:

> The vulgar little street, in this view, offered scant relief from the vulgar little room; its main office was to suggest to her that the narrow black house-fronts, adjusted to a standard that would have been low even for backs, constituted quite the publicity implied by such privacies. One felt them in the room exactly as one felt the room—the hundred like it or worse—in the street. (21)

The syntactical parallels ("vulgar little street . . . vulgar little room"; "one felt them in the room exactly as one felt the room . . . in the street") and the condensed expressions of reversal ("the publicity implied by such privacies") point to the strangely inside-out topography of this room (the topography, in condensed form, that Eve Kosofsky Sedgwick traces in the novel: a turning inside out that is also a merging of front and back). Sticky, slippery furniture, or Lionel's insinuating power to make you feel, while visiting him, that you are the one compromised by his apartment: both might be read to figure an experience of dependence. Kate's gaze into the mirror at her collected beauty—and the larger plot she concocts—attempt to ward off this power of insinuation and, of course, the poverty it reflects.

Other psychological and thematic readings would be possible. The thematic resonances, however, are perhaps less crucial than (and may even be the aftereffects of) the coming together of conceptual questions of identification with the effect of narrative "proximity" and "distance" in free indirect style. "She waited, Kate Croy": the effect of that syntactical repetition, linked, moreover, to an exchange between Kate and the room in which we first encounter her, might represent the expropriating potential of identification. The inside-out topography of Lionel's rooms thus marks not the predicament of one particular character, but a generalizable predicament of character, or identity, as such. The "vulgar little room" simply provides an image for the syntactical structures of extraposition, which, notably, are not tied to any particular character but mark the style as a whole. "Extraposition" is, in this sense, the syntax of identification; indeed, Sedgwick's reading of the novel also suggests that we see in the novel's opening a figure of identification writ large. Tracing the identificatory effects of Lionel Croy's ostentatiously unspeakable crime, Sedgwick shows an identification with (the refused possibility of) male homosexuality at the heart of gender and sexual "identity" in the novel. Emphasizing the "urgency in understanding queer people as not only *what the world makes* but *what makes the world*" (93), she sees in the novel the possibility of recasting in the mode of "queer tutelage" certain psychoanalytically inspired narratives of subjective genesis. Thus, for instance, Lionel's "preterited homosexual disgrace" (86) is, she suggests, central to the novel, but it is not, properly speaking, a paternal or Oedipal effect; his disgrace forms Milly's desire and gender identity, too. Sedgwick's reading captures in an exemplary way the tendency of identificatory effects to exert an influence not only beyond any (drearily) predictable Oedipal orbit, but also according to logics that are perhaps more properly textual and linguistic than psychological—even if psychological effects travel in their wake.

A series of moments, Sedgwick notes, has "Milly [respond] to the sight of Kate's splendor by experiencing her own visual faculty as demonically possessed by a man and alienated from herself" (Sedgwick, 86).[16] Milly, that is, suddenly sees Kate through Merton's eyes:

What was also, however, determined for [Milly] was, again, yet
irrepressibly again, that the image presented to her, the splendid
young woman who looked so particularly handsome in impatience,
with the fine freedom of her signal, was the peculiar property of

somebody else's vision, that this fine freedom in short was the fine freedom she showed Mr. Densher. Just so was how she looked to him, and just so was how Milly was held by her—held as by the strange sense of seeing through that distant person's eyes. (157; see also 122, 133, 166)

Yet another moment of apposition, the coalescence of gazes also emerges through—one may even dare say because of—a particular syntax in the novel, the tendency of different subjects to converge ambiguously on a single pronoun. That convergence is thematized by the (almost) parallel syntax, which makes active and passive forms mirror one another: "just so was how she looked . . . , and just so was how Milly was held." The mirroring seems to fracture in the second clause, creating a stutter: "just so was . . . just so was . . . was," or "was how . . . was held." (As with Kate's gaze into the mirror, the question is perhaps whether the syntactical structure reflects or creates the identificatory one.) On the level of character, the habitual fracturing of Milly's gaze offers several alternatives for interpretation: that Milly, for whatever reason, can experience her desire for Merton only by way of Kate, for instance, or that Merton allows her to experience her desire for Kate ("'If I were a man, I should simply adore her. In fact I do as it is.' It was a luxury of response" [275]). The alternatives would depend, that is, on one's particular parsing of the relation between identification and desire.

A third interpretation, however, would see not opposed alternatives but the structure of Milly's desire *tout court*; her desire is from the outset circuited through their relation (a desire not for either Kate or Merton but rather for their desire for each other). Seen in these terms, it is not clear that Milly is the "victim" of money-seeking aspiration. It isn't just Milly, though, whose desire can be described this way. Desire in the novel is not the provenance of a couple: the various people who intervene between the desiring and ostensibly thwarted pair—Milly, Aunt Maud, Lord Mark, even Sir Luke Strett and Susan Stringham—are perhaps less impediments to the desire of Kate and Merton than constitutive elements of it. Desire in the novel is always crossed with various forms of identification, and it is always circuited through one or more others who are therefore never "outside" the desire they ostensibly interrupt. Densher might be said to misconstrue this relation; the narrative of betrayal and guilt through which he moralizes Milly's death (followed in this, as he is, by many of the novel's critics) would depend on seeing his desires for Kate and Milly as alternatives, on seeing desire as sheltered only in a couple. Kate's burning of Milly's letter is, in these terms, a mistake if we see in it an effort to possess (Merton) and exclude (Milly); if instead it is an effort to make Milly a permanent part of her relation to Merton, it is once again Densher who fails to be adequate to Kate's lucidity. (This structure extends outward in the novel. One thinks, for instance, of Susan Stringham's "passion" for Milly and one's sense that her desire extends to Densher, and not merely for Milly's sake. The violence of Lord Mark's Venetian demystification would be, in part, its forcible insistence that desire be legible in the form of an erotic couple.) To put all of this another way, if (to return to the terms above), we reverse our perspective and see the blurrings of identification and desire as generated by—or as secondary to—the syntactical inversions, we begin to perceive an unnerving potential in the psychological readings themselves. The terms, therefore, are ostensibly psychological, but the disruptions of the tyranny of the couple pursue an antipsychological logic that turns consciousness inside out. (Jacques Lacan's dictum that there is no sexual relation, which interrupts the understanding of sexual difference as complementary, not only disrupts normative understandings of sexuality but also presents a potentially antipsychological understanding of desire.) To moralize the novel in terms that depend on the redistribution of couples—who is inside, who out—serves, perhaps above all, to protect the "insides" of characters, to protect character and psychology as such.

Taking Milly's fractured gaze as neither (necessarily) a feint nor an evasion or a disavowal, but as an intimation of the structure of desire in the text also makes some sense of perplexing moments—difficult to explain psychologically—that suggest Milly's cognizance of Merton and Kate's engagement. Thus, for instance, Milly asks Kate to accompany her on her first visit to Sir Luke Strett because, we are told, "she had wanted to prove to herself that she didn't horribly blame her friend for any reserve; and what better proof could there be than this quite special confidence? If she desired to show Kate that she really believed Kate liked her, how could she show it more than by asking her help?" (142). The curious transition is that between Milly's wanting "to prove to herself" and her desiring "to show *Kate* that she really believed Kate liked her." The question, in terms of plot and psychology, of why Milly might "horribly blame her friend"— the possibility at least emerges that Milly's invitation registers an intuition of the lovers' intimacy—is here posed through a leveling of difference between Kate and Milly. The question of what Milly "knows" encounters the puzzle, first, of why Milly should have to perform an action in order to persuade herself of her own feelings (as if, like Kate in Lionel's apartment, her internal states were externalized and cognizable only as external perceptions—an effect redoubled by the attributed need to prove that Kate's "liking," too, is visible), and, second, of why proving her feeling to herself is synonymous with showing it to Kate—why, relatedly, Kate's "reserve" can be compensated by Milly's "confidence."

If such identificatory blurrings mark a structure of desire, they also describe, simply, the way the novel is narrated. "She waited, Kate Croy," like the scenario of the gaze into the mirror that is there described, might figure structures not only of desire and identification, but also of the novel's mode of narration. The novel habitually renders the exposition of characters' backgrounds through conveyed reports to third parties, usually of what has by then already been told: the story of Lionel Croy, or as much as we learn of it, is presented less in the initial description of Kate's visit to his rooms than later, through Densher's view of it; Densher's background, too, is given by way of his report to Kate of what he has told Aunt Maud (70–71). The reader—like, often, the characters involved—arrives at such information belatedly. That temporal lag is linked to a point of view fractured, or made vicarious. For both Kate and Milly, the first mention of Densher (as, presumably, an object of desire) comes from someone else (for Kate, Marian, and, for Milly, Susan Stringham), and Milly, of course, enters the novel with her back to us, first appears in Susan's gaze at her. Kate's expropriated gaze at the beginning of the novel is all the more striking in light of the consequent intimation that she comprises this externalized view "in" herself. However one reads James's famous habit of "going behind" his characters, Kate seems able to "go behind" herself;[17] the novel's opening thus unites a structure of narration with structures of identification and desire "within" the text. Desire and identification are, curiously, narrative rather than psychological effects—or are psychological categories shown to be produced as secondary effects of narrative logics. To put this another way, the narration of the novel is caught up in the desire it depicts (or, rather, desire is caught up in the narration that depicts it); desire in *The Wings of the Dove*, it might be said, takes shape as free indirect style rendered *en abîme*. The kind of topographies we encounter in *The Golden Bowl* as a consequence of the novel's figurative language— and, for that novel, the global trope of zeugma, culminating in the visible emergence of the house of fiction in Maggie's garden—is here the result of a narration turned as it were inside out.

Evoking Kate's initial gaze into her father's mirror, the emphasis when Densher first appears is on a dislocated perspective, here implicitly identified with that of a reader:

> Merton Densher, who passed the best hours of each night at the office of his newspaper, had at times, during the day, to make up for it, a sense, or at least an appearance, of leisure, in accordance with which he was not infrequently to be met in different parts of the town at moments when men of business are hidden from the public eye. More than once during the present winter's end he had deviated toward three o'clock, or toward four, into Kensington Gardens, where he might for a while, on each occasion, have been observed to demean himself as a person with nothing to do. (45)

The emphasis as the passage continues is on visibility: "his behaviour was *noticeably* wanting in point. . . . *Distinctly* he was a man either with nothing at all to do or with ever so much to think about," and we are told of "the impression he might often thus easily make" (45). Emphasized, on one level, is a body exposed, displayed as other male bodies are not (those of "men of business . . . hidden from the public eye"). (This sense of exposure, we might speculate, could have something to do with the transition between "demean himself" as it is used here—to behave with an eye toward social decorum or the observation of others—and the sense of degradation audible in the phrase now. The literal use of "deviate" follows, as it were, a similar path.) His frustration of a taxonomical gaze is a consequence of his visibility: "it was almost impossible to name his profession" (46).

The passage also dramatizes equivocalities of distance between him and the narration. Reading that his behavior is "noticeably wanting in point," one hesitates between an externalized view of him (he is, unlike the businessmen, wandering aimlessly, exposed, moreover, to public view) and a rendering of his own imagining of how he ought to appear. He is headed, in other words, to meet Kate, and so his aimlessness has a certain theatrical quality to it. Thus, when we are told that Densher "had, at times, . . . a sense, or at least an appearance, of leisure," the hesitation between internal sense and external perception presents, in terms of narrative distance, (at least) two options: a distancing (asserting that we can know his appearance, but not

his "sense"—a withdrawal from narrative omniscience); or a closer proximity (where the gap between inside and out renders Densher's own self-
conscious projection or self-awareness, which, in turn, can have the effect
either of drawing a reader closer to Densher's predicament or of distancing
the reader by exposing Densher's calculation in the theatricalizing of that
predicament). As with "She waited, Kate Croy" and the depiction of her
gaze into the mirror, the possibility emerges of a character's gaze at himself
coinciding with a free indirect rendering of his consciousness. The character's consciousness presents, as it were, a free indirect gaze at itself, which
compels us to think about a character's mind at a greater or lesser distance
from, taking a more or less ironized perspective on, "itself." The minimal difference necessary for this relation implies, in short, that the character cannot
coincide with himself; narration, in this sense, alienates the perspective it
renders. (That also means that it is perhaps difficult to talk about free indirect style at all insofar as the uncertainty extends not only to the distance
between narrator and character but also to the discrete existence of anything
like a "character" whose view is to be distanced from, or, on the contrary,
assimilated to, that of the narrator.) When one then attempts to read Densher's presenting "the sense, or at least the appearance, of leisure" as itself
a "rendering" of consciousness—deciding, for instance, the proximity or
distance of the narration from the depicted consciousness—the question
becomes undecidable, abyssal. (More simply, if a character's thought centers on the difference between his thoughts and the appearance he creates,
the registering of that difference puts the free indirect equipoise of proximity and distance *en abîme*.) As with Milly, the question is, too, the difficulty
of determining what Densher "knows"—and of what the narration at that
moment can be said to "know" about him. The paradoxes of knowledge in
the text are at the same time questions of proximity and distance in free indirect narration, even if these questions also subvert the terms through which
one would locate free indirect style "in" the text.

The dispropriated perspective that marks Kate's gaze at herself at the
beginning of the novel recurs at many other moments. Here, for instance,
is Densher, after his return to London, contemplating, in conferences with
Aunt Maud, his life in Venice and his last interview with Milly:

> He himself for that matter took in the scene again at moments as
> from the page of a book. He saw a young man far off and in a rela-
> tion inconceivable, saw him hushed, passive, staying his breath, but

half understanding, yet dimly conscious of something immense
and holding himself painfully together not to lose it. The young
man at these moments so seen was too distant and too strange for
the right identity; and yet, outside, afterwards, it was his own face
Densher had known. He had known then at the same time what
the young man had been conscious of, and he was to measure after
that, day by day, how little he had lost. (369)

Densher's view of "the young man" replays the gaze of "She waited, Kate
Croy"; initially "too distant and too strange for the right identity," when
brought closer, it enables a form of self-recognition, but its expropriating
phrasing attests to the alienation implicit in that consolidation: "it was his
own face Densher had known." Moreover, the highlighted temporality—
the recognition lags behind itself—explicitly leaves a temporal gap separating knowledge not only from the recognition but also (the past perfect
suggests) from the later state that reflects on that knowledge. The depersonalizing "it," which makes the consolidating moment of recognition also
one of objectifying alienation, replays the sealing off of the verb *to know*
from any present tense—too late for realization, it seems to pass away too
soon for cognition or narration.

The obliquity and potential alienation describe both Densher's view of
the mysterious "event" and the need to suppress details in his telling of it
to Aunt Maud: "He had been, in his recovered sense, forgiven, dedicated,
blessed; but this he couldn't coherently express. It would have required an
explanation—fatal to Mrs. Lowder's faith in him—of the nature of Milly's
wrong. So, as to the wonderful scene, they just stood at the door" (370).
The distance and strangeness thus register both that he tells the story to
a particular, invested listener and, perhaps, that he evades his own guilty
conscience. Both the asserted immediacy and the effect of alienation are
captured by the particular quality of absorption—namely, the experience
of reading: "He himself for that matter took in the scene again at moments
as from the page of a book." As with Kate, the possibility emerges (as the
redoubled naming—"he himself"—suggests) of his viewing himself as
narrated in a free indirect mode. It is perhaps also unclear where and when
"outside" and "afterwards" are located: the description that follows, by
figuratively positing a scene that Densher and Aunt Maud visit together,
leaves open the question of whether realization takes place "outside" this
constituted fictional space or "outside" Aunt Maud's house after Densher

leaves it (conflating two levels of narration while reminding us, too, that Aunt Maud's is no less fictional a space). A similar equivocation marks Densher's sense that "he had been, in his recovered sense, forgiven, dedicated, blessed." "In his recovered sense" leaves unresolved whether the statement is a constative or a performative one, whether he remembers the forgiving, dedicating, blessing (or realizes that it had occurred), or whether the sanctifying moment occurs in his remembering of the earlier time. The temporal quandary of "*in* his recovered sense" is rendered as an indeterminate space, an uncertain enclosure or interior. Wherever it is, the interior is identified with a consciousness that is, or that has been, out of synch with itself: "his *recovered* sense." The equivocations of the event "too beautiful and sacred to describe" (370) mark, perhaps, what it means for Densher to view himself in a scene taken "from the page of a book."

Such moments of externalized gazes repeatedly evoke identification: for instance, "As she saw herself, suddenly, he saw her" (304)—where, moreover, the gaze identified with is itself already an externalized one. The later moment with Densher thus returns us to the novel's opening, where what initially seems a conventional gesture of characterization (a character's gaze into a mirror supplies the opportunity to describe her) becomes a figure for identification—and for its unsettlingly dispropriating potential. It seems possible (and this might be implicit in her account) to emphasize in Sedgwick's assertion that "no role model, no ego ideal, Lionel Croy presents the most demeaned and demeaning figure imaginable in the novel" not only the "shaping pressure" Lionel brings to "bear on his world" by transforming it "in the image of his specific queer stigmatization" but also a certain groundlessness in identification (Sedgwick, 79). Lionel's queerness, in other words, registers as a tangible effect of a refusal of "models" as such—a particular groundlessness that perpetually marks the novel's meditations on identification.[18] In one of the moments where Milly sees Kate through Densher's eyes, "Milly found herself seeing Kate, quite fixing her, in the light of the knowledge that it was a face on which Mr. Densher's eyes had more or less familiarly rested and which, by the same token, had looked, rather *more* beautifully than less, into his own" (122). The fracturing of Milly's perspective is paired with the odd effect of the adverb *beautifully*, which describes how Kate looked looking—depicting her gaze, too, as it is seen, from the outside, by Densher. The effect is compounded by the implied parallel between *familiarly* and *beautifully* (not only the morphological homology, but the implied parallel quality, emphasized by the italics, that both terms are subject to intensification or reduction, can be "more" or "less"), which conflates a gaze or way of looking with an appearance or object seen. Compared, too, are Densher's *eyes* and Kate's *face*, which is thereby given a gaze only to be rendered a beautiful surface to be looked at looking. To *look* beautifully: the moment brings out the potential for both uncanny exchange and depersonifying objectification as a look turns to "looks"—a surface depersonified and potentially reanimated, looking back. All of these circuits could be described in terms of identification—including Milly's seeming identification with identification as such (beyond any particular figures to be identified "with")—but in a curiously recursive, reflexive form.

Even the names in the novel return us to potentially groundless structures of reflection—effects of assonance, consonance, and alliteration marking paired syllables in every name: Kate Croy, Merton Densher, Milly Theale, Susan Stringham (or Shepherd).[19] The proliferation of Ms has a similar effect: Milly, Merton, Maud, Mark. (Milly's is the only name not metrically paired as well—as spondee [Kate Croy, Lord Mark, Aunt Maud] or paired trochees [Merton Densher, Susan Stringham, Susan Shepherd].) Such effects traverse the entire novel and bring together disparate registers—the name "Kate Croy," for instance, with the syntax of "She waited, Kate Croy," with the questions of identification thematized there, with the novel's free indirect narration. One is therefore but following the text's own mode when one moves from the names to another famous moment that presents an instance of reflection that might be paired with Kate's gaze into Lionel's mirror: Milly's encounter with the Bronzino painting in the second chapter of Book Five. The curiously recursive form taken by identification is here explicitly (as it is elsewhere implicitly) linked to the belated structure of identification as an anticipation of what one will have been. Leaving uncertain where one "is" in that play of reflection, identity is suspended in a temporal lag. An uncertain temporality and a to-be-constituted object of reflection: such is the frame for Milly's intimations of mortality. Her self-recognition—and the constitution of her illness—takes shape as she sees herself in a painting, then sees herself as others see her, and, finally, imagines how someone she sees will look to someone else looking at her. (The moment leads to her fracturing sight of Kate as seen by Densher and then to her inviting Kate to accompany her to the doctor.) The scene has been read many times; I would emphasize in it just a few details. In "the pink dawn of an apotheosis coming so curiously soon," Milly discovers that "it was she herself who said all":

She couldn't help that—it came; and the reason it came was that she found herself, for the first moment, looking at the mysterious portrait through tears. Perhaps it was her tears that made it just then so strange and fair—as wonderful as he had said: the face of a young woman, all splendidly drawn, down to the hands, and splendidly dressed; a face almost livid in hue, yet handsome in sadness and crowned with a mass of hair, rolled back and high, that must, before fading with time, have had a family resemblance to her own. The lady in question, at all events, with her slightly Michael-angelesque squareness, her eyes of other days, her full lips, her long neck, her recorded jewels, her brocaded and wasted reds, was a very great personage—only unaccompanied by a joy. And she was dead, dead, dead. Milly recognized her exactly in words that had nothing to do with her. "I shall never be better than this." (137)

The "apotheosis" that marks Milly's intuition of her mortality is figurally an assumption of her body into art.[20] This apotheosis seems almost to constitute Milly's disease, and her fading into art is curiously rendered as her later discovery of having spoken, of having "said all."

That Milly's gaze at the Bronzino might be paired with her gaze at Kate is suggested by the adjective "handsome" that describes both of them, and, indeed, the exchange with the painting evokes (with the terms reversed) an earlier description of Kate: "the handsome girl from the heavy English house had been as a figure in a picture stepping by magic out of its frame" (111). Milly's Matcham encounter with the painting also evokes the novel's opening description of Kate because of the similar trouble it presents for specifying a locus of perception, and the apotheosis into art, taking shape through a fracturing of vision, might likewise be read to figure a relay between the novel's identificatory and narrative logics.[21] The first difficulty for this scene of "recognition" is introduced by Milly's tears. The self-recognition is blurred from the outset, leaving open the possibility that the recognition is possible because her vision is blurry. More important, though, is the assertion of causality: "the reason it came was that she found herself, for the first moment, looking at the mysterious portrait through tears." On one level, the moment seems to assert that "recognition" has outpaced cognition, that Milly has seen the resemblance which her tears then allow her to cognize. But a more unsettling possibility also emerges of a groundless relation: her tears make possible the recognition that they are also generated by. Milly's recognition, moreover, repeats a series of waverings "in" the painting: "splendidly drawn," for instance, describes both the fact of representation ("drawn" as in well-executed or depicted) and the model's (and Milly's) appearance ("drawn" as in haggard). The "wearing" of illness (its effects on a body) is made analogous to the effect of representation in art. That overlap, in turn, is figured by the implied parallelism of the artist's and the model's work of representation: "splendidly drawn . . . splendidly dressed."

Likewise, the description equivocates on where (in time) to locate the wearing away described. That the woman's hair "must, before fading with time, have had a family resemblance" to Milly's leaves in question whether the fading took place before or after the painting was created—did it occur, that is, to the woman's hair or to the paint that captured it?[22] Similarly, her "eyes of other days" leads us to wonder whether the days are "other" to Milly or to the moment in which they were painted. (Such effects are also captured in the transition to past participles in the description of the painting—"her full lips, her long neck, her recorded jewels, her brocaded and wasted reds"—where the parallel forms [recorded . . . brocaded . . . wasted] intimate a link between the wasting exacted by time and the fact of representation [recorded . . . wasted] and intimate, too, a collapsing of temporal difference [between the "past" of (in relation to) the painting, the past where the "brocading" would have taken place and where the model herself would have wasted away to her depicted state, and the painting as the past, where the jewels have become "recorded jewels" and the painting itself has been subject to "wasting"].) Part of the appeal of the painting's subject—and her capacity to excite recognition on Milly's part—seems to be the way she is already, the moment she is painted, strangely posthumous. Beyond a temporal gap separating various loci of identification, what is described here seems to be an identification with a temporal gap. Milly's recognition, then, is framed in particularly disorienting terms: "Milly recognized her exactly in words that had nothing to do with her. 'I shall never be better than this.'"

The moment presents a number of ambiguities: first, who is the second "her," Milly or the woman in the painting? Context might favor the painting, but the ambiguity that nevertheless remains condenses the (potentially groundless) structure of identification in the scene; like the relation between the tears and the recognition, the possibility of deciding which "her" is meant recedes at the moment that the realization (and, with it, the

subsequent modalities of Milly's illness) is established.[23] Indeed, this literally is the form of Milly's identification: *I shall never be.* Similar, I think,
is the effect of the "exact" recognition that takes place "in words that had
nothing to do with her." To recognize "exactly" seems to be something
other than representative adequation or possession or the correlation of
objectifiable presences—whatever the appeal for the gathered spectators,
this does not seem to be a matter of Milly's looking "like" the painting.
If the second "her" is the woman in the painting, and the "this" refers to
Milly (though, as with "her," the "this" remains ambiguous enough for
Lord Mark to mistake its reference—"than she?"), then the "recognition"
links two entities by asserting that they have "nothing" to do with each
other. (The expected relation, moreover, is reversed, moving not from the
painting to Milly's self-recognition, but in the opposite direction, to words
about herself in which she "recognizes" the painting.) It seems to me, too,
that one ought to hold on to the oddity of a recognition "in" words—having nothing or everything to do with her. Idiomatically, the meaning might
be more like "Milly acknowledged her" (as a queen might, or anyone else
might, too, according to social decorum—or parliamentary etiquette), but
because the passage is about self-recognition, the phrase shades toward
the more unidiomatic sense that gives an interior to words and suggests
the possibility of vision being circuited through that space. In other terms,
the passage asks the reader to reconsider what is meant by perception or
"recognition," suggesting that it might occur in externalized (and, in this
sense, expropriating) form—and externalized, moreover, "in words."[24]

The groundlessness that marks the recognition from the outset in the
tears that blur the vision they make possible would then mark, too, the
recognition "in" words—and, by implication, might extend that groundlessness to the words of the novel itself. The recognition "in words" might
also be read in relation to the film of tears and to the temporal equivocation of the portrait's fading. Read in that context, the tears mark the
mediation of a gaze, the intervention of a narrative "voice"—the intervention that, by inserting a third time between the painting and Milly's recognition, to this extent forms the temporal equivocation. (Insofar as Milly
"recognizes" her mortality here, the moment implicitly links the time of
narrative and the time of death.) The tears, and the intuition of mortality
to which they bear witness, move between a psychological meaning and a
sort of becoming-visible "in" the text of narrative questions animating the
novel. Milly's particular predicament—to which I will return—consists, in

this sense, of a character's taking cognizance of the novel's narrative logic. As with the earlier moments involving Kate at the mirror and Densher demeaning himself, free indirect narration seems here to become an element of plot and theme. The moments that present turning points for character psychology also present a mixing of register like that of zeugma, the mode of narration becoming an "object" of narration. Free indirect "impersonal intimacy," Kate's turn from the indeterminate topographies of Lionel's room to a gaze at her own reflection, the novel's equivocal gaze at Densher's equivocal gaze at himself, and Milly's habitually fractured vision: the uncertain topography of this realization "in words" connects Milly's gaze at the Bronzino (and with it, her illness) to these narrative and identificatory logics.

The scene, moreover, presents a series of embedded "recognitions"; part of what Milly can recognize "in" the painting is her own gaze at it as a redoubling of everyone else's gaze at her. "Lady Aldershaw meanwhile looked at Milly quite as if Milly had been the Bronzino and the Bronzino only Milly" (139); Lady Aldershaw's gaze has been prepared by Kate, who has brought her to see the resemblance: "she had brought a lady and a gentleman to whom she wished to show what Lord Mark was showing Milly" (138). (The redoublement is again redoubled if one considers that "what Lord Mark was showing Milly" is, in a sense, the showing of Milly; the phrase perhaps also makes clear that the ambiguity of the object—insofar as "what Lord Mark was showing Milly" could name the painting, Mark's "point" to her about the resemblance, or the fact that others are seeing a resemblance—does not matter because the options boil down to the same thing.) This moment, moreover, leads to one of the characteristic fracturings of Milly's vision:

> It had come up, in the form in which she had had to accept it, all suddenly, and nothing about it, at the same time, was more marked than that she had in a manner plunged into it to escape from something else. Something else, from her first vision of her friend's appearance three minutes before, had been present to her even through the call made by the others on her attention; something that was perversely *there*, she was more and more uncomfortably finding, at least for the first moments and by some spring of its own, with every renewal of their meeting. "Is it the way she looks to *him*?" (140)

As Sedgwick points out, "something else" is also the closest the novel comes to defining Milly's illness: "'It's only that it isn't *the* case she herself supposed' [says Susan to Maud], 'It's another?' 'It's another.' 'Examining her for what she supposed he finds something else?' 'Something else.'" (246). The moment of Milly's realization of her illness is, simultaneously, her internalization (as themselves indifferent) of an overlapping series of gazes at her. Milly finds herself contemplating the painting to escape from "something else," just as the doctor, "examining her for what she supposed . . . finds something else." The groundlessness of the scene may therefore extend, too, to the "realization" depicted. As Cameron notes,

> Milly's illness is introduced here as if it were a consequence of—at
> any rate it directly follows from—her having been shown the
> Bronzino. (Her illness, though alluded to earlier, is dismissed by
> being treated as trivial, or inconsequential.) It is as if, after Milly
> has looked at the Bronzino and thought of the girl as dead, her own
> life is put in jeopardy. As if, to put it glibly, the thought of death
> could kill. (130)

Cameron's emphasis is on the externalization of "thought" and its consequent uncanny power in the novel; also implied here, however, is a peculiar receding of causality. Like Milly's tears that enable the recognition they in turn respond to, her illness seems to be the result of her realization of it. Cognition in such a scenario is at once belated and ahead of itself.

On the level of plot and character, the Bronzino moment and the interaction with Kate that follows it eventually lead to Milly's asking Kate to accompany her to see Sir Luke Strett—with all of the mediations of consciousness that the logic of Milly's request entails. One of the central moments in the plot is thus generated by a series of interacting, groundless reflections. In addition, therefore, to the link that Sedgwick notes between Milly's illness and Lionel's disgrace—and the consequent possibility of reading both in relation to the closet (concealing homosexual desire, or simply as a structure of occlusion that Sedgwick and others have taught us to view in relation to homosexuality and homophobia)—I would also dwell on the queer sense of "something else," "something that was perversely *there*," that emerges in these scenes of reflection. Such scenes recur at crucial moments: we have noted, already, the opening of the novel, Densher's first appearance, Milly's confrontation with the Bronzino painting, and Densher's retrospective gaze at his time with Milly in Venice. The reflection presented by these moments—literally or figuratively— extends beyond the characters' psychological modes of self-examination to intimate a reflection on the "impersonal intimacy" of free indirect style; examining themselves, the characters seem uncannily to "narrate" themselves as characters. The characters' gazes at themselves coincide with the novel's own gaze at itself, and "something else" emerges, at many different levels, from that reflexive gaze. Once again, such structures are legible even in the smallest syntactical units—for instance, in names, as we have noted, in the repeated forms of extraposition, and in sentences such as the following: "She might learn from *him*," the text tells us of Milly and Lord Mark, "why she was so different from the handsome girl—which she didn't know, being merely able to feel it; or at any rate might learn from him why the handsome girl was so different from her" (101). The implication is that Milly's difference from Kate might itself differ in some essential way from Kate's difference from Milly. Introducing a difference between each girl and herself, as if the parallel syntax that sets up the comparison between them had migrated "inside" each character, the moment also presents a kind of reflection that isn't one—a sentence, here, with mirroring syntax that announces nonreciprocity. Similarly, "He was mixed up in her fate, or her fate, if that should be better, was mixed up in *him*, so that a single false motion might either way snap the coil" (322). As in "she waited, Kate Croy," the trope of chiasmus offers ostensibly identical syntactical terms that turn out to be nonidentical. Also like the novel's opening, this instance of mirroring raises the question of interiority.[25] By making explicit the metaphorical ground of the expression "mixed up in," the specification of a relation of containment renders asymmetrical the two ways that "he" and "her fate" might be intertwined.

Character, in such effects, turns inside out,[26] pointing both toward (on the one hand) the questions of identification and self-dispropriation that animate the scenes of Kate at the mirror, Milly and the Bronzino, and Densher demeaning himself, and (on the other) toward the role of the narration in the novel, toward its relation to the events it depicts. The alienation legible in these scenes might then register, as a psychological effect, what is entailed in inhabiting the locus of what Banfield calls "unspeakable sentences"—what it means for a character to "identify," paradoxically, with the uninhabitable locus of free indirect speech. It is perhaps in part this potential in free indirect style that leads Frances Ferguson to turn to this mode of narration in her reading of Jeremy Bentham. Against Foucault's famous reading of Bentham, Ferguson resists subsuming objectification under interiorization; the objectification of persons in the Panopticon does not necessarily issue in the forming of determinate identities. (Where Foucault sees a scene of disciplinary subject formation, Ferguson sees the potential for the proliferation of determining contexts: the world's third-best figure-skater in one context, for instance, and the fifth-worst speller in Mrs. Smith's fourth-grade class in another, with no necessary connection between the two.) In Flaubert's *Madame Bovary* and "the objectifying mode" signaled by *style indirect libre*, Ferguson traces the thoroughgoing objectification of oneself in action.[27] The novel, she writes, makes "individuality look like a mistaken conclusion" (114). Where identity is generated from immediate context, and where there is no necessary continuity linking various contexts to one other, the possibility emerges of losing track of oneself:

> In arguing that individuals might really derive different kinds of value from their associations with different kinds of persons, utilitarianism seemed to deprive characters of themselves by making all their actions so reliant upon our connections with other people that they could scarcely recognize themselves as tied to their own actions. The importance of this detachment from even the actions in which they have most completely participated manifests itself throughout the novel—most notably in the way Flaubert uses *style indirect libre*. Flaubert does more than simply give the narrator privileged access to the thoughts of the characters; he makes it clear that their experience requires as much representation to themselves as it does to other people. . . . The Emma who says to herself, "I have a lover!" is not simply marveling at her situation but is also narrating it to herself and producing the emotions to go with that situation.[28] That feature of the novel—the way characters are shown describing the effects of their actions and deducing the emotions that they come to have—makes it possible to understand Flaubert's celebrated claim that he *was* Emma Bovary in a slightly different fashion from the one in which it has commonly been understood. For the fact is that lots of people *are* Emma Bovary. Moreover, this identity between the character and the legion of others who *are* Emma does not reflect a similarity of circumstance

or a deep psychological identification. It is, rather, an inevitable product of the fact that as it as easy for many to occupy Emma's emotions as it is for her, since others come to her emotions the same way that she does—through deducing them from the effects that she sees around her. (112–13)

The present chapter attempts, in part, to think about what happens when the effects of self-objectification and externalization Fèrguson describes appear in a novel ostensibly invested in a model, if not of psychological depth, then of a possible lucidity about such effects. What happens when it isn't a novel that "knows" these things, but a character in a novel? At the limit, I have suggested, Kate's lucidity is less a psychological characteristic that an inhabiting of a point of view—specifically, that of a narrator. One way to read the novel's groundlessness—the "something else" to which it recurs at crucial junctures—is as an effect of the narrative turning back on itself, free indirect style rendered, as it were, reflexive.

This might be the moment (if, indeed, it isn't rather too late) to register some of the idiosyncrasy of my use of the term "free indirect style."[29] The concept is very illuminating, it seems to me, for thinking about *The Wings of the Dove* because of the effects that writers such as Ferguson, Miller, and Banfield have located in it. Equivocalities of proximity and distance, speakerless sentences, an identity that tends to disappear into the multiple contexts that determine it: the conceptual effects of free indirect style seem to describe narrative effects in late James even though as a formal element of the novel, "free indirect style" may be very difficult to locate in specific sentences. One primary reason for that is what David Kurnick calls "house style": characters in late James all tend to talk alike and to talk remarkably like a Jamesian narrator.[30] There isn't the difference that one finds in Jane Austen, for example, between the vocal inflections of particular characters and the prose of an imperturbably removed narrator. In relation to specific moments, therefore, I sometimes shuttle uncertainly between the terms "free indirect style" and "focalization," but rather than, in despair of narratological rigor, purging the term entirely, I continue to refer to free indirect style because of its relevance for the narrative of *The Wings of the Dove*. It is as if the dynamic of proximity and distance that can be marked in specific sentences in Jane Austen had migrated to the text as a whole, as if the grammatical indeterminacy of assignable voice that can be seen in particular sentences of free indirect style had come to describe the ontology of character "in" the text, and as if the locus of the "objectifying mode" of free indirect style had moved to the "interior" of the text, to plot and theme and character.

Moreover, one implication of the effects I have traced in the novel's syntax—the syntax of extraposition, for example—and in the mode of characters' self-narration in James's "perspectivism," is to make "perspective" and "narration," which is also to say "focalization" and "free indirect style," curiously difficult to hold apart. In other terms, the relation of character to narrator has been distributed "inward," marking characters' relation to themselves and becoming an element of theme and plot "within" the text. This redistribution turns both character and narration inside out—character, in the externalized view of "itself," and, "narration," insofar as its "object" coincides with its mode of narration. As a dynamic of narrative distance from and proximity to characters, free indirect style would thus be difficult to locate in specific instances. What the narration moves closer to and farther from is a narrative dynamic of proximity and distance; free indirect style is put *en abîme*, which makes measuring "distance" in particular instances akin to trying to measure the distance between points on facing mirrors. At the limit, free indirect style names a dynamic that undermines the possibility of locating it. Or, in other terms, the inside-out topography that is its effect on character extends to the narrative itself. (The question of whether characters have "insides"—thematized in many of the moments in the text examined so far, and in many others as well—extends to the text itself. And vice versa.) Free indirect style offers a way to talk about viewpoint—as a principle of individuation instead of an individual view—as it is bound up with, even indistinguishable from, the role of narration. Viewpoint, too, marks the disappearance of "character" (as does the "perspectivism" of James); free indirect style links effects of focalization to the turning inside out implicit in zeugma and *The Golden Bowl*. It links the effect, for example, of Maggie's traveling round and round a vase and round and round her strange garden pagoda to questions of identification in *The Wings of the Dove* (Milly's recognition of herself "in words that had nothing to do with her," Kate's gaze into the mirror, the uncertain interior marked for Densher by "in his recovered sense," and the incoherent spatial relation of "he was mixed up in her fate, or her fate . . . was mixed up in him")—links it to the hall of mirrors that results when free indirect style takes itself as its object and to the expropriating effects of extraposition: "She waited, Kate Croy."

Another reason to maintain the concept of free indirect style is that however unknowable the distance between character and narrator, however much both may seem for multiple reasons to turn inside out, and however much the "surface" of the style may come to inhabit the "depth" of characters' psyches, the novel nevertheless does not assimilate characters' perspectives to that of the narrative. (This is partly to say that one finds *perspectives* in this novel even if one does not find *characters*.) The crossing of the narrative's and the characters' points of view—which leaves the characters in the place of a perspective inhabited by no one[31]—draws one's attention to otherwise seemingly conventional interruptions of presumed continuities between the perspectives of the narrative and of particular characters. Parenthetical reminders of a filtering voice also often implicitly group the reader with the narrator in an ostensibly knowing relation to the events of the novel:

His business, he had settled, as we know, was to keep thoroughly still. . . . (328)

Perfect tact—the necessity for which he had from the first, as we know, happily recognised. . . . (322)

[T]hey might have struck themselves, or may at least strike us, as coming back from an undeterred but useless voyage to the North Pole. (150)

Add that he again knew she knew, and yet that nothing was spoiled by it, and we get a fair impression of the line they found most completely workable. (323)

Whatever their many other differences, such reminders have a distancing effect: the assertion that "we" know what the narrative has already told us, the implicit assumption of an "us" to be differentiated from the characters, and the implicit assertion that the "line" taken by Milly and Merton can be distinguished from our "fair impression of it" all interrupt, by reminding us of narrative filtering, any illusion of unmediated access. They remind us, most simply, of the fact of perspective. Other moments distance the narrative from the perspective of the characters in gestures of removal often built upon the inhabiting of that perspective:

[H]e mooned for a minute, as he would have called it, at a window. (339)

Never yet so much as just of late had Mrs. Stringham seen her companion exalted, and by the very play of something within, into a vague golden air that left irritation below. That was the great thing with Milly—it was her characteristic poetry, or at least it was Susan Shepherd's. (124)

"Oh!" said Lord Mark again—and again it was just as good. That was for Densher, the latter could see, or think he saw. (217)

He didn't, none the less, know, and, at last, thank goodness, didn't care. (321)

The diagnosis of the investments—either, as in the moment about Susan Shepherd, in a desired other, or, as in the moments with Densher, in an image of oneself—that, implicitly, result in characters' misperceptions is itself enabled by a similar investment on the part of the narrative, a drawing closer to the character's perspective made possible by free indirect style. That it can then, suddenly, pull away interrupts any presumed transparency between the narrating voice and the mind of various characters, leading one to question, for instance, where to place "thank goodness" in relation to the narrator and Densher. (This last instance perhaps comes closest to an example of free indirect style— insofar as an indirect rendering of what may be Densher's thought has an effect similar to that of the parenthetical asides.) To put this another way, the narrative "reflects" the perspective of a character, and thereby generates something other than a reflection of the character's own point of view.

Striking in this regard is a discussion between Densher and Susan Stringham about Lord Mark's motives for denouncing Densher to Milly:

"He [Lord Mark] saw you received, as it were, while he was turned away."

"Perfectly," Densher said—'I've filled it out. And also that he has known meanwhile for *what* I was then received. For a stay of all these weeks. He had had it to think of."

"Precisely—it was more than he could bear. But he has it," said Mrs. Stringham, "to think of still."

> "Only, after all," asked Densher, who himself somehow, at this
> point, was having more to think of even than he had yet had—
> "only, after all, how has he happened to know?" (340)

The curious thing, to my mind, is the narration's picking up of Susan's
and Merton's terms to describe Densher in turn: "who himself somehow, at this point, was having more to think of even than he had yet
had." The effect is both to draw the narrative voice closer—because of
the intimated inhabiting of Densher's own thought, his own turning of
the conversation's terms back on his own predicament—and to distance
it—because of the potential for ironizing comment. Free indirect style
has the same potential for narcissistic reassurance and satirical deflation
that a mirror on a dance floor has: the perfect reflection of a character's
mode of expression makes possible an ironizing or distancing effect.[32]
It therefore also condenses effects—"inside" and "outside" the text—of
affiliation, of who is "in," as it were, and who is "out."[33] If this moment
in *The Wings of the Dove* is perhaps atypical for the novel insofar as it
locates a dynamic between (therefore, at this moment) differentiable
"voices" of character and narrator (and, notably, unlike Austen, or Benson, the effect is very local, which is to say the narrative mirrors a phrase
used by Densher, not a *characteristic* expression, as if the novel had
to generate, for this nonce use, a differentiated voice), the movement
"outward" (toward a reader) that is the effect of a gravitating "inward"
of these effects of voice is also implicit in Austenian free indirect style
and focalization. The potential for shame in such effects emerges in the
movement toward a reader; Miller has shown the way that the disavowal
of an investment in Austen's style is internal to that style, and also how
the effects of shame within the text always have the potential to spiral
out to implicate a reader.[34] Effects of characterization thus often have
an ancillary effect—or, perhaps, the establishing of character might be
ancillary to the implicit threat to the reader.

One thinks in this regard of Mrs. Elton's presumptuous "we" in *Emma*,
which dramatizes these questions of affiliation and which, unlike *The
Wings of the Dove*, achieves its satirical effects largely through the ventrilo-
quizing of highly idiosyncratic voices:

> My dear Miss Woodhouse, a vast deal may be done by those who
> dare to act. You and I need not be afraid. If *we* set the example,

many will follow it as far as they can; though all have not our situations. *We* have carriages to fetch and covey her home, and *we* live in a style which could not make the addition of Jane Fairfax, at any time, the least inconvenient.[35]

The first-person plural pronoun is no doubt the stupidest pronoun in English—if also the one that offers the most seductive of pleasures. In Mrs. Elton's case, whatever its other determinants—presumptions of equality in class, taste, education, and so on that betray, in being asserted, their falsity—the stupid pronoun derives its charge in part from the obliviousness it betrays to its vulnerability to, even demand for, a withdrawal of sympathy or community: "whom, exactly, do you mean by *we?*"—or, more subtly, a nearby Emma's quiet refusal to join in the chorus of we. Mrs. Elton's infraction is potentially shaming and stands as a warning to a reader: just as the bond uniting characters and narrator is subject to sudden abrogation by the narrator, so, too, is that of the reader's with the narrator, which threatens, in turn, not only a puncturing of intimacy but an exposure of presumption.

Notably, *Emma* at this moment distinguishes between two different types of affiliation:

Emma had not to listen to such paradings again—to any so exclusively addressed to herself—so disgustingly decorated with a "dear Miss Woodhouse." The change on Mrs. Elton's side soon afterwards appeared, and she was left in peace—neither forced to be the very particular friend of Mrs. Elton, nor, under Mrs. Elton's guidance, the very active patroness of Jane Fairfax, and only sharing with others in a general way, in knowing what was felt, what was meditated, what was done. (284)

However else one might understand the difference between "exclusive" and "more general" forms of affiliation, the difference seems to turn on being *addressed*, and therefore on the kind of coercive affiliation exercised, for example, by a text. In contrast—but also in somewhat perilous proximity—are Mrs. Elton's crassly presumptuous "we" and the unstated "we" linking Emma and narrator in the expression of Emma's relief. If such moments as the one with Mrs. Elton register (for a reader) as more pleasure than threat, it is perhaps because they manage—among other things—to transmute the question of whether characters (or texts) have "insides" to a question of who is "inside" a particular group, a question that is then moralized.

It is therefore striking that *The Wings of the Dove* troubles a moral reading of its central plot by presenting emphatic moral judgments that are emphatically groundless; the difficulty of locating a character in a circuit of reflection finds its analogue in the difficulty of locating a voice in such assertions. Such effects are, perhaps not surprisingly, especially visible around Lionel Croy. At the end of the first chapter appears this withering judgment: "And then came up the spring that moved him. 'If it only displeases you, you can go to Marian to be consoled.' What he couldn't forgive was her dividing with Marian her scant share of the provision their mother had been able to leave them. She should have divided it with him" (33). This censorious tone floats indeterminately between the narrator and Kate—consolidating, in one sense, our sympathy with Kate (by aligning her with "our" perspective and the narrator's knowledge).[36] The effect, however, is also to bring to the fore a certain groundlessness in the moral judgment presented by leaving open the perspective (and, with it, the degree of more or less interested distortion) from which it is "spoken." Similar is one of the first thematizations of Lionel's "preterited homosexual disgrace" (Sedgwick, 86):

> It always struck him [Densher] that she [Kate] had more life than
> he to react from, and when she recounted the dark disasters of her
> house and glanced at the hard odd offset of her present exaltation—
> since as exaltation it was apparently to be considered—he felt his
> own grey domestic annals make little show. It was naturally, in all
> such reference, the question of her father's character that engaged
> him most, but her picture of her adventure in Chirk Street gave him
> a sense of how little as yet that character was clear to him. What was
> it, to speak plainly, that Mr. Croy had originally done? (56)[37]

This crucial question is not rendered in Merton's voice but somewhere between Merton's and the narrator's—and is presented not as direct quotation (no matter how "plainly" it is spoken) but as a free indirect report. Kate answers as if Merton has asked it, but the question itself is not in fact given as quoted, nor even as reported, speech. The moment thus at once raises Lionel's crime and an indeterminate voice. To that extent, the central question of that unspecified sin—and its identificatory effects, which, as Sedgwick shows, traverse the novel—is explicitly bound up with the question of narrative "proximity" and "distance"; Lionel's disappearance as a legible character is paired with the vanishing, in the narration, of a determinate locus of voice. The parenthetical "since as exaltation it was apparently to be considered" further prepares us for this movement toward free indirect style by making it difficult to locate the perspective of the commentary: where, for example, in the various relations among Kate, Densher, and the narrator (including the narrator's view of Densher's view of Kate) are we to locate that "apparently"? As such moments pile up in the text—especially if one considers them in the light of the many explicit thematizations of perspectives vacated or divided against themselves by being circuited through other gazes—one is led to suspect that these moments are there not to be resolved (here speaks Kate, here Densher, and here the narrator), but rather to disrupt the workings of perspective that are, at the same time, central to the novel's moral mechanisms. Thus, to the queer effects around Lionel Croy that Sedgwick traces, I would add this tendency of the free indirect style to erode perspective and thereby to introduce into the narration an effect of groundlessness. Kate's effort to ward off Lionel's presumptuous encroachments, which enacts the blurring it hopes to evade, desire in the text as a constitutively vicariating structure that blurs identification and desire, and the free indirect narration in its disorienting effects on character made explicit in repeated scenes of reflection: the foundational role of Lionel's queerness traced by Sedgwick through the novel's identificatory logic also marks the novel's reflections on the modalities of its free indirect style. To put this another way, free indirect style in *The Wings of the Dove* is queer.

Yet again, these effects traversing the novel are legible in small details in the prose—in a sense leveling distinctions among theme and psychology, narrative perspective, and syntax. Another striking characteristic of the style of *The Wings of the Dove* is a sort of parallel subordination stretched almost to the point of syntactical suspension:

> Her father's life, her sister's, her own, that of her two lost brothers
> —the whole history of their house had the effect of some fine
> florid voluminous phrase, say even a musical, that dropped first
> into words and notes without sense and then, hanging unfinished,
> into no words nor any notes at all. (21)

> He recalled, on his bench in the Regent's Park, the freedom of
> fancy, funny and pretty, with which she had answered; recalled

> the moment itself, while the usual hansom charged them, during which he felt himself, disappointed as he was, grimacing back at the superiority of her very "humour," in its added grace of gaiety, to the celebrated solemn American. (192)

> While, for this first week that followed their dinner, she drank deep at Lancaster Gate, her companion was no less happily, appeared to be indeed on the whole quite as romantically, provided for. (111)

> It was born, for that matter, partly of the conditions, those conditions that Kate had so almost insolently braved, had been willing, without a pang, to see him ridiculously—ridiculously so far as just complacently—exposed to. How little it *could* be complacently he was to feel with the last thoroughness before he had moved from his point of vantage. (281)

"Say even a musical" enacts the trailing off of sense that the sentence describes—"musical" hesitating between an adjective and a noun because of its distance from the noun it modifies.[38] ("American" in the next example presents perhaps analogous difficulties; if the phrase "the celebrated solemn American" names, as it seems to, Milly [and not, for instance, the American style of humor], the grammatical clarification comes at the expense of a certain conceptual asymmetry: compared, then, are Kate's humor and Milly [herself].) The adverbs "complacently" and "romantically" present perhaps less striking instances, but they, too, suggest a syntactical suspension because a parallel (or simply repeated) element is left implied. The moment when Kate's face is said to have "looked, rather more beautifully than less, into his own" presents a similar effect, explicitly linking, in this instance, these effects of syntactical quasi-suspension to identificatory and narrative structures of reflection.

Such effects of syntactical suspension mark the syntax of the novel with the uncertain topographies of identification and narrative distance, and repeatedly force one to question a sentence's capacities to "contain" meaning. Sentences no less than characters' psyches are turned inside–out; it may be rather more accurate to say that part of what turns psyches inside out is their structuring by this syntax. Another stylistic characteristic of the novel has a similar effect: its tendency to expand parts of a sentence through interlocking series, often in apposition, delaying syntactical closure until the very end. An effect perhaps not unrelated to syllepsis and zeugma in *The Golden Bowl*, it presents long series that seem to point toward possibilities of both syntactical dissolution and syntactical elasticity:

> The smallest things, the faces, the hands, the jewels of the women, the sound of the words, especially of names, across the table, the shape of the forks, the arrangement of the flowers, the attitude of the servants, the walls of the room, were all touches in a picture and denotements in a play; and they marked for her moreover her alertness of vision. (99)

Sentences similarly pile up other syntactical units of various size—adverbs or gerunds, for instance:

> [H]e would somehow wear the character scientifically, ponderably, proveably—not just loosely and sociably. (143)

> She [Milly] had no time at all; she was never at her best—unless indeed it were exactly, as now, in listening, watching, admiring, collapsing. (168)

With larger units, series are drawn in parallel, often with other parallel (or quasi-parallel) elements intercalated:

> They had exchanged vows and tokens, sealed their rich compact, solemnized, so far as breathed words and murmured sounds and lighted eyes and clasped hands could do it, their agreement to belong only, and to belong tremendously, to each other. (72)

> They were on the edge of Christmas, but Christmas this year was, as in the London of so many other years, disconcertingly mild; the still air was soft, the thick light was grey, the great town looked empty, and in the Park, where the grass was green, where the sheep browsed, where the birds multitudinously twittered, the straight walks lent themselves to slowness and the dim vistas to privacy. (370)

> [H]e wondered if he were afraid. Yet it wasn't of Sir Luke, who was coming; nor of Milly, who was dying; nor of Mrs. Stringham, who was sitting there. (338)

Other rhetorical forms—such as anaphora—emphasize the parallelism:

> She [Milly] won't show for that, any more than your watch, when
> it's about to stop for want of being wound up, gives you convenient
> notice or shows as different from usual. She won't die, she won't
> live, by inches. She won't smell, as it were, of drugs. She won't taste,
> as it were, of medicine. No one will know. (215)

> The cold breath of her reasons was, with everything else, in the air;
> but he didn't care for them any more than for her wish itself, and
> he would stay in spite of her, stay in spite of odium, stay in spite
> perhaps of some final experience that would be, for the pain of it,
> all but unbearable. (330)

> He had come to say he had saved her—he had come, as from Mrs.
> Stringham, to say how she might *be* saved—he had come, in spite
> of Mrs. Stringham, to say she was lost: the distinct throbs of hope,
> of fear, simultaneous for all their distinctness, merged their identity
> in a bound of the heart just as immediate and which remained after
> they had passed. (350)

On the level of syntax, the novel shows a sort of mania for parallel elements,
and parallel forms seem to beget further elements branching off from
various parts of the sentence and drawn, likewise, in parallel.

The enthusiasm for parallelism also seems to generate forms that (only)
look as if they were parallel—"*to* belong only, and *to* belong tremendously,
to each other." As many of these moments suggest, moreover, the most crucial part of such series is often when the parallelism gives way. Perhaps most
striking, then, are parallel grammatical elements that diverge conceptually:

> Milly, from the other side, happened at that moment to notice
> them, and she sent across toward them in response all the can-
> dour of her smile, the luster of her pearls, the value of her life, the
> essence of her wealth. (310)

> [I]t was neither Kate nor he who made his strange relation to Milly,
> who made her own, so far as it might be, innocent; it was neither of
> them who practically purged it—if practically purged it was. Milly her-
> self did everything—so far at least as he was concerned—Milly herself,

and Milly's house, and Milly's hospitality, and Milly's manner, and Milly's character, and, perhaps still more than anything else, Milly's imagination, Mrs. Stringham and Sir Luke indeed a little aiding. (314)

As with zeugma in *The Golden Bowl*, such sentences align unlike elements: "the candour of her smile, the luster of her pearls, the value of her life, the essence of her wealth." The description of the Bronzino painting presents, of course, just such a series: "The lady in question . . . with her slightly Michaelangelesque squareness, her eyes of other days, her full lips, her long neck, her recorded jewels, her brocaded and wasted reds, was a very great personage— only unaccompanied by a joy" (137). The appearance here of this syntactical effect encourages us to read the novel's recurrent series—its parallelism, its anaphora, its yoking of unlike things—in relation to its trope of reflection, in relation, that is, both to its understanding of identification and to its linking of identificatory concerns to questions of proximity and distance in the narration. Forms of mirroring that disrupt a mapping of the prose in terms of inside and out, these stylistic effects might be said to mark the novel's syntax with its ostensibly larger preoccupations. Or, put another way, the novel's concern with identification—and its groundlessness—is to be perceived even on the minute level of its style, and, indeed, such stylistic effects further encourage one to read the identificatory vicissitudes as, in the first instance, questions of the syntax, from which psychological questions emerge as secondary byproducts.

Parallel series in fact often emerge at moments of characterization, where a sort of exhaustiveness signaled by the series gives way to an evocation of "something else":

> She [Kate] was handsome, but the degree of it was not sustained by items and aids; a circumstance moreover playing its part at almost any time in the impression she produced. The impression was one that remained, but as regards the sources of it no sum in addition would have made up the total. She had stature without height, grace without motion, presence without mass. (22)

> She [Milly] had arts and idiosyncrasies of which no great account could have been given, but which were a daily grace if you lived with them; such as the art of being almost tragically impatient and yet making it as light as air; of being inexplicably sad and yet making it as clear as noon; of being unmistakeably gay and yet making it as soft as dusk. (82)

The sense of exhaustiveness—as if saturating the descriptions with more and more detail, and detail, moreover, that all seems to converge (in different modes) on a single point—pulls against the aesthetic ideal that is, at the same time, asserted in such passages.[39] In the latter description, it is perhaps unclear whether it is "great" or "account" that is negated, and the ostensibly contrary proposition ("but which were a daily grace") provides an alternative not clearly opposed to either. Likewise, the parallel similes work by negating—in asymmetrical ways—both the adjective and the adverb: "light as air" is opposed not only to "impatient" but to "tragically," just as "clear as noon" negates both the sadness and its inexplicable nature. A syntactically unifying effect relies on a fracturing or asymmetrical form of reflection. Both descriptions assert, in different ways, a resistance to representation, a gap between the listed elements and the categories through which they might be classified. (The description of Densher as unclassifiable—"it was almost impossible to name his profession" (46)—makes the effect explicit.) "No sum in addition would have named its total": the aesthetic principle is perhaps the inverse of the Croy family failure, its fine florid voluminous phrase lapsing into "no words, or any notes at all." A series of parts that fails to make a whole and a whole that is not to be accounted for by the sum of its parts: these moments signal a gap between appearances and categories of cognition that is also made explicit in Kate's description of Milly's death. The signs of her illness will not be legible—"she won't smell, as it were, of drugs. She won't taste, as it were, of medicine"—or, in other words, "no one will know."[40] The groundlessness in the novel's structures of reflection—the recurrence of structures of identification, for example, where the formation is not legible, or appears to proceed reflexively, or backwards in time—evokes the argument against formalization that James presents in his essays on the novel. The virtuoso suspension of meaning in the sentences that add parallel element to parallel element, and resolve unexpectedly, and only at their end, enacts at a stylistic level what is asserted in these descriptions. Meaning cannot be added up—is not subject to a logic that would allow Kate's beauty or Milly's death to be expressed in a series of parts; they cannot be represented but can only be invoked through a "something else" that exceeds exhaustive description. Kate's felt need to differentiate herself from Lionel is therefore perhaps also an intimation of this structure's proximity to its inverse, the senseless phrase. However *Kate* might feel about that, for the novel Lionel's centrality might lie in the queer effects of representation that he embodies and that traverse the rest of the text at many different levels.

"No sum in addition would have made up the total": the gap marked here also emerges in other registers. One might wonder, for instance, about the coincidence of Kate's nickname for Aunt Maud—"Britannia of the Marketplace" (37)—and the accidental drowning of her beloved brother: "the flower of the flock, a middy on the *Britannia*, dreadfully drowned" (55).[41] There is something ominous, it seems to me, in this form of "reflection," something not fully explicable in psychological terms (which might see in the moniker a form of mourning, for instance, or an unconscious return of that lost brother). However compelling such terms might be, I would be tempted to emphasize, instead, the seeming links among financial qua national power—Britannia of the Marketplace—a certain contingency, the implacable stroke of accident, and an abyssal causality registered in linguistic terms: the pecuniary determinants that set in motion the plot, chance, and an extra-psychological causality that might appear, for instance, in an unexpected pun—or in the paranomastic effects in the novel's various names, a sort of unmeaning, mechanical agency internal to language that produces effects of reflection and symmetry without necessarily "meaning" them.

Such moments make explicit a nonpsychological agency that is likewise not determined by exigencies of meaning, and they might also be linked to the text's dwelling on obscure forms of causality.[42] "He has somehow an effect," Kate says of Lord Mark, "without his being in any traceable way a cause" (219). The emphasis here is on Lord Mark's "grandeur"—Kate is trying to explain to Merton his appeal for Aunt Maud—but this vexing of causality reappears at the crux of the plot, when Lord Mark travels to Venice to inform Milly of Kate and Merton's engagement.[43] Seeing Lord Mark in a café in Saint Mark's Square, Densher sees that "he had already made the difference." This explanation

> made him no less restless. But it explained—and that was much, for with explanations he might somehow deal. The vice in the air, otherwise, was too much like the breath of fate. The weather had changed, the rain was ugly, the wind wicked, the sea impossible, *because of* Lord Mark. It was because of him, *a fortiori*, that the palace was closed. (328)

The moment is legible in various psychological registers. It figures in a particularly striking way Merton's sudden illumination, for instance, his understanding of why he has been barred from Milly's Palazzo, and, as the subsequent paragraph makes apparent, Lord Mark's serving to embody that insight also allows Merton to shift blame to the "cause"—and thereby to feel himself "remarkably blameless" (328). In another register, Lord Mark's "causing" the weather is perhaps also an instance of the external- ized consciousness Sharon Cameron traces in the novel. The text at times encourages us to moralize Lord Mark's intervention—Densher and Susan call him an "idiot of idiots," "the inevitable ass" (340)—and, perhaps, to moralize the evasions that this intervention affords Densher. However compelling each of these explanations might be, I think it is also worth dwelling on the exorbitant casuality in Densher's assertion: "The weather had changed . . . *because of* Lord Mark. It was because of him, *a fortiori*, that the palace was closed." The pairing implies a relation—of degrees of inten- sification, if not even of consequence—between the two registers of cau- sality: the claim that a psychological explanation of Lord Mark's effect on Milly is still more conclusive than his asserted power to shape the weather undermines the psychological register, if only through the implied link. The abyssal quality of the moment might be contained through psycho- logical terms—through the suggestion, for instance, that the exorbitance of the first assertion's causality is meant to figure Densher's sense of the predicament signaled by the second. If the abyssal causality is to be tamed, however, the logic seems rather to be a narrative one; the moment inti- mates that the weather is horrible because of the *novel's* plot, because it forms a suitable background to this climax. (Again, too, it is parallelism that makes the conclusion feel inevitable. It is as if, moreover, the con- clusion and the plot were driven by the syntax.) And in fact Lord Mark's brutal actions also have the artificial weight of a plot twist—or *deus ex machina*—to bring the plot to an "inevitable" close. Densher's specula- tions on causality, then, resonate in a different register, as a metareflection on the making of plot.

The novel's reflections on causality are further complicated by the tem- poral register they introduce, a temporality proper to narrative. Milly and Merton, like Merton and Kate (and like, for that matter, John Marcher and May Bartram at the beginning of "The Beast in the Jungle"), have more of a relation than they can trace a cause for:

> At the same time, while many things in quick succession came up
> for them, came up in particular for Densher, nothing perhaps was
> just so sharp as the odd influence of their present conditions on
> their view of their past ones. It was as if they hadn't known how
> "thick" they had originally become, as if, in a manner, they had
> really fallen to remembrance of more passages of intimacy than
> there had in fact at the time been quite room for. (229)

The "as if" highlights the fictional, which is therefore also to say the metafictional, quality of their remembrance; the result, notably, is an expansion of
time, and an assertion of the shaping force of what they did *not* experience:
Combray appears as it was never experienced, as it was never viewed. Going
on to compare their speculation to the mythmaking through which "prosperous states place their beginnings," what comes into focus is the reversal of cause
and effect proper to narrative retrospection, which results here in the discovery of unknowingness: it was as if they hadn't known.[44] This effect at other
moments points to the fact of the narration, blurring, in a sense, its "inside"
and its "outside" and pointing to the temporal lag internal to narrative:

> These things were of later evidence, yet Densher might even then
> have felt them in the air. (221)

> It may be declared for Kate, at all events, that her sincerity about
> her friend, through this time, was deep, her compassionate imagi-
> nation strong; and that these things gave her a virtue, a good con-
> science, a credibility that were later to be precious to her. (262)

> When Milly had settled that the extent of her good will itself made
> her shy, she had found for the moment quite a sufficient key, and
> they were by that time thoroughly afloat together. This might well
> have been the happiest hour they were to know. (112)

These are perhaps not unprecedented markers of omniscience in realist
fiction. However, the suspension of certainty in the conditional statement
in the past perfect ("might have been"), like the registered uncertainty, in
the second example, about what Densher sensed ("might even then have
felt") suggests instead an emphasis on a temporal blurring as the statement
straddles two times: "might have been . . . were to know." The last instance

is perhaps the most striking because of the interaction of tenses, interjecting a sense of contingency into the backward glance: the statement hesitates between the sense that the moment might have been that at which, in retrospect, they were to know themselves as having been happiest, and the sense that, at that moment, they were to have been happiest—but fate made things turn out otherwise.

Thematically, this temporal structure emerges in the novel through Milly's death. In the New York Edition preface, James remarks that "the way grew straight from the moment one recognized that the poet essentially *can't* be concerned with the act of dying" (4). In this sense, the various forms of interrupted reflection enact or give an image for what James calls the "great smudge of mortality across the picture, the shadow of pain and horror" (347). The preface seems to make the withdrawal of narrative perspective a moral question, noting that

> Milly's situation ceases at a certain moment to be "renderable"
> in terms closer than those supplied by Kate's intelligence, or, in a
> richer degree, by Densher's, or for one fond hour, by poor Mrs.
> Stringham's . . . ; just as Kate's relation with Densher and Densher's
> with Kate have ceased previously, and are then to cease again, to
> be projected for us, so far as Milly is concerned with them, on any
> more responsible plate than that of the latter's admirable anxiety. It
> is as if, for these aspects, the impersonal plate—in other words the
> poor author's comparatively cold affirmation or thin guarantee—
> had felt itself a figure of attestation at once too gross and too blood-
> less, likely to affect us as an abuse of privilege when not as an abuse
> of knowledge. (12)

The "merciful indirection" through which the novel presents Milly's plight describes the narrative's mediation through various "centers" of focalization, which eschews the direct presentation—of Milly's death, but also of "Kate's relation with Densher and Densher's with Kate"—that is called an "abuse." The moral questions that have guided many readings of the novel are effects of narrative perspective; to note this fact is simply, as I suggested at the outset, to bring out the relative or interested nature of such moral judgments on the novel. It might also bring us to the implications of the externalization of consciousness that Cameron notes. At the end of her account of the power of thought in James to act on the world, she dwells on the consequent indeterminacy of mind and world introduced by thought's externalization:

> Thought as psychologized implies a crossing of mind and world. Thought as pictured doesn't. Thus, as I have argued, the effect of the psychological novel, as James writes it, is to divorce thinking from psychologizing, to depsychologize it. Because in *The Wings of the Dove* thought is objectified—is, as pictured, even made material—it is perfectly clear how thought has power in the world, but to see it this way, as the novel insists we do, questions the idea, the intelligibility, of what we recognize as mental states. (168)

This picture of consciousness leads Cameron to the "torture of the extreme case" where "'being in the same place' does not mean 'being the same thing'" (168). At risk of alienating Cameron's argument from its theoretical orientation, this last possibility might link the de-psychologizing of thought to James's novelistic project as I have traced it in this study: a form of representation for whose object "being in the same place" does not mean "being the same thing." Consciousness, in one gloss of that statement, does not coincide with itself; in this, it is the "object" *par excellence* for Jamesian representation. (James looks like a "psychologizing" novelist if one reverses the temporal perspective as Walter Besant does in his "art of fiction," if one assumes the existence of consciousness and asks how to render it. Or, analogously, if one understands perspective and viewpoint as functions of the individual and not the other way around.) Thus James's insistence that the poet "*can't* be concerned with the act of dying" (4) might be read less in moral terms than as a linking of Milly—and her death—to this principle of representation.[45]

The groundlessness that appeared in Milly's confrontation with the Bronzino portrait adumbrates, I noted, a temporal predicament. That temporality is a sort of "straddling" of two times (like "might have been . . . were to know"). Here is James's Paterian description of Milly's condition:

> The idea, reduced to its essence, is that of a young person conscious of a great capacity for life, but early stricken and doomed, condemned to die under short respite, while also enamoured of the world; aware moreover of the condemnation and passionately desiring to "put in" before extinction as many of the finer

vibrations as possible, and so achieve, however briefly and bro-
kenly, the sense of having lived. (3)

The Paterian aspect of this passage is not simply the echoing vocabulary—
"short respite" and "finer vibrations," for instance—but the verb tense:
Pater's aesthetic moment makes present not life but its vanishing; to live,
for Milly, is here similarly cast not as a sense of life but as a "sense of having
lived."[46] This returns us to what is meant by the life Milly wants not to have
missed, and the preface, like the novel, repeatedly puts that life in a tense
that defers it until after it is over: "the sum of her experience, . . . what she
should have *known*" (5). Milly's confrontation with the Bronzino painting
marks not only a receding gaze but a receding temporality: "Lady Aldershaw meanwhile looked at Milly quite as if Milly *had been* the Bronzino
and the Bronzino only Milly" (139, emphasis added). The collocation of
tenses—"looked . . . had been"—isn't, strictly speaking, necessary; the
meaning could have been conveyed by a subjunctive or a past indicative.
Milly's assertion that "I shan't . . . have missed anything" points to a peculiarly posthumous (because future anterior) tense (I shan't have missed
anything; she won't have loved you for nothing): the moment that negates
or redeems the "missing" is delayed beyond the horizon of one's existence.
The life not to be missed and the moment in which one can be conscious
of not having missed it do not overlap in time; "enjoying life" or even "living while one can" clearly will not do to gloss that temporality. Milly's
formulation points again to *belatedness,* which, as we will see in chapter
four, *The Ambassadors* connects to the experience of Jamesian style, a disorienting of any simple opposition between "life" and "art" in that novel's
meditation on the relation between "missing" and representing experience. (The injunction given Milly is strikingly similar to that given Little
Bilham by Strether and invokes, too, the younger man's rendering of "to
live" as "to see": "see all you can," says Luke Strett, ". . . isn't 'to live' exactly
what I'm trying to persuade you to take the trouble to do?" [151].)

Belatedness in the novel is not only its fundamental experiential or
psychological "theme"; it also marks a rendering, on a quasi-psychologi-
cal or thematic register, of many different elements: extraposition and
parallel series, on the level of syntax; structures of reflection, on the level
of imagery; a certain groundlessness in identification, on the level of the
novel's conceptualizations of identity; free indirect style and focalization,
on the level of narrative. Milly's "I shan't . . . have missed anything" also

links temporal noncoincidence to a structure of representation that is simultaneously a structure of desire. Her ability to "live" is thus tied to a text's ability to touch (as it were) its object, to "capture" what it represents. For Susan, Milly is "the real thing" (78), just as Susan notes at another moment, Kate—"deputed flower-strewing" damsel, "chosen daughter of the burgesses" to Milly's princess—is, for Milly, the "real," "the wondrous London girl in person" whose attraction is its contrast to Milly's "plane of mere elegant representation," to her "effigies, processions, and other stately games" (111). Desire, such moments suggest, casts the beloved other as "the real thing" and thereby constitutes one's own contrasting—and thereby merely "representative"—state. Thus Milly's assertion that "I shan't . . . have missed anything" suggests that she will have experienced life, will have had her desire ("She won't have loved you for nothing. . . . And you won't have loved me" [364]), not only in the sense that desiring Densher will have been her passion, but also in the sense that, because, as we have noted, her desire was always constituted by her relation to Kate and Densher's relation to each other, it was always, in this sense, *representative*. (Kate's "you won't have loved me" can therefore be read less as a diagnosis of their doomed love than an intuition that "me" misnames what Densher loved, or "will have loved.") The rendering explicit of their engagement is, according to this logic, deflating because it is the consummation of Milly's desire. The posthumous structure of Milly's life is also the structure of desire in the text. And, once again, that particular predicament asks to be read less in psychological terms (as a "sad" one, for instance, capitalized upon or redeemed by opportunistic or beneficent lovers) than as a realization of a form of desire that is at the same time a reflection on the novel's mode of narration.

It is therefore striking that a similar verb tense marks the preface's discussion of the novel's putative aesthetic failures. The preface's emphasis on "failure" (a word that appears in the preface's final sentence) returns over and over to evince aesthetic beauty that "was to have been":

Yet one's plan, alas, is one thing and one's result another; so that
I am perhaps nearer the point in saying that this last strikes me
at present as most characterised by the happy features that *were*,
under my first and most blest illusion, to have contributed to it. I
meet them all as I remount the stream, the absent values, the palpable voids, the missing links, the mocking shadows, that reflect,
taken together, the early bloom of one's good faith. (9)

Missing links and palpable voids emerge from a temporal structure evocative of what comes to define Milly's life. Lionel Croy—along with the foundational "preterited homosexual disgrace" that Sedgwick traces in the novel—might also be read in relation to the missing links and voids of this temporality.[47] The registered regret (which, as Sedgwick notes, potentially attempts to suppress Lionel's structural place in the novel) also serves to link that disgrace to Milly, and to a certain structure of writing:

> The image of her so compromised and compromising father was all effectively to have pervaded her life, was in a certain particular way to have tampered with her spring; by which I mean that the shame and the irritation and the depression, the general poisonous influence of him, were to have been *shown*, with a truth beyond the compass even of one's most emphasised "word of honour" for it, to do these things. But where do we find him, at this time of day, save in a beggarly scene or two which scarce arrives at the dignity of functional reference? He but "looks in," poor beautiful dazzling, damning apparition that he was to have been. (10)

Lionel's queer disgrace might thus be read in terms of the pattern it establishes for the rest of the novel (not as a theme but as a temporal structure): a representation that "was to have been"—like Milly's life, and like Kate and Densher's marriage.[48] Such moments in the preface are less crucial, it seems to me, for any implied authorial judgment on the novel's aesthetic success or failure than for this temporal structure, a future locked, but also preserved, unrealized, in the past. Densher's "situation," James writes,

> personal, professional, social, was to have been so decanted for us that we should get all the taste; we were to have been penetrated with Mrs. Lowder, by the same token, saturated with her presence, her "personality," and felt all her weight in the scale. We were to have reveled in Mrs. Stringham, my heroine's attendant friend, her fairly choral Bostonian, a subject for innumerable touches, and in an extended and above all an *animated* reflexion of Milly Theale's experience of English society; just as the strength and sense of the situation in Venice, for our gathered friends, was to have come to us in a deeper draught out of a larger cup, and just as the pattern of

Densher's final position and fullest consciousness there was to have
been marked in fine stitches, all silk and gold, all pink and silver,
that have had to remain, alas, but entwined upon the reel. (10–11)

The achieved form of the novel is something that *was to have been*; the
preface's evocation of misplaced centers, its recurrent emphasis on failure,
whatever else it does, also links Milly's Paterian appreciation of life to the
very structuring of the narrative.

Perhaps more precisely, it links Milly's predicament to the backward
glance at writing James calls "revision." It ought to be read, therefore, not
in the (implicitly psychological) register of a regret for opportunities left
unrealized but in the (in my sense, stylistic) register of recovered potentiality. Later in the preface, that temporality appears in a more neutral context signaling not thwarted ambition but mere narrative sequence—as a
way of expressing what came to pass while gesturing toward the retrospective gaze at those events:

> They are far from a common couple, Merton Densher and Kate
> Croy, as befits the remarkable fashion in which fortune was to way-
> lay and opportunity was to distinguish them. . . . (14)

> But as I was to find it long since of a blest wisdom that no expense
> should be incurred or met, in any corner of a picture of mine,
> without some concrete image of the account kept of it, that is of its
> being organically re-economised, so under that dispensation Mrs.
> Stringham has to register the transaction. (15)

The verb tense is not exactly the same, and yet the temporal perspective
remains that of a past potential—even if the shift from the past perfect to the
infinitive suggests a future not necessarily left unrealized seen from the (recovered) perspective of the past. Yet even in the infinitive, the construction comprises a contingency (or at least the possibility that it gives a statement not of
what happened but of what didn't) in its distance from a mere past participle
("fortune waylaid" versus "fortune was to waylay"). Revision seems able to
recover the novel before it was written—and thus, perhaps, what looks like
missed opportunity recovers nothing short of writing as such.

Such contingency structures from the beginning the reflections on the
novel's putative failures:

> He places, after an earnest survey, the piers of his bridge—he has
> at least sounded deep enough, heaven knows, for their brave posi-
> tion; yet the bridge spans the stream, after the fact, in apparently
> complete independence of these properties, the principal grace
> of the original design. *They* were an illusion, for their necessary
> hour; but the span itself, whether of a single arch or of many, seems
> by the oddest chance in the world to be a reality; since, actually,
> the rueful builder, passing under it, sees figures and hears sounds
> above: he makes out, with his heart in his throat, that it bears and is
> positively being "used." (9)[49]

"Failure" might thus name the gap between design and construction, the resistance to formalization that, as we noted in "The Art of Fiction" and "The Future of the Novel," marks the queerness of James's theory of the novel. If death, too, might name the interruptions of reflection in the novel, it enters by way of this temporality—of Milly's "I shan't have missed anything" (271), for instance, or Kate's "She has had *all* she wanted. . . . She won't have loved you for nothing. . . . And you won't have loved *me*" (364).[50] (If the poet, as James writes, "essentially *can't* be concerned with the act of dying" (4), the injunction is perhaps to preserve this temporality from becoming an *object* of representation.) Such moments ask to be read less for the pathos of a particular relation between characters than for the intimation that the psychological predicaments follow from narrative structures. That reversal and the temporal asynchronicity of narrative intimated by Milly's predicament—more than any thematic evidence one might adduce of Milly's love for Kate, Kate's for Milly, Susan Stringham's for Milly or Maud, or of the queer nonmarriage of Merton and Kate, or even of the slighted (if therefore all the more compelling) forms of masculinity in the novel—account for the queerness of *The Wings of the Dove*. Like the structure of desire in the text, "life"—and the question of what one "will have had"—emerges through the novel's reflecting on its mode of free indirect narration, which takes the form of nonpsychological identification.[51] In this regard, we might note in passing the end of James's preface, and its final evoked "failure": "I become conscious of overstepping my space without having brought the full quantity to light. The failure leaves me with a burden of residuary comment of which I yet boldly hope elsewhere to discharge myself" (16). A load to bear, the *burden* is perhaps also a refrain. Reminding one of Eugenio, compared at one point to a "residuary legatee" (259), "comment" does not take place in the novel or the preface but remains after, as it were, the settling of an estate, or, perhaps, after the vanishing of character into nonpsychological forms of externalized consciousness, into (if such a topography even applies) "something else"— that future anterior time when Milly won't have missed anything, or when she won't have loved for nothing. The time, in short, of "the future of the novel."

CHAPTER 3

Hover, Torment, Waste: Late Writings
and the Great War

Why does poetry matter to us? The ways in which answers to this question are offered testify to its absolute importance. For the field of possible respondents is clearly divided between those who affirm the significance of poetry only on the condition of altogether confusing it with life and those for whom the significance of poetry is instead exclusively a function of its isolation from life. . . . Opposed to these two positions is the experience of the poet, who affirms that if poetry and life remain infinitely divergent on the level of the biography and psychology of the individual, they nevertheless become absolutely indistinct at the point of their reciprocal desubjectification. And—at that point—they are united not immediately but in a medium. This medium is language. The poet is he who, in the word, produces life. Life, which the poet produces in the poem, withdrawals from both the lived experience of the psychosomatic individual and the biological unsayability of the species.

—Giorgio Agamben, *The End of the Poem*
(translated by Daniel Heller-Roazen)

THE LAST ESSAY THAT HENRY JAMES prepared for publication was an introduction to Rupert Brooke's *Letters from America*. This remarkable tribute to a beautiful dead young poet, killed by blood poisoning while serving in the British Army, offers various enticements to biographical reading. It joins a series of James's essays written during World War I—many of them collected in Pierre Walker's important collection *Henry James on Culture*[1]—which tempts one to read them as radically distinct from, if not opposed to, the other late fictional and critical writings. Here, at last, so a reader might think, is the writer in his own voice, bereft of a narrator's ironical remove, speaking about the real world without the subtleties (or evasions) of fiction—a revelation that might inspire, depending

on one's attitude toward the late style, regret or vindication, disappointment or relief, embarrassment or gratification. At last we are allowed
behind the curtain. Often implicit in accounts of this period of James's
work is an assumption that his writing here turns both referential and
autobiographical—pointing to the war and to a life—and these strange
essays are assimilated to the larger oeuvre by referring them to the author's
biography. In Leon Edel's account of James's life, for instance, these essays
often appear—quoted or summarized—as statements of James's attitude
toward the war. So conscious, before the war, that his American birth
made him an outsider in England, James, Edel writes, "began to speak
of 'we' and 'us'"; James's taking of British citizenship in July 1915 and the
energy he devoted to various humanitarian activities during the war suggest that this claim of (for Edel, valorized) identification and community
might be to a certain extent justified, biographically speaking.[2] To Edel
and other biographers, the psychobiographical interest of the essays—
and what further links them to the coherent story of a life—lies in the
mystery of James and the Civil War.[3] The castration thematics that have
to a large extent oriented discussion of James's "obscure hurt" has allowed
critics to unite unexamined understandings of the relation of "art" to "life"
with unexamined attitudes about masculinity (the contempt, vicarious
shame, or the restraint of queasy delicacy about treating another's evasion
of the "choice" to fight manfully in war, for instance, that implicitly cast
deviations from conventional masculinity in terms of lack or failure). The
desire of scholars to vindicate James's not serving in the Civil War attests
to a felt, if also a more or less disguised, need to vindicate his style from a
lack of direct "engagement," thereby tied, through the pull of the particular
thematics about which one might or might not be direct, to an implied
effeminacy, even sexual deviance. Redemptive understandings of James's
later "war record," therefore, give readers reason to cringe, even apart from
the grotesque puffery through which a certain kind of writing inevitably
seeks to overcome its distance from the war (or even sporting event) it
would celebrate through the blind adulation of the writer's asserted identification with it. Hence the hidden pity, contempt, and the vindication of
vicarious pride asserted in Fred Kaplan's summary of James's World War
I activities are not the less striking for their being implicitly attributed to
James himself: "At last he did his Civil War service."[4]

   To read these texts for their homoeroticism is perhaps not sharply to be
distinguished from reading them for evidence of redeemed cowardice. Edel's

suggestion that James, "appalled by war," nevertheless "thrilled to human endurance and strength"—"the sense of power and glory in James made him an admirer always of the solider"—makes all but explicit the undertone of homoeroticism that runs through Edel's account of the war years.[5] That eroticism is more explicit in Edel's retelling (in a note to his edition of the letters) of James's prewar meeting with Rupert Brooke at Cambridge. James was "smitten by Brooke's physical beauty," Edel writes, glossing James's remark to Charles Sayle after that famous Cambridge weekend: "For their share in these generous yet so subtle arts please convey again my thanks to all concerned— . . . with a definite stretch toward the insidious Rupert—with whose name I take this liberty because I don't know whether one loves one's love with a (surname terminal) *e* or not."[6] Whatever James's attitude toward "the soldier," Rupert Brooke did inspire his playful encomia: "Splendid Rupert—to be the soldier that could beget them [the sonnets that would be Brooke's final poems] on the Muse! and lucky Muse, not less, who could have an affair with a soldier and yet feel herself not guilty of the least deviation!"[7] (It might go without saying, but it is difficult to imagine such lines written by someone paralyzed with panic at the thought of same-sex attraction.) Reading Marsh's memoir of him, it is indeed easy enough to imagine falling in love with Rupert Brooke, whose wit, in his writing, exerts a magnetism even apart from his reportedly astonishing physical beauty.[8] Like Marsh's memoir, James's tribute bears witness to this magnetism in terms that are at moments frankly homoerotic: "our unspeakably fortunate young poet of today, linked like [Byron], for consecration of the final romance, with the isles of Greece, took for *his* own the whole of the poetic consciousness he was born to, and moved about in it as a stripped young swimmer might have kept splashing through blue water and coming up at any point that friendliness and fancy, with every prejudice shed, might determine."[9] The eroticism, it seems to me, is constituted by a crossing of literal and figurative registers, a wavering between metaphors' vehicles and tenors, which creates a sort of striptease, covering and revealing Brooke's young body as he splashes boyishly around in the blue waters of Greece and in the fullness of his poetic consciousness, shedding his clothes and his prejudices alike.

Brooke had the "art," as James wrote to Gosse, "of inspiring personally (as well as otherwise) an interest," and he was a particularly invested figure as England began to reckon the enormous cost of war.[10] "A voice had become audible," wrote Winston Churchill (then First Lord of the Admiralty) upon news of Brooke's death,

a note had been struck, more true, more thrilling, more able to
do justice to the nobility of our youth in arms engaged in this
present war, than any other—more able to express their thoughts
of self-surrender, and with a power to carry comfort to those who
watched them so intently from afar. . . . During the last few months
of his life, . . . the poet-solider told with all the simple force of
genius the story of youth about to die, and the sure triumphant
consolations of a sincere and valiant spirit. He expected to die; he
was willing to die for the dear England whose beauty and majesty
he knew; and he advanced towards the brink with perfect serenity,
with absolute conviction of the rightness of his country's cause,
and a heart devoid of hate for fellow-men. . . . Joyous, fearless,
versatile, deeply instructed, with classic symmetry of mind and
body, he was all that one would wish England's noblest sons to be
in days when no sacrifice but the most precious is acceptable, and
the most precious is that which is most freely proffered.[11]

Most troubling—if perhaps also most affecting—is the placidity with
which Churchill ventriloquizes a voice now silent and animates a consciousness now vanished. James's preface and Marsh's memoir both
appear against the background of the investment to which Churchill's
eulogy attests and which it perhaps helped to foster. The distance separating James's tribute from Churchill's, however, points to concerns beyond
even James's own relation to the war, and to Brooke and to other beautiful
young men it killed; the complexity of James's response asks to be read
in the context of his late reflections on the literary life and on literary language, asks to be read in relation to "style." With Brooke, moreover, James
might be said to reflect on the poet's "own" relation to his work, on "a life"
devoted to art—and thus on the claims of the "biographical" in readings
of a writer's corpus.

    With Churchill's eulogy in mind, then, consider James's arresting
account of Marsh's "infinitely touching record" of Brooke's life seen from
the perspective of his premature death:

What could strike one more, for the immense occasion, than
the measure that might be involved in it of desolating and heart-
breaking waste, waste of quality, waste for that matter of quantity,
waste of all the rich redundancies, all the light and all the golden

store, which up to then had formed the very price and grace of life? Yet out of the depths themselves of this question rose the other, the tormenting, the sickening and at the same time the strangely sustaining, of why, since the offering couldn't at best be anything but great, it wouldn't be great just in proportion to its purity, or in other words its wholeness, everything in it that could make it most radiant and restless. Exquisite at such times the hushed watch of the mere hovering spectator unrelieved by any action of his own to take, which consists at once of so much wonder for why the finest of the fine should, to the sacrifice of the faculty we most know them by, have to become mere morsels in the huge promiscuity, and of the thrill of seeing that they add more than ever to our knowledge and our passion, which somehow thus becomes at the same time an unfathomable abyss. (766)

"Waste" names an unredeemable loss, the obscene profligacy bound to sicken any observer not irremediably corrupt when faced with the spectacle of war. We might begin to measure James's distance from Churchill's redemptive strains by noting how the striking phrase "rich redundancies" opts out of any calculus of profit or exchange, refusing to domesticate the unredeemed fact of loss by tallying it against a cause, just or unjust, achieved or baffled in the event. "Waste" here refers, straightforwardly enough, to the waste of life: "this is too horrible and heart-breaking," he wrote to Edward Marsh on news of Brooke's death. "If there was a stupid and hideous disfigurement of life and outrage to beauty left for our awful conditions to perpetrate, those things have been now supremely achieved, and no other brutal blow can better them for making one just stare through one's tears."[12] "This is indeed a dismal damnable stroke," he wrote to Gosse, "the barren extinction of so beautiful a being and so distinguished a young poet as R.B. It wrings the heart & makes the time still more hideous."[13] "The war," he wrote elsewhere, "has used up words."[14]

"Waste," however, brings in another register, which might begin to explain the ambiguously redemptive tonalities at the end of the passage. Next to the statesman's eulogy, James is markedly equivocal; in contrast to Churchill's stress on nation, knowledge ("he expected to die"), "conviction," "serenity," and—through his gesture of ventriloquism and through the progression toward closure in his peroration—an identification (available to patriotic standers-by) with the "poet-soldier" and his "precious"—because "freely proffered"—sacrifice, James turns to an unsettling "thrill," to an "unrelieved," isolated spectator, and, finally, to "an unfathomable abyss." Redemption is posed precisely as a problem—as a lure, even a danger that might not be avoidable. To begin to spell out that claim, the passage is, from the outset, self-consciously poetic, rendering loss through a well-worn poetic trope: "all the light and all the golden store." Honey laid away by industrious bees as hidden (but golden, luminous) treasure becomes a figure for the harvest and for fall, for the holding in reserve of the fruits of human labor. In Christopher Pitt's 1753 translation of Virgil's *Aeneid,* for instance, Aeneas looks down on Carthage, on the construction of its walls and towers, and the founding of its civic institutions:

> Thus to their toils, in early summer, run
> The clust'ring bees, and labor in the sun;
> Led forth, in colonies, their buzzing race,
> Or work the liquid sweets, and thicken to a mass.
> The busy nation flies from flow'r to flow'r,
> And hoards, in curious cells, the golden store;[15]

Pope has "Th' industrious bees neglect their golden store"; Keats writes of "golden store / In Autumn's sickle"; in Shelley, we read, "The vines and orchards, Autumn's golden store, / Were burned"; and various other poets use the phrase in forms and contexts more or less distant from the original topos.[16] Linking, by analogy, the course of the seasons to that of a human life, that golden store, wasted, can therefore figure a life ended before its due season. James thus renders the waste of life as a waste of poetic promise, the waste of poems left unwritten; a life cut short long before the autumnal harvest, its golden store laid uselessly away with no future provisioned winter coming to make use of it severs the thread of meaning as temporal continuity. The redemptive turn is similarly rendered through a traditional poetic locus: "out of the depths themselves of this question rose" evokes, of course, the opening of Psalms 130—"Out of the depths have I cried unto thee, O Lord"—as well as the long tradition of literary conceits built upon that anguished cry.[17]

Thus far, the turn to poetry seems relatively conventional: the "golden store" is both poetry and the young life wasted, and an observer, faced with this "waste," calls—"out of the depths"—for redemption. (The bad faith of Churchill's persuasive peroration is the redemption it asserts through a quasi-syllogism that implicitly works in reverse: "in days when no sacrifice but the most precious is acceptable, and the most precious is that which is most freely proffered" makes an unspeakable sacrifice "acceptable" by fiat, and by linking its recuperation to the preciousness of what has been lost. One senses that the preciousness is evoked to establish that the sacrifice was in fact "freely proffered," that it appears, in other words, to establish the premise as a given—thereby redeeming it, too, perhaps, through a metonymic logic linking the freely relinquished life to the freedom the sacrifice would ostensibly protect.) For a reading of James, the initial complication is the term *waste* in the larger context of his writings, a context signaled here by "rich redundancies" as a particularly moving rendering of "life" that refuses, as I suggested, to understand death in terms of economics or exchange. It disrupts this calculus because it renders life as, precisely, waste.[18] To waste life's rich redundancies is to waste the golden store of its wastefulness.

To my mind, the central Jamesian text on the relation of "life" to "waste" is *A Small Boy and Others,* where *waste* brings together the (auto) biographical (as memory, as the narration of artistic development) with the question of art's relation to the world. Early in the memoir, James's reflections on the perpetual belatedness to which he was doomed by William's sixteen-month head start in life frame a meditation on waste:

> I lose myself in wonder at the loose ways, the strange process of
> waste, through which nature and fortune may deal on occasion
> with those whose faculty for application is all and only in their
> imagination and their sensibility. There may be during those bewil-
> dered and brooding years so little for them to "show" that I liken
> the individual dunce—as he so often must appear—to some com-
> mercial traveler who has lost the key to his packed case of samples
> and can but pass for a fool while other exhibitions go forward.[19]

"I lose myself" is a striking phrase in an autobiography, and a recurrent one in this text, where the narration of development overlaps with curiously productive refinements of self-loss. This description of what might, in psychoanalytic terms, be called "latency," renders "waste" in terms reminiscent of the temporal structure of "The Art of Fiction" and "The Future of the Novel." That structure makes the writer's "life" unrepresentable or unobjectifiable just as, in the earlier essays, "fiction" and the "novel" are: the "waste" of having nothing to show, no salable items to exhibit, thus names a life told (and lived) according the principles of that antimimetic theory of novelistic representation. The contingent fact of Henry's belatedness consigns his life itself to the temporal structure of its later narration; the predicament of the boy arriving belatedly on the scene of his brother's learning overlaps with the novelist's belated return (in autobiography) to his childhood. That overlap links "life" and writing as, precisely, "waste."[20]

The text returns at several moments to Henry James (Sr.) and his unconventional experiments in education; William is represented as having regretted the randomness, the lack of pedagogical method, while Henry (Jr.) defends them by a *nachträglich* logic of development reminiscent of his discussions of the form of the novel. The small boy proved, in retrospect, to have been educable by dint of having later developed as he did. And James over and over again insists on the strange productivity of a consciousness exposed to the contingent effects of its experience. "It may be asked," he writes,

> of the root of "what" matter I so complacently speak, and if I say,
> "Why, of the matter of our having with considerable intensity
> *proved* educable, or, if you like better, teachable, that is accessible
> to experience," it may again be retorted: "That won't do for a
> decent account of a young consciousness; for think of all the
> things that the failure of method, of which you make so light,
> didn't put into yours; think of the splendid economy of a real—or
> at least of a planned and attempted education, 'a regular course
> of instruction'—and then think of the waste involved in the so
> inferior substitute of which the pair of you were evidently victims."
> An admonition this on which I brood, less, however, than on
> the still other sense, rising from the whole retrospect of my now
> feeling sure, of my having mastered the particular history of just
> that waste—to the point of its actually affecting me as blooming
> with interest, to the point even of its making me ask myself how in
> the world, if the question is of the injection of more things into the
> consciousness (as would seem the case,) mine could have "done"
> with more. (113)

James's rendering of development wryly parodies a model of consciousness as a container into which experience or education "puts things." Like
the novel form in the essays on fiction, education cannot be objectified or
measured in this way. Contrasted with the "economy of a real—or at least
of a planned and attempted education," the "method" of the small boys'
educations overlaps with the method of the autobiography; "waste" is the
(unrepresentable) material, the life upon which that belated consciousness broods, to its infinite profit.

The lack of method brings to the fore a groundlessness in autobiography that is, again, reminiscent of the earlier essays on fiction:

> I see my critic, by whom I mean my representative of method at
> any price, take in this plea only to crush it with his confidence—
> that without the signal effects of method one must have had by an
> inexorable law to resort to shifts and ingenuities, and can therefore
> only have been an artful dodger more or less successfully dodging.
> I take full account of the respectability of the prejudice against
> one or two of the uses to which the intelligence may at a pinch
> be put—the criminal use in particular of falsifying its history, of
> forging its records even, and of appearing greater than the trace-
> able grounds warrant. One can but fall back, none the less, on the
> particular *un*traceability of grounds—when it comes to that: cases
> abound so in which, with the grounds all there, the intelligence
> itself is not to be identified. I contend for nothing moreover but the
> lively interest of the view, and above all of the measure, of almost
> any mental history after the fact. Of less interest, comparatively,
> is that sight of the mind *before*—before the demonstration of the
> fact, that is, and while still muffled in theories and presumptions
> (purple and fine linen, and as such highly becoming though those
> be) of what shall prove best for it. (113–14)

Returning again and again to the "*un*traceability of grounds," the autobiography, which tends to vaporize the subject whose coming into being
it narrates, resists formalization just as the earlier essays do, insisting on
the purely retrospective interest of the boy's development. The potentially "criminal use" to which the intelligence may be put—"of falsifying
its history, of forging its records even, and of appearing greater than the
traceable grounds warrant"—figures the project of autobiography; the

writer thus recovers "that capacity of childhood for making the most of its adventures after a fashion that may look so like making the least" (35).²¹ The gap between a life and what it "looks like" might define, simply, autobiography.

To my mind, this gap provides for the central interest of the anticommercial refrain that runs through the text, the insistence that two generations of the James family never did anything, never went into "business"—father, siblings, cousins, uncles, aunts, all like the seeming "dunce" of a child likened to "some commercial traveler who has lost the key to his packed case of samples" (5).²² This insistence extends to the very stories James's father told:

> The truth was indeed that we had, too, . . . our sense of "dissipation"
> as an abounding element in family histories; a sense fed quite
> directly by our fondness for making our father . . . tell us stories
> of the world of his youth. He regaled us with no scandals, yet it
> somehow rarely failed to come out that each contemporary on his
> younger scene, each hero, had, in spite of brilliant promise and
> romantic charm, ended badly, as badly as possible[;] . . . everyone
> without exception had at last taken a turn as far as possible from
> edifying. (25–26)

Just as the James cousins could not turn their experience to monetary profit, even the stories—of promise squandered, of lives failed to turn to "profit"—do not themselves have morals, cannot be put to "edifying" use. (In another register, in these useless stories about wasted promise, the charisma exerted by that spectacle of waste also makes them all the farther "from edifying.")

Waste in *Small Boy* therefore connects a number of registers linking the (belated) narration of a life to James's antimimetic understanding of literary language, and the term forces a reconsideration of, among other things, the role of loss in the memoir. The text is a testament to a mourned loss—of William, whose death in 1910 occasioned it. Autobiography—the recovery of "the full treasure of scattered, wasted circumstance" (1), its recovery *as* wasted, and, with that paradoxical recovery, the narration of authorial emergence—is, simultaneously, the writing of a memorial. It is a text that is in many ways transfixed by loss: from the outset, his father's family presents "a chronicle of early deaths, arrested careers, broken promises, orphaned children" (7). Thus, the glamorous dancing cousins of Albany all die young:

> It is at all events to the sound of fiddles and the popping of corks that I see even young brides, as well as young grooms, originally so formed to please and to prosper . . . vanish untimely, become mysterious and legendary, with such unfathomed silences and significant headshakes replacing the earlier concert; so that I feel how one's impression of so much foredoomed youthful levity received constant and quite thrilling increase. (23)

His "red-headed kinsman Gus Barker . . . as by a sharp prevision, snatched what gaiety he could from a life to be cut short, in a cavalry dash" (90); of Gus's older brother Bob—"a handsome young man, a just blurred, attractive illusive presence, who hovered a bit beyond our real reach"—James writes, "it was all in the right key that, a few years later, he should, after 'showing some talent for sculpture,' have gone the hapless way of most of the Albany youth, have become a theme for sad vague headshakes (kind and pitying in his case) and died prematurely and pointlessly, or in other words, by my conception, picturesquely." The "sharp prevision" of these lives seems to make them anticipate not only their too early ends but also their later narration. The recurrent verb tense—"should . . . have gone . . . have become"—makes for a curiously posthumous prolepsis that is particularly suited to narrative. "The headshakes were heavier and the sighs sharper," James continues,

> for another slim shade, one of the younger and I believe quite the most hapless of those I have called the outstanding ones; he too, several years older than we again, a tormenting hoverer and vanisher; he too charmingly sister'd, though sister'd only, and succumbing to monstrous early trouble after having "shown some talent" for music. The ghostliness of these aesthetic manifestations, as I allude to them, is the thinnest conceivable chip of stray marble, the faintest far-off twang of old chords. (98–99)[23]

The ghostly dead cousins and the ghostliness of unrealized aesthetic potential are brought together in this figure for vanished time as "waste," as a disunified fragment (itself attenuated to the almost imperceptible) of a lost aesthetic whole, "the thinnest conceivable chip of stray marble, the faintest far-off twang of old chords."[24]

Whatever else is suggested by these moments, read with the passages about his father's wasteful (non)system of education, loss in the memoir begins to seem curiously productive. And perhaps the central (non)object of loss in the text is nothing other than the narrating voice itself, the consciousness whose development would be narrated. That loss is marked in the text's very title: a memoir begun as a memorial, an attempt "to place together some particulars of the early life of William James and present him in his setting, his immediate native and domestic air" (1). It is unclear, from the outset, who is the small boy and who the others. The uniting "and," moreover, resists subordinating other lives to the story of the small boy, whoever he may be, and merges him with those others whose identities are made to seem, from the title on, part of the boy himself. "I lose myself": the repeated phrase delineates with particular economy the central movement of this memoir by rendering the rapture, absorption, interest of a gaze back in time and the composition it inspires—and the subsequent vanishing of the narrative voice in the narrating of its development. Striking in this regard is the tendency of the text's point of view to fracture, enacting in its prose the dividing of its central consciousness, its constitutive ceding of perspective to the others surrounding it. Thus, the "and others" of the title makes of particular interest, perhaps, an effect the autobiographical texts share with the rest of the late prose—most strikingly *The American Scene*—namely, ventriloquism and thrown voice. Evident in the ventriloquized debate with the partisan of educational method (where the author's apologia, too, is ventriloquized), such effects of thrown voice now extend to the very scenery as formative of the small, gaping (later to be authorial) pilgrim:

> The further quays, with their innumerable old book-shops and print-shops . . . must have come to know us almost as well as we knew them; . . . we moved in a world of which the dark message, expressed in we couldn't have said what sinister way too, might have been "Art, art, art, don't you see? Learn, little gaping pilgrims, what *that* is!" Oh we learned, that is we tried to, as hard as ever we could. . . . Style, dimly described, looked down there [the outer vestibule to the Palace], as with conscious encouragement, from the high grey-headed, clear-faced, straight-standing old houses— very much as if wishing to say "Yes, small staring *jeune homme*, we

are dignity and memory and measure, we are conscience and proportion and taste, not to mention strong sense too: for all of which
good things take us—you won't find one of them when you find
(as you're going soon to begin to at such a rate) vulgarity." This was
an abundance of remark to such young ears. (176–77).

The effects of expropriated consciousness demonstrated by Sharon
Cameron in her reading of *The American Scene* here uncannily mark the
narration of James's aesthetic development.[25] The fracturing of the narrating voice as the aesthetic sensibility comes into being is enacted by the narrative's curious effects of thrown voice and is figured by the giving of a face
to the scene described.[26] The anthropomorphic effect of Style "look[ing]
down, as with conscious encouragement" and of "grey-headed, clear-
faced, straight-standing old houses" figures—through the "recognition"
of a posited face—the giving of voice to the viewed city. But that anthropomorphic effect potentially extends to the "gaping pilgrims" themselves,
suggesting a literalization of the assertion that the visited shops "must
have come to know us almost as well as we knew them"; their "young ears"
are alike constituted by the exchange between spectator and viewed spectacle. The personification of the small boy and others—the recovery of
past selves and of vanished loved ones—is a similar textual effect.

When, then, James describes the origin of his aesthetic gift, he wryly
turns to a little French boy, Louis de Coppet; James's gift is imputed to
him by Louis, with no outward signs to warrant the presumption. Working
together one summer "in the production of a romance" that Louis "*se fit
fort* to get printed, to get published," the effort, "alas, failed of the crown":

> I think of my participation in this vain dream as of the very first
> gage of visiting approval offered to the exercise of a gift—though
> quite unable to conceive my companion's ground for suspecting a
> gift of which I must at that time quite have failed to exhibit a single
> in the least "phenomenal" symptom. It had none the less by his
> overtures been handsomely *imputed* to me; that was in a manner
> a beginning—a small start, yet not wholly unattended with
> bravery.... If I drop on his memory this apology for a bayleaf it is
> from the fact of his having given the earliest, or at least the most
> personal, tap to that pointed prefigurement of the manners of
> "Europe," which, inserted wedge-like, if not to say peg-like, into my

young allegiance, was to split the tender organ into such unequal
halves. His the toy hammer that drove in the very point of the
golden nail. (18–19)

The reassertion of the metaphor's ground—the shift from wedge to peg
in naming the object that was "inserted . . . into my young allegiance"—
makes playfully explicit the penetrative erotics of the scene. That Louis's
"tap," moreover, is "the earliest, or at least the most personal" also makes
explicit the relay between temporal narrative (and origination) and erotic
proximity—the earliest as the intimate, which makes the "earliest" a drawing closer to one (figuratively) in space. James's (proleptically) figured
split in allegiance (between "Europe" and "America") as a split in origins
replays the division implicit in the narrative of the artist's genesis (both
his origination as an organ split into unequal halves and a talent originat-
ing in another's ungrounded imputation). Such a split is also enacted by
the ambiguity of the relative clause: it is perhaps unclear whether it is the
manners of Europe or their "prefiguration" that is "inserted"; if the subsequent future anterior tense leads one to side with "manners," the verb
tense, combined with that "prefiguring," leaves us with an initiation that is
constitutively belated, a split that *was to occur*—even if, strictly speaking,
consciousness is not literally split by a prefigurement. The emphasis on
the lack of "phenomenal" evidence also links the splitting implicit in that
structure of (temporally shuffled, vicarious) imputation to the strands of
dereification and antiformalization in his novel theory, and to the fracturing of the narrative voice and point of view in the text.[27]

This memoir, which begins as a memorial to William James and ends
with a "lapse in consciousness," thus narrates an authorial voice coming
into being through its division from itself. The origin of the writer's gift is
"failure," an unwritten, unachieved "romance"; his voice comes into being
by losing itself, his talent, imputed, by failing to present the least "phenomenal" symptom. This curiously productive self-loss cannot but inflect
the memoir's recurrent thematics of loss, shifting the "waste" those losses
present to the more productive forms of "waste" through which his consciousness comes into being.[28] We might therefore find in Vernon King—
another dead cousin (this time on his mother's side)—a precursor to
Rupert Brooke. Vernon—whose cultural achievements are represented as
far exceeding those of young William and Henry, and who is the focus of
the latter half of the penultimate chapter of *A Small Boy and Others*—died

in the Civil War. Casting about for an identity, Vernon finally "found him-self" as "the American soldier":

> As strange, yet as still more touching than strange, I recall the sight,
> even at a distance, of the drop straight off him of all his layers
> of educational varnish, the possession of the "advantages," the
> tongues, the degrees, the diplomas, the reminiscences, a saturation
> too that had all sunk in—a sacrifice of precious attributes that
> might almost have been viewed as a wild bonfire. . . . To this all the
> fine privilege and fine culture of all the fine countries (collective
> matter, from far back, of our intimated envy) had "amounted"; just
> as it had amounted for Vernon to the bare headstone on the
> Newport hillside where, by his mother's decree, . . . there figured
> no hint of the manner of his death. (204–5)

Vernon's self-discovery is a narrative of dehiscence, and the description of his at-last discovered identity is at the same time a description of his death. This life, whose sacrifice is unmemorialized even on the boy's tombstone (if not, we note, in James's prose), read in relation to a generation immune to commerce, to the educational system whose programmatic refusals are to the having of programs and to the having of anything to show for itself, to "that capacity of childhood for making the most of its adventures after a fashion that may look so like making the least" (35), to the narrative's own possibly "criminal" forging of its documents and falsifying of its history, might figure "waste" as a term for the memoir's depiction of authorial genesis and the late style made into a mode of narration there. And at the crux of that is "waste," at the same time, as the death of a beautiful boy of exquisite promise—the com-ing-to-naught of all the fine privilege and fine culture of all the fine countries.

That "wild bonfire" of precious, envied gifts is therefore not most illu-minatingly to be read as James's investment in the spectacle of Civil War masculinity or as any oblique confession of penance for a writerly life achieved by the evasion of service. The various modalities of "waste" in *A Small Boy and Others* evoke Rupert Brooke and the "desolating and heart-breaking waste" his death presents, the "waste of quality, waste for that matter of quantity, waste of all the rich redundancies." We might therefore also be in a better position to gloss the perplexing turn taken by James's description of that later wild bonfire:

Exquisite at such times the hushed watch of the mere hovering spectator unrelieved by any action of his own to take, which consists at once of so much wonder for why the finest of the fine should, to the sacrifice of the faculty we most know them by, have to become mere morsels in the huge promiscuity, and of the thrill of seeing that they add more than ever to our knowledge and our passion, which somehow thus becomes at the same time an unfathomable abyss. (766)

Seen from the perspective of *A Small Boy and Others,* war presents a difficulty that is perhaps the inverse of that which the description initially intimates. It is less that the "war has used up words" than that the "waste" it wreaks threatens to overlap with the "waste" that might define, simply, the infinitely productive ways of consciousness.[29] "The liveliest lesson," he writes in *Small Boy,*

I must have drawn . . . makes in any case, at the best, an odd educational connection, given the kind of concentration at which education, even such as ours, is supposed especially to aim: I speak of that direct promiscuity of insights which might easily have been pronounced profitless, with their attendant impressions and quickened sensibilities—yielding, as these last did, harvests of apparitions. (194–95)

The problem, then, is that this promiscuity—the "profitless" impressions that yield "harvests of apparitions"—overlaps with the "huge promiscuity" that makes of beautiful young poets "mere morsels," and, we note, mere apparitions; the finest of the fine thus sacrificed "add more than ever to our knowledge and our passion." That, it seems to me, is the "unfathomable abyss" of our thus supplemented knowledge and passion that the death of Rupert Brooke has James face.

A Small Boy and Others and its account of authorial origination, read against the war essays, suggest that the "biographical" enters James's late writing through its meditations on the relation of literary language to its time and place, which is, moreover, explicitly the concern of the Rupert Brooke preface. It begins with the soliciting interest of the poet's relation to circumstance:

Nothing more generally or more recurrently solicits us, in the light of literature, I think, than the interest of our learning how the poet, the true poet, and above all the particular one with whom we may for the moment be concerned, has come into his estate, asserted and preserved his identity, worked out his question of sticking to that and to nothing else; and has so been able to reach us and touch us *as* a poet, in spite of the accidents and dangers that must have beset his course. (747)

The precarious "estate" is the "clear safe arrival of the poetic nature . . . at the point of its free and happy exercise" able, furthermore, "to reach us and touch us"; the attaching question is thus at once that of the poetic gift's self-realization and that of literary transmission, mysteries, both, of "how, in a world in which difficulty and disaster are frequent, the most wavering and flickering of all fine flames has escaped extinction." "We are at any rate," James continues, "in general beset by the impression and haunted by the observed law, that the growth and the triumph of the faculty at its highest have been positively in proportion to certain rigours of circumstance" (747). That evasive final phrase—it is unclear how such a "proportion" might be calculated, or of what "certain rigours of circumstance" might consist—leaves open what it is that "haunts" in the poet's relation to his time.

Our interest, he suggests, is perhaps most intense in those poets thwarted by circumstance: "we think of Dante in harassed exile, of Shakespeare under sordidly professional stress, of Milton in exasperated exposure and material darkness; we think of Burns and Chatterton, and Keats and Shelley and Coleridge, we think of Leopardi and Musset and Emily Brontë and Walt Whitman." It is possible, then, to adduce examples of poets not thus thwarted (Byron, Tennyson, Swinburne, Rostand, Hugo),

but it would take more of these than we can begin to set in a row to purge us of that prime determinant, after all, of our affection for the great poetic muse, the vision of the rarest sensibility and the largest generosity we know kept by her at their pitch, kept fighting for their life and insisting on their range of expression, amid doubts and derisions and buffets, even sometimes amid stones of stumbling quite self-invited, that might at any moment have made the loss of the precious clue really irremediable. (748)

That James finds more compelling the becoming visible of circumstance or fortune or contingency than the seeming triumph is suggested by the curious fact that Rupert Brooke is not aligned with either camp, his prosperous public school childhood not making him one of the exempt and his early death in war not tying him to those whose poetic fortunes asserted themselves against circumstance. An exception to these alternatives, he proves "a sudden case in which the old discrimination quite drops to the ground—in which we neither on the one hand miss anything that the general association could have given it, nor on the other recognise the pomp that attends the grand exceptions I have mentioned" (749).

James frames the dropping to the ground of "the old discrimination" by turning right away to Brooke's death: "Rupert Brooke, young, happy, radiant, extraordinarily endowed and irresistibly attaching, virtually met a soldier's death, met it in the stress of action and the all but immediate presence of the enemy" (749). That early death marks the consummation of a paradoxical relation to context that James calls "modern"; Brooke is "a new, a confounding and superseding example altogether" because, "while he is still in the highest degree of the distinguished faculty and quality, we happen to feel him even more markedly and significantly 'modern'" (749). "Modern," Brooke belongs neither to the camp of Chatterton and Milton nor to that of Swinburne and Tennyson because, it seems, he has no relation to his time. Rather, he embodies it and comes to be identified, simply, with the "modern" itself, which may be partly why (aside from the facts of Brooke's death) James equivocates on the "immediate presence of the enemy," and hence on the immediacy of the war at the moment of Brooke's death.[30] Brooke thus lacks the minimal difference that would allow him to have a "relation"—thwarting or enabling his poetic gifts—to his context. Unlike Byron, who fought against the mores of his time (and thereby "looks to us," in his effort to startle the "comfortable faith" of his contemporaries, "comparatively plated over with the impenetrable rococo of his time"), Brooke transcends his time by proving transparent to it (749)—"the exquisite temperament," James writes, "linked so easily to the irrepressible experience" (757). This relation of transparency is achieved at its highest degree of adequation in Brooke's letters from the Pacific: "Never, clearly, had he been on such good terms with the hour, never found the life of the senses so anticipate the life of the imagination, or the life of the imagination so content itself with the life of the senses; it is all an abundance of amphibious felicity" (765).[31] The images of Brooke, stripped and swimming, and the repeated emphasis on his late-found love of the aquatic, recall this "amphibious felicity"—"amphibious," perhaps, in the sense of moving between realms, water and land, imagination and sense perception, poetic consciousness and historical context, and therefore a particular "felicity" that makes of these homoerotic moments figures of Brooke's transparent relation to his time, sustained in the element of his contemporaneity like a young stripped body in the translucent waters of Greece.

The characterization of Brooke's travels in the South Pacific frames the outbreak of war and the fate that awaits him "in the air of so-called civilization." Yet if the war initially seems to be an interruption of that idyll, it also appears in other ways unsettlingly continuous with the description of Brooke's poetic potential: "he came back to England as promiscuously qualified, as variously quickened, as his best friends could wish for fine production and fine illustration in some order still awaiting sharp definition" (765). That "promiscuous" qualification echoes the later "vast promiscuity" in which "the finest of the fine" become "mere morsels" (766); the profligate waste of poetic faculties is emphasized by the echo, but possible, too, is an intimated assimilation of war to an aesthetic "order," or a suggestion, at least, that the war provides the "sharp definition" for the order in which Brooke finds himself promiscuously qualified for production and illustration. (The war might define an "order" in the sense of demarcating a life, or it might provide a vocation for an undefined talent, making Brooke, at last, a poet.) Such a possibility is suggested by a series of words in the essay that, explicitly pointing to the poet's encounter with circumstance, initially register simply as irony: the preface over and over returns to Brooke's "luck," to his "fortune," to the "happy," or to the "felicitous" in a sense that makes manifest that such subjective or affective terms might be rooted in a more psychologically neutral question of adequation—a lack of interference, for instance, between a psyche and its context. (Happy or "felicitous," in other words, in the way that Austin will use that term—or, as one might say, a "happy phrase.")[32] In this sense, like his amphibian love of swimming, Brooke's ebullient good nature overlaps with his "modernity," the "unfailing felicity" of his relation to his surroundings (756): "Our unspeakably fortunate young poet of to-day" (749); "a creature on whom the gods had smiled their brightest" (755); "the young poet with absolutely nothing but his generic spontaneity to trouble about, the young poet profiting for happiness by a general condition unprecedented for young poets"

(753); "this appearance of universal assimilation . . . made each part of his rich consciousness, so rapidly acquired, cling, as it were, to the company of all the other parts, so as at once neither to miss any touch of the luck (one keeps coming back to that), incurred by them, or to let them suffer any want of its own rightness" (753); "these moments of his quick career formed all together as happy a time, in as happy a place, to be born to as the student of the human drama has ever caught sight of" (755). These terms describe his curiously passive relation to experience; he doesn't strive for "development," but, being a child of his time and place, he has it given him:

> [J]ust there was the luck attendant of the coincidence of his course with the moment at which the proceeding hither and yon to the tune of almost any "happy thought," and in the interest of almost any branch of culture or invocation of response that might be more easily improvised than not, could positively strike the observer as excessive, as in fact absurd, for the formation of taste or the enrichment of genius. (757)[33]

And they describe, too, Brooke's harmonizing social presence, his charismatic power to bring his context into agreement with his personality, which, since he carried it with him everywhere, he himself—"so beautifully undesigning weaver of that spell" (763), of "the harmonising benefit that his presence conferred" (764)—seems not to have seen: "it is impossible not to figure him, to the last felicity, . . . presenting himself always with a singular effect both of suddenness and of the readiest rightness; we should always have liked to be there, wherever it was, for the justification of our own fond confidence and the pleasure of seeing it unfailingly spread and spread" (763). In James's last sighting of him in a hospital in London, "it was all auspiciously, well-nigh extravagantly, congruous; nothing certainly could have been called more modern":

> He had never seemed more animated with our newest and least deluded, least conventionalised life and perception and sensibility, and that formula of his so distinctively fortunate, his overflowing share in our most developed social heritage which had already glimmered, began with this occasion to hang about him as one of the aspects, really a shining one, of his fate. (766–67)

The "fortune" that initially describes the privilege of the British public school boy prepared, without effort, for poetry, then, merging with the preface's insistence on Brooke's modernity, comes to describe his relation to the war. One with his time and place, Brooke, "charged" with "our merciless actuality," cannot but embody the "waste" of beauty and promise in World War I:

> Everything about him of keenest and brightest (yes, absolutely of brightest) suggestion made so for his having been charged with every privilege, every humour, of our merciless actuality, our fatal excess of opportunity, that what indeed could the full assurance of this be but that, finding in him the most charming object in its course, the great tide was to lift him and sweep him away? . . . It was as if the peculiar richness of his youth had itself marked its limit, so that what his own spirit was inevitably to feel about his "chance"—inevitably because both the high pitch of the romantic and the ironic and the opposed abyss of the real came together in it—required, in the wondrous way, the consecration of the event. (768)[34]

The "abyss of the real" evokes the "unfathomable abyss" that our "passion" is made, by the contemplation of the "huge promiscuity[,] . . . somehow" to become (766). And the coming together of the "romantic and the ironic" with the "opposed abyss of the real" suggests a convergence of fictional or rhetorical structures with the "real," with factuality as a vanishing of meaning. That, in part, seems to be the "consecration of the event"—the genitive leaving open whether the event itself is consecrated or is rather the agent of consecration, a hesitation that replays, perhaps, the uncertain reference of the *it*, in which the various elements are said to come together (probably "chance," but possibly "spirit" or even "youth"?). The genitive hesitation, especially, equivocates on the sacrilization asserted (or not) by "consecration" (the sanctifying of bread and wine during Communion, like, in another register, the adequation of imagination and context). Unresolved, in other words, is the question of whether the material event is sublimated into something "higher," or whether it simply completes a logic. Does the "consecration of the event" turn death to meaning, or does it merely mark an end (of a narrative, of a logical progression)? The question, perhaps, is the extent to which Brooke's death can be assimilated to the harmonizing felicity of his life—and hence the register in which the "modern" is to be read. The convergence of the fictional and the "real"—the achievement, one might almost say, of true poetic "reference"; the curiously productive ways of consciousness as "waste" in *Small Boy* finding themselves faced with (and doubled by) the "unfathomable abyss" of the preface; a poetic consciousness whose transparency to its time allows for no interference between mind and world, only perfect "felicity," modernity and poetic expression alike realized at last in that gifted poet's untimely vanishing: the death of Rupert Brooke marks the "consecration" of these strands and begins to limn the sense in which the "biographical" shapes these wartime writings.

We might be reminded here of another dead poet; when consciousness merges with "waste" as it is characterized in the autobiography, when the recuperative capacity of "passion" to make the "waste of all the rich redundancies" seem "strangely sustaining" turns that passion into an "unfathomable abyss," the "consecration of the event" evokes Paul de Man's description of Shelley's death in his reading of *The Triumph of Life*. Having read the poem as enacting a repeating series of "disfigurations," delusive forgettings of the "positional" power of language[35]—the "starting, catachretic decree of signification," as he puts it in "Hypogram and Inscription," or "the necessary recurrence of the initial violence," as he writes in "Shelley Disfigured" (119)—that thereby constitute but rupture language's capacity to mean, de Man suddenly turns to Shelley's "actual" death, which functions "as the decisive textual articulation." "This defaced body," he writes,

> is present in the margin of the last manuscript page and has become an inseparable part of the poem. At this point, figuration and cognition are actually interrupted by an event which shapes the text but which is not present in its represented or articulated meaning. It may seem a freak of chance to have a text thus molded by an actual occurrence, yet the reading of *The Triumph of Life* establishes that this mutilated textual model exposes the wound of a fracture that lies hidden in all texts. . . . The rhythmical interruptions that mark off the successive episodes of the narrative are not new moments of cognition but literal events textually reinscribed by a delusive act of figuration or of forgetting. (120–21)

Posing the question of the text's relation to its "outside," and of the particular ways it might be said to be "shaped" by the world, Shelley's death, it seems, leads one to ask not whether the unmeaning interruption of death can be recuperated for meaning (because that interruption, and its forgetting, already constitute meaning) but rather what consequences follow from an unavoidable recuperation, the transformation of "all the other dead bodies that appear in romantic literature" into monuments, "into historical and aesthetic objects" (121):

> [I]t is not avoidable, since the failure to exorcize the threat, even
> in the face of such evidence as the radical blockage that befalls
> this poem, becomes precisely the challenge to understanding that
> always again demands to be read. And to read is to understand, to
> question, to know, to forget, to erase, to deface, to repeat—that
> is to say, the endless prosopopoeia by which the dead are made
> to have a face and a voice which tells the allegory of their demise
> and allows us to apostrophize them in our turn. No degree of
> knowledge can ever stop this madness, for it is the madness of
> words. What *would* be naïve is to believe that this strategy, which
> is not *our* strategy as subjects, since we are its product rather than
> its agent, can be a source of value and has to be celebrated or
> denounced accordingly. ("Shelley," 122)

Prosopopoeia, "which, as the trope of address, is the very figure of the reader and of reading" ("Hypogram and Inscription," 45), makes the dead "have a face and a voice which tells the allegory of their demise and allows us to apostrophize them in our turn"; the disfiguring potential of prosopopoeia, as Cynthia Chase suggests, lies in its making manifest that we are the "product" rather than the "agent" of this strategy, that our "face," as the locus of recognition and human meaning, is figural, and, as such, produced by an act of language, a "starting, catachresic decree" constitutive of, but unassimilable to, meaning.[36] The "abyss" that "passion" becomes in the Rupert Brooke essay seems a consequence, in part, of finding it impossible to avoid making the dead speak, or giving them a face, as well as the possibility intimated by that productivity of consciousness as disfiguration. The "forgetting" that de Man suggests "functions along monotonously predictable lines, by the historicization and the aesthetification of texts" might be read as the forgetting of the disfiguring potential that the

"starting, catachresic decree" makes structural to language, the recuperation of "shape" as form or history.[37]

James himself reflects on the power of death to interrupt consciousness in the curious late essay "Is There a Life after Death?" After defining
life as consciousness and consciousness as the yearning to transcend itself
through the discovery of yet unimagined relations, he seems to argue that
life thus, by definition, entails an "afterlife." The essay ends thus:

> If I am talking, at all events, of what I "like" to think I may, in short,
> say all: I like to think it open to me to establish speculative and
> imaginative connections, to take up conceived presumptions and
> pledges, that have for me all the air of not being decently able to
> escape redeeming themselves. And when once such a mental rela-
> tion to the question as that begins to hover and settle, who shall say
> over what fields of experience, past and current, and what immen-
> sities of perception and yearning, it shall *not* spread the protection
> of its wings? No, no, no—I reach beyond the laboratory brain.[38]

In James's closing assertion that consciousness exceeds its mere material
embodiment—"the poor palpable, ponderable, probeable, laboratory-
brain" (118)—the desubjectifying, antipsychological strains of his late
writing put pressure on the seeming solipsism or idealization, and in fact
the assertion of continuity takes shape through a vanishing of voice: "who
shall say" both asserts (as a rhetorical question) the limitless expansion of
consciousness and bears witness (as a question, precisely, of *who* shall say)
to the vanishing of that consciousness. If it is unclear whether the triumphant claim is for a life after death or for an argument successfully made
on its behalf (independent, that is, of any factual claims), part of what is
disorienting is that the two possibilities seem to amount to the same thing.
The assertion is curiously circular, and the transcendence is identified
with the yearning for it (even with the "conscious" disavowal of knowledge of its impossibility) through an overlapping term that also names a
movement of reference: "I reach" as both an assertion of extension and a
movement of desire (both "my consciousness extends beyond its physical
embodiment" and "my consciousness desires to extend beyond its physical embodiment"). At stake are "conceived presumptions and pledges"
and the power of a "mental relation to the question" to "spread the protection of its wings."[39] Formulating an argument for a life after death, James

seems to reverse the expected hierarchy; what might be seen as the ultimate intrusion of the "real" in the workings of texts becomes a way of questioning the power of literary language to act upon the world, a way of questioning its "reach."[40] That reach, then, asserts the triumph of literary reference over death, over the "consecration of the event" in a paradoxical gesture that also underlines the author's vanishing.

The emphasis throughout the essay is on personal survival—of the investments, passions, desires, and consciousness of a particular personality. Yet the flip side of the assertion of what looks like transcendence is a specter of death that haunts James's discussions of reference and of the relation of literary language to the world. Writing to Robert S. Rantoul on the occasion of the Hawthorne centenary in Salem, James turns an apology for his absence into a meditation on literary fame and on the relation of a writer to his context. His absence from Salem, he suggests, in fact gives him a better view of Hawthorne because, for any author, his fame depends on his vanishing. The temporal structure that in "The Future of the Novel" spelled the novel's resistance to formalization here defines the "posthumous glory" of literary fame:

> [T]here is, unfortunately for the prospective celebrity, no short
> cut possible, on the part of his fellow-townsmen, to the expensive
> holiday they are keeping in reserve for his name. It is there, all
> the while—somewhere in the air at least, even while he lives. But
> they cannot get *at* it until the Fates have forced, one by one, all the
> locks of all the doors and crooked passages that shut it off; and
> that celebrity meantime, by good luck, can have little idea what is
> missing.[41]

Hawthorne's personal loneliness becomes, in James's account, an intimation of his isolation in the future—as he becomes, "unwittingly and unsuspectedly, with an absence of calculation fairly precious for the final effect, the pretext for the kind of recognition you greet him with to-day" (469). "We see," he writes, the streets of Salem as the artist pursues "the *immediate*, the pressing need of the hour," and then we see, "at the other end of the century, these same streets and corners and doorways, these quiet familiarities, the stones he trod, the objects he touched, the air he breathed, positively and all impatiently *waiting* to bestow their reward, to measure him out success, in the great, in the almost superfluous, abundance of the eventual!" (470). These streets measure out his success from the perspective of a world without him in it. This characterization of posthumous glory is further developed by the letter's discussion of the "classic": classics "acquire their final value ... by the manner in which later developments have worked in respect to them—and, it is scarce too much to say, acquire it in spite of themselves and by the action of better machinery than their authors could have set in motion, stronger (as well as longer!) wires than their authors could have pulled" (472). These later developments work "by *contrast*," and "the state of being a classic is a *comparative* state—considerably, generously, even when blindly, brought about by the generations, the multitudes worshipping other gods, that have followed him. . . . He owes it more or less, at the best, to the *relief* in which some happy, some charming combination of accidents has placed his intrinsic value" (472–73). The temporal structure (as with the novel and its formalization, the designation of the classic arrives belatedly for the work, and for the literary life it crowns) anticipates that of T. S. Eliot's "tradition."[42] More radically than in Eliot, the fame that the author cannot know also points to ways that the literary life is out of synch with itself—like Milly Theale, like consciousness in *The Golden Bowl*. The claim of "Is There a Life after Death?" that life entails an afterlife might thus be read in the context of this gap dividing the literary celebrity from his life. The life of the great author is an "afterlife"— much as (we will see in the final chapter) belatedness in *The Ambassadors* makes indistinct the "missing" and "having" of a life. Literary immortality guarantees an afterlife but also ensures that one's life is deferred until after it is over: as Milly Theale says, "I shan't . . . have missed anything," or Kate, "she won't have loved you for nothing." Likewise, the emphasis on the aleatory nature of the fame-consigning future celebrates the author but also brings out the ways that the text's meaning is, finally, not governed by any intention, brings out the lethal or dispropriating consequences of "iterability"—the better machinery than an author could have set in motion, the wires longer than he could have pulled. The "fortune," "luck," and "felicity" of the Rupert Brooke essay appear here as a structural assimilation of the author to the place of death, and even the assertion of the classic's permanence emphasizes the author's "passing" and the mortality sheltered within the longue durée of art: "The grand sign of being a classic is that when you have 'passed,' as they say at examinations, you have passed; you have become one once for all; you have taken your degree and may be left to the light and the ages" (474).

"When once such a mental relation to the question as that begins to hover and settle," James writes at the end of "Is There a Life after Death," and we remember, too, the "slim shade" of a dead cousin in *A Small Boy and Others*, "a tormenting hoverer and vanisher" (99). The syntactical overlap intimates a link between the "mental relation" that "hovers" and the vanishing that James finds in the posthumous nature of literary fame; the verb *hover* brings together the dispropriating spectacle of future fame and the power of consciousness to "reach" beyond its mere material embodiment, "the poor palpable, ponderable, probeable, laboratory-brain." The action of a tormenting, watchful, but distanced presence, *hover* also describes a defiance of rules governing physical bodies—gravity, for instance, or death. (So "hover" can describe both an "object" of thought—a question or a relation—and a ghost.) At least syntactically, then, opposed movements are brought together: an assertion of transcendence that seems to argue for the ultimate gesture of ego consolidation also asserts a radical dispossession of self. (*Hover* can also have a sense of temporizing idleness: one hovers about among people driven by more pressing, and more timely, needs.) We might return again to Rupert Brooke's death to question the specific quality of absence invoked there: "Exquisite at such times the hushed watch of the mere hovering spectator unrelieved by any action of his own to take." It seems clear that the "mere hovering spectator," excluded for whatever reason—by age, by inclination, by circumstance— from war, is left thereby "merely" to observe (and not to take part). That the "unrelieved" spectator who finds no succor or relief is, literally, not raised up again points to an ironic counterpoint with "hovering," and the word's secondary martial meanings (to relieve a sentinel, for instance, or to relieve troops in the sense of replacing in the field soldiers exhausted or killed in battle) link the strain of the spectator's isolated nonparticipation (perhaps ironically, perhaps not) to the unremitting stress on a soldier left unrelieved. "Hushed watch," which suggests not only a sentinel's watchful duty but also a vigil—or a wake—is a striking phrase when the spectator is a writer, as if watchfulness might entail the falling silent of his voice. (In one archaic meaning, *to relieve* means "to bring into relief," as the "charming combination of accidents" brings into relief the talent of the author, makes him a "classic"; hence, *unrelieved* might suggest not brought into relief, not raised up, illegible.) It also is not impossible to read in the sentence an implication that it is open for the spectator to find relief in "taking" someone else's action. Nor is it clear that the sentence in fact valorizes action; it is unclear, in other words, that the spectator of the "great promiscuity" *ought* to be "relieved." What perhaps initially appears as if it would be legible in psychological terms—as regret, for instance, or even guilt—replays in its various equivocations the paradoxes of a writer's relation (or nonrelation) to his time.

The "tormenting hoverer and vanisher" of *A Small Boy and Others* reminds us of another crucial term in the predicament of the "mere hovering spectator" in the Rupert Brooke essay, namely, *torment:*

> Yet out of the depths themselves of this question rose the other, the tormenting, the sickening and at the same time the strangely sustaining, of why, since the offering couldn't at best be anything but great, it wouldn't be great just in proportion to its purity, or in other words its wholeness, everything in it that could make it most radiant and restless. (766)[43]

Here, then, is James in yet another perplexing late text, his introduction to *The Tempest,* which appeared ten years before the Brooke essay:

> If the effect of the Plays and Poems, taken in their mass, be most of all to appear often to mock our persistent ignorance of so many of the conditions of their birth, and thereby to place on the rack again our strained and aching wonder, this character has always struck me as more particularly kept up for them by *the Tempest;* the production, of the long series, in which the Questions, as the critical reader of Shakespeare must ever comprehensively and ruefully call them and more or less resignedly live with them, hover before us in their most tormenting form.[44]

"[O]ur strained and aching wonder" evinces the context in which "torment" often appears in late James: it is the torment (often not unpleasurable) of interest, the force exacted on consciousness by "Questions" in various forms—the flip side, perhaps, of the "magnificent waste" of thought.[45] (The potential pleasure of that torment marks an erotics of cognition. In *A Small Boy and Others,* he uses the term to describe the "almost unbearable intensity" of anticipation, "the scarce tolerable throb," of waiting for the curtain to rise on *The Comedy of Errors* during his first visit to the theater as a child: "the torment of the curtain was mixed" [55].) That the hovering of this "tormenting form" might have something to say about the "tormenting, and yet strangely sustaining" question that haunts the "mere hovering spectator" in the Rupert Brooke essay (and perhaps, too, about the "mental relation" that "hovers" and "settles" in "Is There a Life after Death?") is suggested by what turns out to be the "torment" of the essay on *The Tempest:* the plays' power to "mock our persistent ignorance of so many of the conditions of their birth." Shakespeare thwarts the urge to find or "touch" the "Man" in the "Artist," and torments us, in particular, with the question of how the man—the particular man capable of expressing absolutely everything—could have renounced the artist's gift as he appears to have done. "*How* did the faculty so radiant there contrive, in such perfection, the arrest of its divine flight" (1219); "the fathomless strangeness of his story, the abrupt stoppage of his pulse after *The Tempest* is not, in charity, lighted for us by a glimmer of explanation" (1207).

Contemplating this renunciation, James, as Stanley Cavell writes, is "caught between an insupportable mystery and an insufferable mindlessness" (*Transcendental Etudes,* 235). Among the difficulties this preface presents is what James means by the relation between "the Man" and "the Poet" (or, sometimes, "the artist" or "the Artist"). One possibility that emerges only briefly is that of understanding "the Man" in terms of the material conditions (pecuniary exigencies, for instance) that constrain the Poet's transcendence. In such a view, however, "the Man" is simply uninteresting and would be of no importance to the satisfactions of the poetry:

> For critics of this writer's [Mr. Halliwell-Phillipps] complexion, the
> only facts we are urgently concerned with are the facts of the Poet,
> which are abundantly constituted by the Plays and the Sonnets.
> The poet is *there,* and the Man is outside: the Man is for instance in
> such a perfectly definite circumstance as that he could never miss,
> after *The Tempest,* the key of his piano, as I have called it, since he
> could play so freely with the key of his cash-box. The supreme mas-
> ter of expression had made, before fifty, all the money he wanted;
> therefore, what was there more to express? This view is admirable if
> you can get your mind to consent to it. (1216)

Dismissing the Man makes him independent of the poetry, and there-fore paradoxically allows him to determine it by giving him power over a thereby objectifiable, instrumental gift. Once Shakespeare's renunciation comes into question, dismissing the Man as irrelevant paradoxically reduces the Poet to the Man, defines the Poet entirely by his material context. But Shakespeare, as the "supreme master of expression," represents for James the perfect reconciliation of Man and artist, and *The Tempest*, "the momentous conjunction . . . between his charged inspiration and his clarified experience: or, as I should perhaps better express it, between his human curiosity and his aesthetic passion" (1209). The "sea-change" of Ariel's song ("Full fathom five thy father lies") might serve as an emblem for this effortless movement, from eyes to pearls, from bones to coral, and the "fathomless strangeness of his story, the abrupt stoppage of his pulse," is not to be explained by the mere exigencies of bones and eyes and the material needs of human beings.

The term that resolves the opposition between "the Man" and "the artist" is "style." In the earlier plays, James writes, "the man everywhere . . . is so effectually locked up and imprisoned in the artist that we but hover at the base of thick walls for a sense of him; while, in addition, the artist is so steeped in the abysmal objectivity of his characters and situations." James continues:

> [W]hat we are present at in this fashion is a series of incalculable plunges—the series of those that have taken effect, I mean, after the great primary plunge, made once for all, of the man into the artist: the successive plunges of the artist himself into Romeo and into Juliet, into Shylock, Hamlet, Macbeth, Coriolanus, Cleopatra, Antony, Lear, Othello, Falstaff, Hotspur; immersions during which, though he always ultimately finds his feet, the very violence of the movements involved troubles and distracts our sight. In The Tempest, by the supreme felicity I speak of, is no violence; he sinks as deep as we like, but what he sinks into, beyond all else, is the lucid stillness of his style. (1209)

"Style" brings us closer to the man because, in its triumph, the "artist" is "consummate," because "style" effects the "momentous conjunction" James writes of, which thus brings us closer to the man by merging him completely with (rather than "plunging him into") the artist. "Style" can be opposed to two sorts of logics: the agonistic or oppositional (the Man *versus* the Poet, the claims of poetry *versus* those of material existence) and the identificatory (the "plunging" of the man "into" the artist succeeded by

that of the artist "into" his characters). Against the agonistic and the identificatory, James describes a merger whose keynote is tranquility or "lucid
stillness." *Lucid* here suggests a suffusion of light and hence a transparency
that figuratively renders a cognitive clarity—and hence tranquility—of a
mind unthwarted by material constraints and a medium so consummately
expressive that it is as if it isn't one. "Supreme felicity," as in the Rupert
Brooke essay, seems to index a relation of perfect transparency, with no
interference between inspiration and realization, mind and world, idea
and matter. To sink into the lucid stillness of style is hence to experience
the perfect merger of Man and Poet.

James figures this tranquil merger as the artist performing for his own
pleasure alone:

> I find it pictured for me in some such presentment as that of a
> divine musician who, alone in his room, preludes or improvises at
> close of day. He sits at the harpsichord, by the open window, in the
> summer dusk; his hands wander over the keys. They stray far, for
> his motive, but at last he finds and holds it; then he lets himself go,
> embroidering and refining: it is a thing for the hour and his mood.
> The neighbors may gather in the garden, the nightingale be hushed
> on the bough; it is none the less a private occasion, a concert of
> one, both performer and auditor, who plays for his own ear, his
> own hand, his own innermost sense, and for the bliss and capacity
> of his instrument. (1210–11)

The coming together of "the hour" and "his mood"—that the impro-
vised tune is "for" both of them figures again the perfect concord of
inside and out, "charged inspiration" and "clarified experience"—is tied
to several other unifications. The unity of "performer and auditor" signals art's perfect transmission, with no intervening media or minds. "He"
names an artistic agency distinguishable, at least in the essay's syntax,
from "his own ear, his own hand, his own innermost sense"; the grammatical parallel linking ear and hand to innermost sense (emphasized,
moreover, by the repeated, and repeatedly redoubled, possessives—his
own) enacts, in the perfect accord of the artist's intention and embodiment, conception and extension, the unification in the performer and
auditor of the improvisation at close of day. That, moreover, he performs
for his eye, hand, his innermost sense, and "for the bliss and capacity

of his instrument" signals a further unification, a performer for whom there is no "technique" because his intention, his conception, is one with his instrument. These unities, moreover, are not cast in terms of identificatory consolidation: auditor and performer, he is said to "[let] himself go"—sinking, perhaps, into the lucid stillness of his style. The passage unites "Man" and "artist" through a vocabulary that is at once aesthetic and subjective: "motive," for instance, names both a musical theme (as synonym for *motif*) and a person's "motivating" desire—the impetus putting both "Man" and composition "in motion." "Motive" as the subject of the improvisation is then also tied to James's use of it later in the essay to mean the "subject" of a representation (as opposed to its manner or style). *Expression*—Shakespeare is the "supreme master of expression"—similarly unites two registers: expression as an aesthetic category and "expression" as what gives human meaning to the contours of a face.[46] The term *expression* gives a face to language, and, by uniting Poet and Man, Shakespeare achieves that impossible reconciliation, making linguistic "expression" coincide with a human face.

Thus, Shakespeare

> points for us as no one else the relation of style to meaning and of manner to motive. . . . Unless it be true that these things, on either hand, are inseparable; unless it be true that the phrase, the cluster and order of terms *is* the object and the sense, in as close a compression as that of body and soul, so that any consideration of them as distinct, from the moment style is an active, applied force, becomes a gross stupidity: unless we recognise this reality the author of *The Tempest* has no lesson for us. (1212)

The assertion of this traditional aesthetic unity (in a traditional analogy, moreover, linking an aesthetic ideal to the body's relation to a soul) takes the form of a condition: "unless it be true . . . [Shakespeare] has no lesson for us." (James's sentence asserts not the truth of that unity but the felt necessity of affirming it.) The conditioning unity, moreover, is a "reality" to be "recognized," suggesting that at issue, too, is the question of reference, of a text's power to touch the reality to which it refers. Also striking is the genitive circumlocution—"the author of *The Tempest*"—which, on the one had, makes visible the conjoining of "Man" and "Poet." On the other hand, making such conjoining visible by subordinating the author to his work also suggests that the phrase offers a circumlocution for "the Man." The lesson of "the Man" depends on "style."

The condition asserts not unity but its necessity, and the phrasing of style's power of unification is wily: the analogy of parallel, close "compressions" of body and soul, manner and meaning, implies a minimal distinction between the terms "compressed," without resolving, moreover, how tight the compression is—of body and soul—to which the aesthetic unity is compared. "Manner" and "motive" may be inseparable, but it is an inseparability that has to be asserted—by "style" as "an active, applied force." To the precise extent that it makes visible this unity as an ideal, then, style makes it visible as yet to be achieved and is, in that sense, disfiguring. The unity of body and soul, "Man" and "Artist," "charged inspiration" and "clarified experience": *The Tempest* is "our Poet's high testimony to this independent, absolute value of Style" (1212). For Shakespeare to sink into the lucid stillness of his style—with no violence—is thus the achievement of the impossible, of a union posited as an ideal. On the one hand, the artist alone at the harpsichord is an image for expression completely unconstrained—unthwarted by circumstance, by any limits to inspiration, or by any interference intervening between inspiration and expression. "It is for Shakespeare's power of constitutive speech quite as if he had swum into our ken with it from another planet"; *The Tempest* is a finding of "tone . . . beyond any register of ours" (1211, 1212). Realized, the aesthetic ideal of Style is a transcending of human limits, the discovery of a language unconstrained by its constitutive unmeaning. "The tormented task James attends to," Cavell writes, "is seriously to conceive how *any* mortal could have achieved" what Shakespeare did. On the other hand, unconstrained expression brings to the fore just those human limits, makes visible how constrained language can be for those of us not composing "beyond . . . any register of ours," not from another planet. Quoting Emerson's assertion that Shakespeare "of all men best understands the English language, and can say what he will," Cavell notes the unsettling implication that "the rest of us are in various states of ignorance of our language and are unable to say what we will, chronically inexpressive, as if we are all to some extent aphasic" (Cavell, 237).[47] Such a possibility is intimated, too, by de Man's Shelley; intervening to interrupt his text, Shelley's death might be said to body forth (and, perhaps, delusively to contain) the impossibility of any supreme mastery of expression that would allow us "to say what we will."[48] The loss of "the Man" in James's essay is thus the loss of the possibility of such mastery—hence, the urgency, and the torment. In Cavell's gloss of Wittgenstein's reaction to Shakespeare, what Shakespeare makes visible is "the continuous threat of chaos clinging to his creation, an anxiety produced as the sense that it is something miraculous that words can mean at all, that there are words" (237).

The torment of Shakespeare's renunciation of his faculty of expression, "his inconceivable act of sacrifice" (*Tempest*, 1214)—"the eternal mystery, the most insoluble that ever was, the complete rupture, for our understanding, between the Poet and the Man" (1215)—is less the contingent historical question of the particular writer's career, less that, even, of his unaccountable decision willingly to renounce his gift, than that, in it, the lapse into silence appears not as a boundary to human life but as internal to it, internal, indeed, to the greatest capacity for linguistic expression the world has ever seen. The frontiers separating silence and speech, life and death, may not coincide, and "the Man" may not be what limits or what constitutes "the Poet." Nor can that silence be understood as a consequence of a lapse of time, of the centuries that seem, initially, to make for the torment of historical research's failure to turn up any but the most meager knowledge of Shakespeare's life. The loss inherent in historical transmission becomes one case among others of the rupture of Poet and Man, and the temporal lag of history, internal to expression itself.

There are moments, James writes, when we find ourselves "willing to let it pass as a mystery. But there are others when, speaking for myself, its power to torment us intellectually seems scarcely to be borne" (1215). What is the relation of this "torment" to that of the "mere hovering spectator unrelieved by any action of his own to take" when faced with the death of Rupert Brooke?[49] The later "tormenting" question is that of the sacrifice of "the finest of the fine" made "mere morsels in the huge promiscuity" (766), and one might therefore be tempted to read the rupture of Man and Poet as intimating the depressing realization that the spirit is merely its material embodiment, a "mere morsel" or "poor palpable, ponderable, probeable, laboratory-brain" ("Life," 123). Yet the question is more tormenting. The search for "the Man" is, in the essay's terms, a refusal to consent to "bewildered credulity" in the face of Shakespeare's renunciation (1214). The effort to discover what infinite capacity meant for a human being—" the effect on him of being *able* to write *Lear* and *Othello*" (1218)—is, however, not figured as the potential to heal a violent rupture

of Poet and Man. One's refusal to consent to bewildered credulity's renunciation of any search for "the Man" is itself figured as a form of violence,
as an unwillingness "to ignore any impulse, in presence of Play or Sonnet
(whatever vague stir behind either may momentarily act as provocation)
to try for a lunge at the figured arras" (1216). "The secret that baffles us,"
James writes,

> Being the secret of the Man, we know, as I have granted, that we
> shall never touch the Man *directly* in the Artist. We stake our hopes
> thus on indirectness, which may contain possibilities; we take that
> very truth for our counsel of despair, try to look at it as helpful
> for the Criticism of the future. That of the past has been too often
> infantile; one has asked one's self how it *could,* on such lines, get at
> him. The figured tapestry, the long arras that hides him, is always
> there, with its immensity of surface and its proportionate under-
> side. May it not then be but a question, for the fulness of time, of
> the finer weapon, the sharper point, the more extended lunge?
> (1220)

"Indirection" leads Cavell back to "mood"; "indirection thus negates
the active direction of knowing and names the direction in which an
approach is awaited from an object." Reading, he suggests, is "a surprise,
an accident, something you did not see coming" (245); in this, it evokes
the aleatory quality, the "felicity" of Rupert Brooke's modernity. Also
perplexing, however, are the references to *Hamlet:* it is Polonius who
proposes to Reynaldo that, spying on Laertes, he "by indirections find
directions out" (2.1.63), and he who, hidden "behind the arras" (3.3.28),
is killed by the lunge of Hamlet's sword (3.4.23).[50] For Polonius, as for
Rosencrantz and Guildenstern, whose story parallels his, spying by indirection proves lethal. What would the "more extended lunge" reach? One
possibility is that intentions and actions could coincide—that Hamlet
could kill the king instead of Polonius. The "indirection" through which
we might "touch" the Man, however, also suggests that that lunge might
redound upon us. Our effort to catch the Man in the Artist, to get behind
the arras, might leave us in the position of Polonius, skewered, thereby
by indirections having found, at last, directions out. Could this be the
"unfathomable abyss" of our "passion," and the infinite productiveness of
consciousness as "waste"?

The search for a queer Henry James is, perhaps unavoidably, one caught in tension between the two opposed senses we might give to a search for the Man in the artist. The disfiguring potential in what we have called the queerness of style is perhaps inevitably recuperated by the posited face—the psychologizing, biographical, and reifying reading of queerness as person and language as object. "Figured arras" and "figured tapestry" name, on the one hand, a distance from reference—they are fabrics that exist only in writing. On the other, they name a fabric, text, or textile that has become a face: a *figured* arras. The lunge through the figured arras is perhaps an effort to rend the reifications of the posited face, but a reminder, too, of the difficulty of achieving such a feat without further personification (a body behind the curtain—can James's image be read without seeing one there?). James's image also serves as a warning about the violence and dispropriating effects of such an effort of reconciliation. The death of Rupert Brooke and James's late meditations on literary language in its relation to context thus frame the queerness of style—and the difficulty of sustaining (maintaining, but also enduring) it. Such are some ways of considering the "abyss" of our "passion" when faced with "waste"—and the various hovering torments of that consideration.

In a chapter of *Profanations* entitled "The Author as Gesture," Giorgio Agamben considers a series of movements in the writing of Michel Foucault that evoke the torment of James's search for the Man and the Poet in Shakespeare.[51] Reading Foucault's "What Is an Author?" and "The Lives of Infamous Men," Agamben brings together Foucault's assertion that "the trace of the author is found only in the singularity of his absence" (61)[52]—the potential tension in Foucault's account whereby "the same gesture that deprives the identity of the author of all relevance nevertheless reaffirms his irreducible necessity" (62)—with his account of subjectivity, visible in "The Lives of Infamous Men." In the latter essay, the consigning of individual life to the terms of medical or juridical judgment (and hence its vanishing as anything but the expropriating judgment of it, as anything but its submission to disciplinary regimes of power) at the same moment preserves a life that would otherwise have vanished, makes it in a paradoxical sense legible. "At least for a moment in these pages, these lives shine blindingly with a dark light" (66): they become visible not as mere psychologizing, medicalizing, or otherwise punitive glosses, and still less as a recoverable empirical or "biographical" reality. The mode of being of these infamous lives—queer lives, we might say, that appear only in the singularity of their vanishing—is also that of the author. "It is possible that the infamous life . . . constitutes the paradigm of the presence-absence of the author in the work"; "the author is not dead," he comments, glossing Foucault, "but to position oneself as an author means occupying the place of a 'dead man'" (64).

In the author and the infamous life, Agamben finds a paradoxical mode of presence and a model of what he terms "ethics"—a risking or putting into play of life, without reserve. "The Author as Gesture" suggests what it might mean to "occupy the place of a 'dead man'" as a way of putting life in play—as a confronting of a central emptiness that cannot be assimilated to meaning or representation, cannot be owned or made substantial. "If we call 'gesture' what remains unexpressed in each expressive act," Agamben writes, "we can say that, exactly like infamy, the author is present in the text only as a gesture that makes expression possible precisely by establishing a central emptiness within it" (66). "The infamous life" in the archive is "played"—but not by anyone; it "is only played, it is never possessed, never represented, never said—and that is why it is the possible but empty site of an ethics, of a form of life." "A life is ethical not when it simply submits to moral laws but when it accepts putting itself in to play . . . irrevocably and without reserve"; "the author," he writes, "marks the point at which a life is offered up and played out in the work. Offered up and played out, not expressed or fulfilled. For this reason, the author can only remain unsatisfied and unsaid in the work. He is the illegible someone who makes reading possible, the legendary emptiness from which writing a discourse issue" (69–70):

> The place of the poem—or rather, its taking place—is therefore neither in the text nor in the author (nor in the reader): it is in the gesture through which the author and reader put themselves into play in the text and, at the same time, are infinitely withdrawn from it. The author is only the witness or guarantor of his own absence in the work in which he is put into play, and the reader can only provide this testimony once again, making himself in turn the guarantor of the inexhaustible game in which he plays at missing himself. . . . [T]he author and the reader enter into a relationship with the work only on the condition that they remain unexpressed in it. And yet the text has no other light than the opaque one that radiates from the testimony of this absence. (71–72)

Recent novelizations of James's life might be said to respond, knowingly
or not, to this structure; it may not be a coincidence that the search to
recover vanished or erased queer lives and the search for the particular
"life" that happens to be the author's alight on the same object. The mistake is to think that the author's same-sex desire determines, or exhausts,
his queerness—or to think that the life of a heterosexual author would not
be queer. The author and the infamous man are alike tormenting hover-
ers and vanishers. This opaque light testifying to a constitutive authorial
absence might thus offer a way to understand the torment James finds in
Shakespeare—and in the death of Rupert Brooke. "No, no, no—I reach
beyond the laboratory brain": it seems possible to read in this equivocal
assertion—as in the lunge through the figured arras that might at once
reach, at last, the author, and redound upon the reader hidden, Polonius-
like, in discovery's way—such a risking or a putting in play of life, such
an entry of the author's "life" into the text as "unsaid" or inexpressible, as
the limitless subtracting of itself, the "illegible someone who makes reading possible, the legendary emptiness from which writing and discourse
issue" (Agamben, 69–70).

For James writing on *The Tempest*, we noted that the term that resolves
the opposition between the "Man" and the "artist" is "style"; the mode of
that resolution is not unlike the effect of "style" in Deleuze's writing on
Proust: "it is style that substitutes for experience the manner in which we
speak about it or the formula that expresses it, which substitutes for the
individual in the world the viewpoint toward a world, and which transforms reminiscence into a realized creation."[53] Like Barthes listening
to himself playing the piano, style in this sense marks not an individual
signature but a sort of subtraction, one that in the "resonance machine"
severs subjective associations as the individual is subtracted from a
viewpoint, leaving "Combray in its essence, as it was never experienced;
Combray as Viewpoint, as it was never viewed" (Deleuze, 152). (A hoverer and vanisher might also describe, simply, a Viewpoint, or a figure
with a pair of eyes at its aperture, perched aloft, hanging over the spreading scene of life.) *Hover, torment,* and *waste* present different modes of the
self-subtraction through which author and reader meet, unexpressed and
unfulfilled, in the "taking place" of the text. These terms, notably, remain
in crucial ways unresolved, and the becoming impersonal that is a consequence of an experience of style moves toward both an infinitely productive cartography[54] and a redoubtable falling-silent, just as "torment" is

left hovering before the curtain—either the one that will rise for the small boy's theatrical initiation or the one that hides the unfathomable abyss of Shakespeare's renunciation—or just as "waste" names both the infinitely productive ways of a consciousness that can redeem, for its own uses, any event, even the death of a beautiful boy, even, at the limit, its own vanishing, and the disconsolate realization of the irremediable consequences for a life thus played. "Reading must come to an end," writes Agamben, "at the place where the reading of what has been poetized encounters in some way the empty place of what was lived. It is just as illegitimate to attempt to construct the personality of the author by means of the work as it is to turn his gesture into the secret cipher of reading" (72).

Several obsolete meanings for "torment" are perhaps worth noting: "an engine of war worked by torsion, for hurling stones, darts, or other missiles" or "an instrument of torture," like the "rack" on which "our strained and aching wonder" is stretched by Shakespeare's plays, the twisting that these meanings share (at least implicitly) with their modern acceptations (and, for that matter, with the term *trope*) are also shared by their most surprising precursor, a violent storm, tornado, or, in other words, a "tempest" (*Oxford English Dictionary*).

CHAPTER 4

Lambert Strether's Belatedness: *The Ambassadors* and the Queer Afterlife of Style

Body, remember not only how much you were loved,
not only the beds you lay on,
but also those longings for you that
shone clearly in the eyes,
that trembled in the voice—and some
random obstacle put them off.
Now that everything is in the past,
it almost seems that you have also given
in to those longings—how they shone,
remember, in the eyes that gazed at you;
how they trembled in the voice, for you, remember, body.

—Cavafy, "Remember, body . . ."
(translated by Anna Seraphimidou)

CRITICS OF JAMES'S WORK have been less circumspect about the search for "the Man" in "the Poet"—less attentive to the search's paradoxes and perils—than is the author himself in the late essays. And thus the tale of belatedness and equivocal aesthetic recompense offered by *The Ambassadors* has often served to reinforce a current in James studies that—more or less explicitly and to vastly different effects—understands James's style in biographical terms: its opacities or seeming evasions point to the way the man himself diffused, postponed, avoided, sublimated, or more or less missed "life." The novel is particularly available to such readings because of Strether's strikingly rigorous—and, for many critics, frustrating—renunciation, which has often been read as a failure to be adequate to his experience: Strether, the "exemplar of the life of the senses," Richard Blackmur argued, is "not finally up to that life," a diagnosis that is often extended to the author who created that temporizing American pilgrim.[1] F. W. Dupee suggested that if James "drew on Howells for Strether's sentiments, he drew far more on himself"; F. O. Matthiessen wrote that the "passive rather than active scope" of Strether's desire "is one of the most striking consequences of James's own peculiar conditioning" as he describes it in *Notes of a Son and Brother* and *A Small Boy and Others*.[2] Strether, according to Matthiessen, speaks for James as well (28), and "neither Strether nor his creator," he argued, "escape a certain soft fussiness" (39). For Arnold Bennett, he is like the provincial damsel taken to task by Walter Besant for daring to write about barracks life, and his claim that James knew a lot about "cultured" people but very little "about life in general," that his "fastidiousness" led him to "[repudiate] life," leaving him unmarried and "ignorant of fundamental things to the last," is echoed by more subtle readers.[3] Allon White's *The Uses of Obscurity* argues that James's style allowed him to evade sex, the vulgarity of which distressed him; Maxwell Geismar's immoderate condemnation of James's suspicion of passion, his fear of women and sex, finds a more sophisticated rationale in White's reading.[4] Even writers who do not assume the synonymity of passion, life, and "satisfied" heterosexual desire make similar assumptions about art's relation to life when they attempt to redeem James's homosexual desires from a repression attributed either to his critics or to him (aspiring to undo the repression, and to redeem both the shame ostensibly felt by artist and critic, and, I suppose, the shame of having ever submitted oneself to shame). However noteworthy the homophobia animating the more or less cultivated obliviousness to the evidence of gay eroticism in James's self-understanding, as in his relations with men, that has often marked considerations of James's life, later antihomophobic readers risk taming the queerness of James's style by countering such considerations merely with new accounts of that life. When Colm Tóibín's *The Master* rewrites Strether's gaze from the street at Little Bilham on Chad's balcony as James's own longing vigil under the windows of Paul Zhurkovski, in the translating (after the fact) of art "back" into a life understood to be originary, the revised account of James's biography, and even the attention to the homoerotic aspects of *The Ambassadors*—whatever their value in themselves—are of perhaps less moment than what the recovery, precisely as recovery, misses: the erotics of belatedness, the power of style to create life by submitting individual existence to an impersonal becoming.

In the logic of substitution or obfuscation that, for both of these types of readings, links an opaque style to a missed experience, "life" stands in—implicitly or explicitly—for direct representation, for the mimetic capturing of experience. At some level, both types of readings respond, more or less unconsciously, to James's style rather than to the known facts, such as they are, of his life. It is the "virtuality" of the writing that makes for the interest on both sides; that virtuality, however, is immediately transcribed into psychology.[5] The indirection of James's style is thereby made a (mimetic) representation of a "missed" life, which is in turn interpreted in psychological terms of repression, inhibition, or, more simply, loneliness. The complementary understandings of life and style are perhaps more troubling than the idea—which is troubling enough—that James is to be pitied for failing to make the most of his life.[6] In other terms, however one might object to the implicit portrayal of James's life in terms of a lack and evasion sufficient to occasion various refinements of critical pity, what is more crucial, perhaps, is that the compensations of this pathos allow critics to avoid confronting the disorienting effects of James's style: to avoid, for example, the complications both of the antimimetic understanding of representation set forth in the essays on the novel, and of the understanding of "life" animating the late fiction, the autobiography, and the late essays.[7] I would therefore follow critics such as Julie Rivkin, Mary Cross, and Shelia Teahan,[8] who suggest that the novel's plot be understood in relation to its linguistic practices, and critics such as Leo Bersani and Sharon Cameron, whose readings of late James suggest the possibility of perceiving something disruptively antipsychological in texts often seen as being among the most profound soundings of psychological depths in the tradition of the novel.[9] In my view—in terms indebted to, but theoretically divergent from, Cameron's rereading of Jamesian consciousness—Strether's relation to "life" is most interestingly a linguistic, and not a psychological, question. The narrative of *The Ambassadors,* and the critical tradition with respect to the text, raises the question of the linguistic representation of a life, including James's own—which brings into view, among other things, ways in which the recent resurgence of critical interest in that life, however salutary and illuminating it may be in many respects, can serve to contain or repress the more challenging aspects of his style.[10]

Read in these terms, the narrative of *The Ambassadors* offers a reflection on the theory of novelistic representation that James outlined in "The Art of Fiction" and "The Future of the Novel," and on the consequences for "a life" of the effects of style we traced in *The Golden Bowl* and *The Wings of the Dove.* If the "subject" of *The Golden Bowl* is in some sense the trope of zeugma, and of *The Wings of the Dove,* perspective and focalization in free indirect style, then the "subject" of *The Ambassadors* is the "life" produced by a writer's self-subtraction "in" the text;[11] it is the relation of writer to work, and work to world that James confronts in Rupert Brooke's death and in Shakespeare's renunciation made, as it were the experience of a character. Like recent novelizations, we are in a sense moving backward—not only chronologically but also genetically—but we move not from the life to the novel but from *a* life (in Deleuze's sense) to the novel. Recovered, then, is not the traces of an early transmuting of life into fiction (as Tóibín perhaps finds, in tracing the scene from *The Ambassadors* back to its authorial source) that give flesh to a biography, but the traces of an inverse movement, a reflection, in the novel that anticipates the later considerations of the writer's life. As when attempting to describe the figural language in *The Golden Bowl* turning into a reflection on the novel's own taking place, or the reflexivity of the characters in *The Wings of the Dove* seeming to narrate themselves as characters, one turns to impossible spatialities to describe the effect of the prose—characters turned inside out, viewing themselves from the outside, or, in a voiding of psychic depth, seeming to flatten to the same plane as the narration; the surface of the prose, as it were, turns inward, creating an interior (a vase, a strange garden pagoda) visible "within" the novel, impossibly "within" the novel's surface—as style in *The Ambassadors* moves "inward" to become the dramatized experience of the text. Lambert Strether's experience of belatedness might be read as a further refinement of the novelistic theory, and, in its variously ambivalent depiction of the experience of a life within the style whose disorientations we have traced in the course of this book, as a meditation on the difficulties of sustaining the insights of that theory—of living up, as it were, to James's style.

The premise of *The Ambassadors* is therefore not, perhaps, as simple as it might initially appear. Lambert Strether, James writes in the novel's "Project,"

> has had a life by no means wasted, but not happily concentrated; and rather makes on himself the impression of having come in for many of the drawbacks, even perhaps for the little of the discredit, of an incoherent existence, without, unfortunately, any of the accompanying entertainment or 'fun.' He feels tired, in other words, without having a great deal to show for it; disenchanted without having known any great enchantments, enchanters, or, above all, enchantresses; and . . . is vaguely haunted by the feeling of what he has missed, though this is a quantity, and a quality, that he would be rather at a loss to name.[12]

Strether has somehow missed out on what the novel might initially seem to imply was unmediated experience: Strether, "burdened" with "the oddity of a double consciousness" (2), subject to "uncontrolled perceptions" (34) and "to an amount of experience out of all proportion to his adventures" (160), and exposed by "his poor old trick of quiet inwardness" (349), has missed out on the opportunity to experience "life"—a failure, as Maria Gostrey diagnoses it, "to enjoy" (11), to catch the "entertainment" or "fun" James notes in the "Project."[13] "He was," the novel tells us, "for ever missing things through his general genius for missing them, while others were for ever picking them up through a contrary bent. And it was others who looked abstemious and he who looked greedy; it was he somehow who finally paid, and it was others who mainly partook" (337). At all these moments, however, the stress is placed not on a missed, unmediated experience but on a missed experience of mediation. Strether looks greedy when he is fact abstemious: the emphasis is perhaps less on missing out without "credit" than on a misrepresentation. In the passage from the "Project," the missed quantity is less experience than its representation—having "a great deal to show" for one's loss. Strether's predicament is an "impression" he "makes on himself," and the missed "enchantresses" seem less to unveil a yearned-for content for his loss than to mark the last of a series of refused reifications or nominalizations, the failure-to-appear of the various nouns that might have bodied forth his disenchantment.

Whatever Strether has missed, it is related in some essential way to a sense of belatedness. The novel's "essence," James remarks in the preface (xxxi), is the scene in Gloriani's garden: "There were some things that had to come in time if they were to come at all. If they didn't come in time they were lost forever. It was the general sense of them that had overwhelmed him with its long slow rush." This general sense inspires Strether's famous speech to Little Bilham:

> It's not too late for *you*, on any side, and you don't strike me as in danger of missing the train. . . . All the same don't forget that you're young—blessedly young; be glad of it on the contrary and live up to it. Live all you can; it's a mistake not to. It doesn't so much matter what you do in particular, so long as you have your life. If you haven't had that what *have* you had? (152–53)[14]

Strether's lesson demands a paradoxical displacement of perspective: for youth not to "forget" that it is young, it must see itself from the perspective of its loss, from the perspective of age—a feat concretely achieved, perhaps, only by Dorian Gray, whom James may well have had in mind, along with William Dean Howells and the advice, according to the *Notebooks*, he gave Jonathan Sturges in Whistler's Paris garden.[15]

Thus Strether's garden exhortation presents an impossible lesson:

> it's as if the train had fairly waited at the station for me without my having had the gumption to know it was there. Now I hear its faint receding whistle miles and miles down the line. What one loses one loses; make no mistake about that. . . . The affair—I mean the affair of life—couldn't, no doubt, have been different for me; for it's at best a tin mould, either fluted and embossed, with ornamental excrescences, or else smooth and dreadfully plain, into which, a helpless jelly, one's consciousness is poured—so that one 'takes' the form, as the great cook says, and is more or less compactly held by it; one lives in fine as one can. Still, one has the illusion of freedom; therefore don't be, like me, without the memory of that illusion. . . . Don't make my mistake. For it was a mistake. Live!
> (153–54)

The repetition of *mistake* underlines the lesson—"gives the measure," the preface tells us, "of the signal warning he feels attached to his case" (xxx)—and seems to present an alternative: either "live" your life or miss it. Yet the "mistake," he argues, is not to know that "what one loses, one loses"; the realization about which one is not to make an error boils down to a tautological definition of loss. Strether's figure of a mold, moreover, throws into question what his "mistake" might have been; it isn't a lost freedom that is to be regretted but the lost "memory" of an "illusion" of freedom.[16] His mistake was not to be able to remember having made a mistake about that illusion (not to have behaved or thought then in a way that would have allowed him the later memory of a mistake). As in Milly Theale's "I shan't . . . have missed anything," the perspective remains retrospective, and belatedness strikes one as both the problem and the solution: the locus of pleasure is not youth, which is only unknowingly mistaken, but age. Nor is the "signal lesson" an easy one to follow, for Strether is a cautionary tale only because he was, if anything, too lucid.

The helpless jelly cannot choose its mould, and Strether's lesson demystifies as an illusion the very freedom it simultaneously asks Little Bilham to embody. He seems to regret missing the train less in the sense of failing to board it than in the sense of failing to know that it was there and that it had left without him. His regret seems less that he was never young than that he was not old soon enough. To live is thus not to be on the train but rather to realize that one should regret having missed it, and to find oneself, perhaps, no longer at a loss to name what one has lost.

The "life" that "our belated man of the world" (xxxvii) thinks he has missed is defined as the vicarious appreciation of Chad and Madame de Vionnet: "I never had the benefit [of youth] at the proper time—which comes to saying that I never had the thing itself.... Though they're young enough, my pair, I don't say they're ... their *own* absolutely prime adolescence; for that has nothing to do with it. The point is that they're mine. Yes, they're my youth; since somehow at the right time nothing else ever was" (240–41). Youth here is constitutively vicarious; one "isn't," one doesn't have, one's own youth. One "is" someone else's youth, which raises the question of what "the proper time" for youth might be; youth in this context is never "proper," never one's own, and, because it is always someone else's, even were it possible for it to arrive for oneself, no particular time could be better—or worse—than any other for its arrival. Chad and Madame de Vionnet "are" Strether's youth, moreover, because "life" for him consists in appreciating Chad's improvement. That "case," he remarks, "was first and foremost a miracle almost monstrous. It was the alteration of the entire man.... All one's energy goes to facing it, to tracking it. One wants, confound it, ... to enjoy anything so rare. Call it then life ... call it poor dear old life simply that springs the surprise" (118). A vicarious structure that constitutes an aesthetic and erotic pleasure, it also makes Chad's "difference" a "sharp rupture of identity." Chad is young because he is not himself: Strether "had faced every contingency but that Chad should not *be* Chad.... You could deal with a man as himself—you couldn't deal with him as somebody else" (96).[17] And he is young because he does not live his life. While Strether admires Chad most for "knowing how to live," knowing how to live is precisely *not* to achieve an unmediated relation to experience. Chad knows how to live because he delegates his life. Initially put in terms of his power to absorb the lives of others, this knowledge indicates a more unsettlingly vicarious relation: "he 'put out' his excitement, or whatever other emotion the matter involved, as he put out his washing"

(355–56). ("It was quite for Strether himself in short to feel a personal analogy with the laundress bringing home the triumphs of the mangle" [356].)
Chad truly lives because he delegates to others the experience of his life.

If Strether's regret is that he is not Chad and that he did not, when
Chad's age, live as Chad does ("I know," he says to Little Bilham, "whom
I should enjoy being like!" [155]), Chad's improvement is a "rupture of
identity," a ceasing to be simply Chad, and a leaving to others the task of
"being" him. In other terms, if to "live" is to appreciate Chad, then to "live"
cannot mean to "be" him: to appreciate Chad requires the perspective of
one who has failed to be him. By truly living, Chad becomes the singular
figure among those characters not irredeemably obtuse who misses his
experience, who proves, in the end, disappointingly inadequate to his own
life. If the lovers are, as Strether says, his "life," the vicariousness that pre-
vents an unmediated access to life defines what it means for him to have a
life; "living," or what the preface calls "reparation" (xxx), cannot overcome
that vicariousness because it is defined by it. The aesthetic and erotic spectacle of Chad suggests that to "live" is not to achieve an unmediated experience but to realize that one has missed it. It may be that to encounter
Chad is to confront the belatedness of one's life, but the example of Chad
also forces a reconsideration of what it means to be belated. Belatedness is
both the obstacle to life and the condition necessary for it: the regret for
the life one missed *is*, paradoxically, the life one missed.

The question, then, is how to understand belatedness and its paradoxical power of recovery, and how to understand its consequences for the representation of a life. As I have phrased it so far, the belated life is perhaps
not opposed to a logic of sublimation: to be belated, one might argue, is to
exchange the lived life for a represented one. Substitution, compensation,
sublimation, exchange: the relation of belatedness to a project of novelistic representation would be understood in these terms. And, indeed, there
are strains in the novel that point to such an understanding, that suggest,
in particular, that Strether's "reward" is the ability to represent to himself
the substance of what he has missed. Strether's epiphany as he waits for
Chad in his empty apartment is thus both a realization of loss and the
recovery of a missed life:

> He felt, strangely, as sad as if he had come for some wrong, and yet
> as excited as if he had come for some freedom. But the freedom
> was what was most in the place and the hour; it was the freedom

that most brought him round again to the youth of his own that he had long ago missed. He could have explained little enough to-day either why he had missed it or why, after years and years, he should care that he had; the main truth of the actual appeal of everything was none the less that everything represented the substance of his loss, put it within reach, within touch, made it, to a degree it had never been, an affair of the senses. That was what it became for him at this singular time, the youth he had long ago missed—a queer concrete presence, full of mystery, yet full of reality, which he could handle, taste, smell, the deep breathing of which he could positively hear. . . . The image was before him when he at last became aware that Chad was behind. (354–55)

Strether's language seems to describe a tryst—he is "as sad as if he had come for some wrong, and yet as excited as if he had come for some freedom." That freedom shifts from a "freedom" he might take to "freedom" in general—and to Chad's freedom, which brings Strether to his own missed youth—the freedom, perhaps, that age, looking back, finds in youth: of attachments yet to be formed, a personality yet to be molded, a life yet to be chosen. A moving evocation of loss, the passage also presents this epiphanic moment as the culmination of a process of aesthetic education: Strether can finally perceive his loss; it is put "within reach, within touch," his youth made a "queer concrete presence . . . which he could handle, taste, smell"; loss and vanished time are made matters for direct perception. At last, perhaps, he is not "at a loss to name" what he has lost ("Project," 375); notably, though, the novel does not at this moment name it. The perception of the fact of loss (and not of any loss in particular) forms the paradoxical content of Strether's aesthetic education—as if the lives one didn't lead could be made present, potentiality actualized, but as potential. (That, more than any literal recovery, seems to be the yearning of belatedness.)

The experience of perceiving loss appears in the same register as the pleasure of perceiving Chad, the text's central aesthetic object. Pedagogical relations in the novel are also erotic ones; to educate a man is—for Madame de Vionnet as for Maria Gostrey—to deck "him out for others" (240), and to experience these pedagogical relations of desire is also to experience betrayal. The betrayal may be structural to the aesthetic value that Strether finds in belatedness. For the aesthetic and erotic pleasure of belatedness dictates that what one recovers one does not perforce possess; its corollary is an experience of sexual exclusion. As every teacher knows, or ought to, the Chads of the world are, by their nature, always marked for someone else. (How could the Chads ever *not* betray? How can one's loyalty, after all, truly be adequate to the investments and desires of those who have formed one?) Sexual exclusion—however riveting as a personal, psychological experience, and however crucial to the often moving effects of identification this novel excites in its readers—is less important for its consequences in a psychological register than for what it suggests about the relation of representation to belatedness. The experience of sexual exclusion ends up putting the narrative of aesthetic recompense (and, with it, the logic of sublimation) to the test, which is explicitly what is at stake in Strether's accidental encounter with Chad and Madame de Vionnet in rural France.

The incident is framed, as it were, by Strether's memory of a painting seen long ago in Boston: "It had been the only adventure of his life in connexion with the purchase of a work of art. The adventure, it will be perceived, was modest; but the memory, beyond all reason and by some accident of association, was sweet. The little Lambinet abode with him as the picture he *would* have bought—the particular production that had made him for the moment overstep the modesty of nature" (380–81). Evoking Strether's relation to Chad—"I know whom *I* should enjoy being like!" (155)—Strether does not want to see the painting again; the possession is more perfect for his not having bought it. "[T]he picture he *would* have bought": his mode of (non-)possession here enacts the ontology of Jamesian fiction—the hypothetical speech of *The Golden Bowl*, for instance, or the action it announces and suspends in an "as if." The past appeals to Strether as virtual. His trip to the countryside thus offers him the chance to recover the lost day in the paradoxical mode of his belatedness:

> [I]t would be a different thing, however, to see the remembered mixture resolved back into its elements—to assist at the restoration to nature of the whole far-away hour: the dusty day in Boston, the background of the Fitchburg Depot, of the maroon-coloured sanctum, the special-green vision, the ridiculous price, the poplars, the willows, the rushes, the river, the sunny silvery sky, the shady woody horizon. (380)

This "restoration to nature" is not a naïve return to a source more "real" than the painting. To return to the ostensible "reference" of the painting, the "natural" elements in the French countryside of which it is made up, is, for Strether, simultaneously to recover the lost day of its contemplated, unrealized purchase: his list of those elements amalgamates the natural scene, the painting, and the remembered Bostonian day. It does so, moreover, in terms that explicitly foreground their linguistic mediation, the lovely alliterative sonority of the evoked loss. (Powerful, too, is the enactment in the sentence of the decomposition of natural elements and their recomposition in syntactically patterned form: the nouns and noun phrases into which the sentence resolves itself move from compound words—*background, Fitchburg*—to hyphenated compounds that make visible their joint—*maroon-colored, special-green*—to unadorned nouns—*poplars, willows, rushes, river*—to recomposed, alliterative, modified nouns in metrically patterned phrases—"the sunny silvery sky," "the shady woody horizon.") The sonority of these phrases also makes language present, available to sense perception; "resolved back into its elements," the lost day reappears, perhaps most notably, as sound. Recovering the remembered mixture resolved back into its elements represents, like Strether's view of Chad's empty apartment, "the substance of his loss, put[s] it within reach, within touch, [makes] it, to a degree it had never been, an affair of the senses."

This paradoxical recovery is evoked in the first part of the chapter as language of fullness and repletion describes an experience of walking into the painting itself:

> The oblong gilt frame disposed its enclosing lines; the poplars
> and willows, the reeds and river . . . fell into a composition, full
> of felicity, within them; the sky was silver and turquoise and var-
> nish; the village on the left was white and the church on the right
> was grey; it was all there, in short—it was what he wanted: it was
> Tremont Street, it was France, it was Lambinet. Moreover he
> was freely walking about in it. He did this last, for an hour, to his
> heart's content, making for the shady woody horizon and boring so
> deep into his impression and his idleness that he might fairly have
> got through them again and reached the maroon-coloured wall.
> (381–82).

The world conforms to a vision of aesthetic plentitude, "falls into a composition," and its enclosing lines mark a bounded whole. "Not a single one of his observations but somehow fell into a place in it; not a breath of the cooler evening that wasn't somehow a syllable of the text." The world becomes a painting, a sky of "silver and turquoise and varnish," and to bore through the representation to reality would be to reach, at last, the "maroon-coloured wall." The seamless fit between text and world writes a lesson of simple existence: "The text was simply, when condensed, that in *these* places such things were" (386–87). That epiphany's echo of the repeated copula linking world and painting—"the sky was silver and turquoise and varnish; the village on the left was white and the church on the right was grey; it was all there, in short—it was what he wanted: it was Tremont Street, it was France, it was Lambinet"—makes this moment of repletion also a moment of elegy, and its seamless recovery, a vanishing: "it was ... it was ... it was ... it was ... it was."

It is at the moment of this asserted recovery, and in the paradoxical repletion of a loss made tangible, that Strether perceives Chad and Madame de Vionnet and thus has to confront undeniable evidence that they are having sex. The lovers unveil a lack, an "emptiness" that—retrospectively—punctures the language of completion and satiety:

> the valley on the further side was all copper-green level and glazed
> pearly sky, a sky hatched across with screens of trimmed trees,
> which looked flat, like espaliers; and though the rest of the village
> straggled away in the near quarter the view had an emptiness that
> made one of the boats suggestive. (388)

The glazed pearly sky hatched across with screens of trees makes the river feel enclosed, an interior space, and the view is described as if it were a painting. The same language of composition that made for repletion now makes for a sudden flatness of view that throws into question the plentitude of the picture, reveals it *as* picture.[18] The unexpected "straggling" of its elements disrupts the harmony of the composition, and the prior fullness of the day is found in retrospect to have been lacking: "it was suddenly as if these figures, or something like them, had been wanted in the picture, had been wanted more or less all day, and had now drifted into sight, with the slow current, on purpose to fill up the measure" (388). As the moment when Strether discovers his exclusion from his friends' erotic relation, it ought to mark the culmination of his education—completing, as their appearance completes the picture, the exclusion dictated by the logic of the belated "life." The sight of Madame de Vionnet and Chad might, like Chad's apartment, represent the substance of his loss, put within touch the sense that it is too late, make manifest the logic of vicariousness, consummate the paradoxical realization of Strether's own belatedness.

The moment, however, is more unsettling; at issue, perhaps, is how to understand this consummation. The painting all the more one's own because one did not buy it; unlived lives recovered as potential: in question is whether such possessions, and such recoveries, can be understood according to a logic of compensation and representation—without thereby becoming mere possession, and mere actualization—whether belatedness ought to be understood as representing the substance of one's loss, as putting loss within reach. It is to protect the paradoxical mode of (non-)possession and potentiality in belatedness, it seems to me, that the novel makes Strether's "lesson" at this moment so searing. The compensatory logic of "reparation"—the painting all the more one's own because one did *not* buy it—is troubled by the unveiling of deceit ("He kept making of it that there had been simply a *lie* in the charming affair" [393]); the moment in the country simultaneously marks the culmination of (one understanding of) the logic that makes the "missing" and "having" of life synonymous and threatens to unravel the fabric of its compensations—threatens the understanding of that logic as having compensations. One of the novel's most moving moments occurs as Strether realizes that Madame de Vionnet is terrified of losing her lover: "she was as much as ever the finest and subtlest creature, the happiest apparition, it had been given him, in all his years, to meet; and yet he could see her there as vulgarly troubled, in very truth, as a maidservant crying for her young man" (409).[19] Put in question is nothing short of the transformation on which the novel rests:

> She had made him better, she had made him best, she had made
> him anything one would; but it came to our friend with supreme
> queerness that he was none the less only Chad. . . . The work,
> however admirable, was nevertheless of the strict human order, and
> in short it was marvelous that the companion of mere earthly joys,
> of comforts, aberrations (however one classed them) within the
> common experience, should be so transcendently prized. (408)

Evoking Strether's earlier sense that he "had faced every contingency but that Chad should not *be* Chad," his perception of Madame de Vionnet's tears throws into question the principle of aesthetic transformation that has underwritten Strether's actions, disrupts his original epiphany of Chad's "sharp rupture of identity" (96)—the very epiphany fueling Strether's own expansion of consciousness, the aesthetic education that leaves him to find himself beautifully, irrevocably altered when he alteration finds. The consequences are serious: if the transformation is an illusion, if Strether has been "silly," then the Pococks were right. And the Pococks are one of the great representatives of stupidity in the history of the English and American novel. In them, James captures the inert, oblivious, disconcertingly insinuating power of stupidity as a force of pure negation—the power to negate one's most treasured, most exquisite perceptions simply by refusing to countenance the existence of complexity in the world. If the Pococks win, the consolation he has constructed may be a delusion; to learn the lesson of Strether's belatedness may be scarce consolation for the loss it recompenses.

Compensation, however, may be the wrong register for thinking of aesthetic transformation and may misrepresent the logic of the belated life. Early on, Strether's guilt over his son's death is put in the same terms as the belatedness he discovers in France to have been his share: he "might have kept his little boy, his little dull boy, who had died at school of a rapid diphtheria, if he had not in those years so insanely given himself to merely missing the mother." This

> was doubtless but the secret habit of sorrow, which had slowly
> given way to time; yet there remained an ache sharp enough to
> make the spirit, at the sight now and again of some fair young man
> just growing up, wince with the thought of an opportunity lost.
> Had ever a man, he had finally fallen into the way of asking himself,
> lost so much and even done so much for so little? (59)

This passage is moving, and not only because the eroticism of the moment—the potential for that "sharp ache" at the sight of some "fair young man" to shade from parental regret to thwarted identification to desire—arises, partly, through its not being able to register for Strether.[20] It is also moving—and jarring—because rendering his boy's vanished future as an "opportunity lost" (seemingly, for Strether) appears to equate the loss of his son with Chad's giving up of the potentially lucrative business venture he must renounce in order to stay in France; the lack of a vocabulary to signal the difference movingly figures the frangibility of the novel's compensatory logic. Strether's question ("had ever a man . . . lost so much . . . for so little?") raises the discomfiting question of what it would mean to compensate a loss, to lose something or someone "for" something else. Like the moment when Madame de Vionnet disconcertingly weeps, this evocation of loss raises the question of whether aesthetic formations should be considered in compensatory terms at all.

In one possible understanding of the novel, such moments bring home to Strether what it really is to miss out—and Strether's watchful vigil after his encounter with the lovers brings a realization familiar, I have to imagine, to many experiencing such momentous events: this is, irrevocably, *my* life—not a rehearsal, and not a novel.[21] Boring through the picture, one reaches the maroon-colored wall. Yet what is punctured in the scenes on the river and with Madame de Vionnet is not the fictional abstraction one achieves through evasion of the "real." It is not that the "real thing" deflates the claims of art. Punctured, rather, is the idea of art or representation substituting or compensating for life, or its lack (or, likewise, the idea that belatedness could become an "object" of representation). Chad's empty apartment and the Lambinet countryside offer the lure of a representable loss, of having, as the "Project" puts it, "a great deal to show for it," or of being able to name what has been missed, to lose something "for" something else. The scene on the river is therefore presented as rupturing not only Strether's illusion, but representation, the painting Strether has been walking around in. The incident, which seems dictated by psychological and aesthetic logics, defies the expectations of realism; what is termed "the general *invraisemblance* of the occasion" (391) punctures the novel's verisimilitude even as it marks its most powerful incident. His enthusiasm for the Lambinet painting is said, we recall, to lead Strether "for a moment to overstep the modesty of nature" (381); the quotation from *Hamlet* links the scene's departure from verisimilitude—"o'erstep not the modesty of nature," Hamlet exhorts the players (3.2.19)—to the "living," the ("modest") "adventure," Strether had through the painting, suggesting that it consists, in part, in a rupture of mimesis. Frustrating the possibility of naming or compensating loss, the novel disarticulates the possibility of conceiving of it in mimetic terms.[22]

I take this to be one reason for the novel's cryptic specification of Chad's opportunity in Woollett; staying in France, he turns down a job in advertising (263), and his disturbing reference at the end of the novel to it as an "art" of at least theoretical interest leads a scandalized Strether to gape as if Chad were dancing a "fancy step" on the pavement. The refusal of advertising's regime, which exchanges representation for compensation or profit,[23] might be one explanation for Strether's refusal to stay with Maria Gostrey at the novel's close. His only logic, he says, is "not, out of the whole affair, to have got anything for myself" (438). If this is an ethical claim, it is not one, I think, of personal or sexual renunciation. For James's preface makes this logic that of the novel itself: Maria, he writes, "is the reader's friend much rather—...; and she acts in that capacity, and *really* in that capacity alone.... She is an enrolled, a direct, aid to lucidity." She, like Waymarsh, belongs "less to my subject than to my treatment of it" (xliii). Her "false position" (xxxv) as a narrative device posing as a character who therefore excites strange effects of sympathy parallels Strether's own false position in relation to Woollet and Mrs. Newsome; the parallel forms of characters' misrepresentations of their function need not be governed by psychosexual determinations of character: Strether's adventure, too, might thus be read primarily in relation to the narration itself. Whatever pathos is generated by the novel's close, James thus seems to suggest, is related less to the pathos of a lost woman, less even to the dynamics of what Eve Kosofsky Sedgwick has called homosexual panic, however resonant her reading of "The Beast in the Jungle" would be for *The Ambassadors*, than to the rigors of dispensing with such aids to lucidity, representability.[24] Such might be the substance of Strether's loss: the final lesson of his belatedness deprives him of representing his loss as a loss, as a substance. In a novel whose erotic and aesthetic pleasure comes largely from gazing on Chad ("handsomer than he had ever promised" [104], looking "so well that one could scarce speak to him straight" [113])—of sensing his new "smoothness" ("for that he *was* smooth was as marked as in the taste of a sauce or in the rub of a hand"), of appreciating his having been "put in a firm mould and turned successfully out" (107)—this confounding of the possibility of representing loss brings out the potential queerness of Lambert Strether's belatedness and the erotics of exclusion it adumbrates.

I would therefore insist that, as moving as the novel can be, Strether's predicament is not sad, that the exorbitant forms of critical investment the text inspires are not to be explained by an identification with the futility of reading; the dominant affect as the novel draws to its close and Strether declines to get anything for himself is not disillusionment or disappointment, not resignation or renunciation, not sadness but joy. Strether gets there by way of those emotions, and through an experience of betrayal and exclusion. His midnight vigil after he discovers the lovers in rural France evokes the disillusionment, even loneliness, that might attend an experience of punctured absorption, a reader's discovery of irremediable separation from a beloved text. Thus to discover a broken spell, as a demystified Strether does when he discovers the relation of Chad and Madame de Vionnet—even, like Strether, to wonder after an experience of rapture if one hasn't been made rather a dupe—is also to discover one's prior absorption. Leavis's claim that he wasn't "in the least tempted" to "identify himself with Strether" thus seems to attest, above all, to his immunity to this text, which he called a "feeble piece of word-spinning."[25] Leavis notwithstanding, the power to exact various forms of critical identification seems to turn on the text's intuition that belatedness is both the obstacle to the "lived" life and its condition of possibility. *The Ambassadors* might therefore be read to detail an "afterlife" such as that in "Is There a Life after Death?"; interpreted in the light of the novel, the afterlife claimed there secures life from vanishing with death by dividing it from itself—by making "life" itself a kind of "afterlife."

Belatedness is a recurrent—and perhaps the primary—figure in the text. "It wasn't until after he had spoken," we read in the first chapter, "that he became aware of how much there had been in him of response" (3), and the pattern is not limited to Strether. Chad's miraculous Parisian transformation makes visible a discontinuity of narrative expectations; "handsomer than he had ever promised" (104), he, like the novel in "The Art of Fiction," is to be appreciated in retrospect. His change, foundational for the novel's principle of aesthetic development, cannot coincide with its representation; like all learning, perhaps, it is unrepresentable. It is therefore scarcely surprising that Maimie—"bridal with never a bridegroom to support it" (311)—finds herself too late "for the miracle" of Chad's transformation (326), and even the Pococks arrive to discover of their effort to turn Chad into Jim that "it's too late" (290). Thus, it is striking that Strether's realization noted earlier ("I know—if we talk of that—whom *I* should enjoy being like!") comes to point to Chad only after the fact. Strether initially indicates Gloriani and only later understands his own declaration: "It was the click of a spring—he saw the truth. He had by this time also met Chad's look; there was more of it in that; and the truth accordingly, so far as Bilham's inquiry was concerned, had thrust in the answer. 'Oh, Chad!'—it was that rare youth he should have enjoyed being 'like'" (155). Consciousness finds itself trailing even its own utterances and arrives belatedly, even to the realization of what it would have wanted to have been. That Strether never had the benefit of youth "at the proper time" (240) thus signals less an avoidable mischance or failure of courage or occasion for pathos than a temporal disjunction, a marker of the ways that consciousness in late James is curiously, and productively, out of sync with itself. This, too, is a modality of what *A Small Boy and Others* and the essay on Rupert Brooke call "waste": more than a thematic concern, and more than a peculiarity of Strether's psychology, belatedness marks the very structure of realization and consciousness in *The Ambassadors*, and, perhaps, in late James in general.

"Live!" Strether exhorts Little Bilham—a self-defeating injunction, insofar as it can be addressed, it would seem, only to one who is not alive—which is to say, in late James, only to those whose consciousness is worth bothering about. "Life" is an "afterlife" because life—and consciousness—do not coincide with themselves, cannot be made objects for representation. As with Milly Theale in *The Wings of the Dove* (the question raised there concerning life missed or possessed, the future anterior tense of Milly's consummated life), and as with the structure of realization and illumination in *The Golden Bowl*, belatedness in late James makes life a form of revision, and links the predicaments that have most often been read in psychological terms to James's theory of the novel—to the antimimetic strands of that theory, and to the self-subtraction through which the author confronts the world "in" a text and thus gives himself over to a created life. For gay readers, *The Ambassadors* might be especially powerful because of the way the novel's discontinuities of consciousness resonate with the experience of the closet, which makes such a discontinuity (not confined, of course, to gay readers, but unavoidable for gay people who have not cultivated a Pocock-like obliviousness to it) *the* principle of one's development. Coming out always occurs too late, no matter what one's chronological age, because it must produce a past that constitutes the identity it asserts: the constituted identity, in other words, remains belated, remains to that degree moored in the constituting past. (By the same token, every coming out also announces, "I shan't . . . have missed anything.") I like to believe that the "obsession" with youth often pejoratively attributed to gay culture—usually chalked up to narcissism or a regressive refusal to grow up—is partly an effort to keep in view life's asynchronicity, to spur eroticism through a continually renewed confrontation with belatedness. If I am talking, at all events, of what I "like" to think, I may, in short, say all: I like to think that life is like *The Ambassadors*. The novel's discontinuities of consciousness—its fundamental narrative of aesthetic development *as* discontinuity and its depiction of the ruptured spell of an absorption like that of reading that makes inevitable a reader's confrontation with cognitive discontinuity—resonates with the closet less because of any thematic concern with repressed sexual possibility than because of the way it makes manifest how the disjunction of the closet's *before* and *after* punctuates a queer narrative of aesthetic education.

The subject of coming out might thus take the paradoxical "form" of discontinuity rather than embodying a *telos* triumphantly unveiled: James's text allows us to see a potential—within the closet's own tendencies toward identity consolidation—for a narrative more thrillingly marked with contingency. In these terms, Eve Kosofsky Sedgwick's reading of the New York Edition prefaces is compelling, among many other reasons, because it allows one to think about the temporality of realization in *The Ambassadors* in what she might call "reparative" terms—in this instance, a way to think of James's relation to this text (and of critical investments in that relation) without generating effects of pathos or pity or condescension.[26] Her argument suggests that belatedness is the temporality of Jamesian revision; to arrive too late at the life one ought to have had transforms that life into the exquisite spell of reading and (re)writing. Shame in Sedgwick's account—as an affect that is put in play and made textually productive—allows one to think "fondly" about one's own prior unknowing or deluded self, to contemplate that past without repudiating it. In the model she takes from Silvan Tomkins, shame emerges from a disrupted circuit of attention, a sudden withdrawal of recognition or response—that of a maternal figure or, she suggests, of an audience or a reader.[27] Rereading James's experiences with *Guy Domville* and the New York Edition, Sedgwick links that threat of withdrawn recognition—which might, after all, be the very condition of absorption—to James's own possibly fragile attention to a younger, less knowing self. That self, in turn, is made the object not of repudiation, nor of elimination through subsequent ego consolidation, but of love, and shame becomes something other than debilitating. If the "queer performativity" Sedgwick finds in the prefaces suggests the possibility of imagining a new, productive relation to the self one was prior to coming out—and I take one implication of her argument to be that, until the abjection of prior unknowingness ceases to attend the triumphalism of coming out and the identity it unveils, queer politics cannot love queer youth, cannot, to this extent, avoid collaboration with homophobic imperatives to punish all signs of queer incipience—it also suggests the possibility of a new relation to Lambert Strether and to the (sexual) life of the author he is often seen to embody.

It also raises the possibility of a new relation to the queerness of the literary. In the poems of Cavafy—to choose one example among many of a poetics, and erotics, of belatedness—one often finds tired (sometimes sleeping) young men with fatigued, haggard faces, and dark circles under their eyes, as if anticipating, in their yet unblemished beauty, the marks of time. His poems at first glance seem to be riveted by a sentimental relation to a missed past. But the passage of time in his writing is an erotic *topos*: arriving too late for desire is a way of rendering it as poetry. Hence his beautiful, exhausted young men embody the passage of time, and the link between his erotics and his poetics.[28] I noted earlier that Dorian Gray may be alone in living his own youth from the perspective of age; he is not, of course, alone in that perception. What makes Dorian Gray compelling is less the fantasy of everlasting youth than his embodying of a recurrent poetic *topos*. His death does not chasten his aspirations so much as provide the paradoxical realization of them by marking his final disappearance into lives unled.[29] It strikes me that if Dorian Gray embodies a recurrent poetic *topos*, it might have less to do with the thematic appeal—of *carpe diem* or *o lente, lente curite noctis equi*—than with the constitution of a poetic voice. To subject a life to that voice is to return it to potentiality.[30] To arrive too late—for Cavafy as for James—is therefore not (sentimentally or despairingly) to wallow in a past irretrievable and irrevocable. To recover Combray as it was never experienced: the self-subtraction of the author in a literary "life" is a recovery of the potentiality of the past, the potentiality sheltered within writing to the precise extent that it is actualized. As Giorgio Agamben writes of Bartleby and the power of "remembrance" to "redeem" the past, "remembrance is neither what happened nor what did not happen, but, rather, their potentialization, their becoming possible once again."[31] The erotics of that redemption underlies the injunction of "Body, remember. . . ." Belatedness is the cipher of this potentialization, and hence of the queerness of style. In the "fortune" of a form little to have been foretold at its cradle, in the definition of the novel as its unforetold future, its refusal of formalization; in the suspension of the novel's taking place in the "as if" and hypothetical discourse of *The Golden Bowl*; in the temporality of Milly's life, an affair consummated in the afterlife of a future anterior tense not unlike the author's own "reaching" beyond the poor palpable, probeable, ponderable laboratory brain; in the out-of-season torment and waste of Rupert Brooke's death and Shakespeare's lapse into silence; and in the curiously posthumous crowning of literary fame: in all these we might find the markers of style's power of potentialization, which is what makes Lambert Strether's experience of belatedness, however searing at moments, something other than sad. And belatedness is queer, not because it renders the sad predicament of gay forms of life in a homophobic context but because of its power to return potentiality to a life. That coming out always occurs too late—whatever mechanisms the politics of normalization turn to in order to obscure or domesticate that belatedness—allows one the sometimes equivocal opportunity to confront the potentiality of identity.

If Strether's life is James's too, it is not because it represents a failed or unachieved life, or even because his love for Chad embodies the homoerotic investments historical research has made an undeniable fact of James's own later (and, for that matter, earlier) years, but because belatedness is an effect of style, because belatedness is an experience of becoming, of the becoming Deleuze calls "a life." Hence, Strether does not "express" his creator's life; the shared concern with belatedness in the late novels and the autobiographical texts suggests something closer to the reverse. The inside-out topographies of the late texts extend to the life of the author. As Ross Posnock points out, James's understanding of his belated arrival after William "blurs his identity with the shadow of otherness"; belatedness, he writes, "defines James and his principal passion."[32] Paired with *The Ambassadors* and the shadow of the author's life that falls on readings of the text, this unusual autobiography might be read, like Strether's tale, as the narration of a life marked by the queerness of style. The fracturing of point of view, often at the moment that a narrating "I" begins to take shape; the recurrent description of the genesis of that consciousness in terms of a "split," enacted, in the largest strokes, by the ceding, from the outset of *A Small Boy and Others*, of the autobiographical "I" to William James, and by the becoming indistinct of "memoir" and "memorial"; the way that "waste" and loss represent a gain in consciousness that cannot be simply accounted for, an experience that defies any simple rendering; the curious patterns of ventriloquism (of landscapes, buildings, scenes, and lost selves) that, as Cameron has pointed out in her reading of *The American Scene,* exteriorize consciousness, projecting James's voice on to the world at large but also thereby rendering incoherent the containing of that consciousness in a singular "I"; the blurring of narrative temporalities that unsettlingly make it difficult to distinguish the narrating from the remembered "I," marking the disappearance of the "I" whose *Bildung* is to be narrated by this autobiography into the disorientations of James's style—all of these aspects of the text suggest ways that the dauntingly opaque, inverted, luxuriantly overstuffed syntax of James's memoirs articulates a relation between James's late style and the representation of a life. It is to these terms—the effect of style on a project of representation—that I would look to understand the biographical investments of criticism of *The Ambassadors,* and the queer potential of Lambert Strether's belatedness.

Acknowledgments

To attempt to acknowledge the debts occasioned by the writing of this book has been inescapably to register the many rich affordances of the intellectual world that has sustained it and me; if the book falls short of the promise of that richness, it can only be that my own capacities have proven inadequate to friends who lead one to wonder what book *could* be adequate to such intelligence. Among those who read chapters of the book, those who helped with the research for it, and those who, knowing little of it, nevertheless provided invaluable, and more or less concrete, support for it and me, I would mention in particular Katherine Biers, Ti Bodenheimer, Chris Bolman, Bob Chibka, Leland de la Durantaye, Matt DeLuca, Lee Edelman, Zach Forsberg-Lary, Jim Giguere, Hollis Griffin, Susan Griffin, Megan Holmberg, Sigi Jöttkandt, Gregory Kenny, Jim Kincaid, Niko Kolodny, Emma Limon, John Limon, David McWhirter, Suzanne Matson, Pat Moran, Joe Nugent, Rob Odom, Mary Ann O'Farrell, Peter Rawlings, Joe Rezek, Melanie Ross, Jake Russin, Ken Stuckey, Laura Tanner, Oleg Tcherny, Andy von Hendy, and Judith Wilt. I am also grateful to my teachers, who—though absolved, at last, of any obligation to read any part of this book and therefore exempt from the remotest blame for any bêtise in it—shaped my readings of literary texts in (for me) unforgettable ways, especially Cynthia Chase, Steve Fix, Ellis Hanson, and Chris Pye. I first read Henry James in a tutorial at Oxford with John Sloan; I mention him here because, though he would have no reason to remember me, I remember him, and fondly. This book was begun with a Research Incentive Grant from Boston College and largely written during a fellowship year at the National Humanities Center. I am grateful to Boston College; to the Humanities Center; to the Research Triangle Foundation, which endowed the Benjamin N. Duke Fellowship that funded my year in North Carolina; to Kent Mullikin; to Lois Whittington; to Marie Brubaker; and to the fellows of the Center that year, especially Tom Cogswell, Lynda Coon, Mary Favret,

Joe Luzzi, Andrew Miller, Cara Robertson, Pete Sigal, Piotr Sommer, and Georgia Warnke. Her death has deprived me of the chance to thank Wendy Allanbrook for the many ways she changed my thinking—about Mozart, inalterably, but also about literature—and for her friendship while I was writing this book; her refusal to countenance sentimentality might have made her cringe to hear me say it, but I miss her.

I would like to thank Richard Morrison for his enthusiasm and for advice that, in its restraint no less than in its acuity, showed his lucid and (to me, flatteringly) comprehensive grasp of my argument. Thanks, too, to Adam Brunner, Erin Warholm, Alicia Sellheim, and to the anonymous readers for the University of Minnesota Press whose responses to my manuscript helped me significantly to reshape it. Thanks also to Anna Seraphimidou for her generous permission to reprint her translation of Cavafy and to Denise Carlson for preparing the book's index.

Attending conferences on James these past few years could not have been the pleasure it was had going to them not also been occasions to see Eric Savoy—and to talk with him about queer style. Frances Restuccia's contribution to the book has been indirect but very far from negligible; her intellectual passion and her indefatigable incitement to thought have no doubt left their mark on my writing and on me. For dinner clubs and walks to Brooklyn, and for the incalculable pleasures of years of friendship, I am grateful to Amy Foerster. I met David Kurnick after most of these chapters had been written; the many ways in which he has improved them since then suggest how much better the book would have been had I only met him sooner, and make for just one, relatively insignificant, reason to regret that lamentable oversight.

It is no more possible for me to imagine the book than it is to imagine myself without Daniel Heller-Roazen serving as every idea's first and most generous interlocutor. From the book's inchoate beginnings, he helped to shape and refine its readings and, indeed, helped me to find value in them I didn't suspect was there; to say that I owe many of its individual formulations and the arcs of several of its larger arguments to him does not begin to describe my indebtedness. In all honesty, unimaginable as it now seems, the book probably could have been written without Milly and Seymour Bergstein, who are, incorrigibly, dogs, and their mention here will not make them know any better what they mean to me. On the other hand, expressing my gratitude to Henry Russell Bergstein (with whom, unlike me, they live) encounters a fittingly complementary inhibition: my grave doubts, not that any words, however felt, could be read, but that any words, once read, could be adequate. I can say only that the book was written in spite of distance, and commuting, and tedious isolation, and that I hope that someday—"Days and Distance disarrayed again"—we can win the argument with separation. Passing time has made me only more aware of my many debts to Jim, Dee, and Kolin Ohi; to begin to enumerate them would be never, with any decency, to finish. For her share in them, this book is dedicated to Dee Ohi, my mother, who was writing a dissertation on Henry James when I was a small boy for whom that name therefore represented, as mere unutterable shibboleth, all the mystical realms of the inaccessible and esoteric, all the undisclosed literary pleasure and knowledge, that I could only dream adulthood would someday hold in store. That would be reason enough, did I not have so infinitely redundant a supply of others, for it to be certain that, for me in this lifetime anyway, she will always be the first Jamesian.

Notes

Introduction

1. D. A. Miller, *Jane Austen, or The Secret of Style* (Princeton, N.J.: Princeton University Press, 2003), 58.

2. Examples of recent queer work on James include John R. Bradley, *Henry James and Homo-Erotic Desire* (London: Macmillan, 1998); Dana Luciano, "Invalid Relations: Queer Kinship in Henry James's *The Portrait of a Lady*," *Henry James Review* 23, no. 2 (Spring 2002): 196–217; Neill Matheson, "Talking Horrors: James, Euphemism, and the Specter of Wilde," *American Literature* 71, no. 4 (1999): 709–50; Leland Person, "James's Homo-Aesthetics: Deploying Desire in the Tales of Writers and Artists," *Henry James Review* 14, no. 2 (Spring 1993): 188–203; Hugh Stevens, *Henry James and Sexuality* (Cambridge: Cambridge University Press, 1998). For biographical work on James and sexuality, see Susan E. Gunter and Steven H. Jobe, eds., *Dearly Beloved Friends: Henry James's Letters to Younger Men* (Ann Arbor: University of Michigan Press, 1991); Fred Kaplan, *Henry James: The Imagination of Genius* (New York: Morrow, 1992); Sheldon M. Novick, *Henry James: The Young Master* (New York: Random House, 1996), and "Henry James's Life and Work," *Times Literary Supplement* (December 20, 1996), 17. For the controversy surrounding recent biographies, see Millicent Bell, "The Divine, the Unique: A Suggestion of 'Active Love' in Henry James's Attachments to Men," *Times Literary Supplement* (December 6, 1996), 3–4; and a series of letters published in *Slate*: Leon Edel, "Oh Henry: What Henry James Didn't Do with Oliver Wendell Holmes (or Anyone Else)," *Slate* (December 12, 1996), http://www.slate.com/id/3124 (December 2, 2002); Fred Kaplan, "Henry James's Love Life," *Slate* (January 7, 1997), http://www.slate.com/id/3633/entry/23774 (December 2, 2002); Sheldon M. Novick, "Henry James's Love Life," *Slate* (December 19, 1996), http://www.slate.com/id/3633/entry/23771 (December 2, 2002). (I cite only the first letter from each participant in what became a lengthy exchange.) For a consideration of the questions of evidence posed by editorial dilemmas in the publishing of James's letters, see Pierre Walker and Greg Zacharias, "James's Hand and Gosse's Tail: Henry James's Letters and the Status of Evidence," *Henry James Review* 19, no. 1 (Winter 1998): 72–79.

3. See Eve Kosofsky Sedgwick, "The Beast in the Closet: James and the Writing of Homosexual Panic," in *Epistemology of the Closet* (Berkeley: University of California Press, 1990), 182–212; Sedgwick, "Is the Rectum Straight? Identification and Identity in *The Wings of the Dove*," in *Tendencies* (Durham, N.C.: Duke University Press, 1993), 73–103; Sedgwick, "Shame, Theatricality, and Queer Performativity: Henry James's *The Art of the Novel*, in *Touching Feeling: Affect, Pedagogy, Performativity* (Durham, N.C.: Duke University Press, 2003), 35–65. See also David Kurnick, "'Horrible Impossible': Henry James's Awkward Stage," *Henry James Review* 26 (2005): 109–29; Kurnick, "What Does Jamesian Style Want?" *Henry James Review* 28, no. 3 (2007): 213–22; Michael Moon, "Sexuality and Visual Terrorism in *The Wings of the Dove*," *Criticism* 28, no. 4 (Fall 1986): 427–43; Moon, *A Small Boy and Others: Imitation and Initiation in American Culture from Henry James to Andy Warhol* (Durham, N.C.: Duke University Press, 1998); Eric Savoy, "'In the Cage' and the Queer Effects of Gay History," *Novel: A Forum on Fiction* 28, no. 3 (Spring 1995): 284–307; Savoy, "Embarrassments: Figure in the Closet," *Henry James Review* 20, no. 3 (Fall 1999): 227–36; Savoy, "The Queer Subject of the 'Jolly Corner,'" *Henry James Review* 20, no. 1 (Winter 1999): 1–21; Savoy, "Theory *a Tergo* in *The Turn of the Screw*," in *Curiouser: On the Queerness of Children*, ed. Steven Bruhm and Natasha Hurley (Minneapolis: University of Minnesota Press, 2004), 245–75; Kevin Ohi, "The Author of 'Beltraffio': The Exquisite Boy and Henry James's Equivocal Aestheticism," *ELH* 72, no. 3 (2005): 747–67; Ohi, *Innocence and Rapture: The Erotic Child in Pater, Wilde, James, and Nabokov* (New York: Palgrave Macmillan, 2005); Ohi, "Narrating the Child's Queerness in *What Maisie Knew*," in *Curiouser*, 81–106.

4. The potential filiations of such an argument would be wide-ranging and would include many critics who might be dismayed to discover themselves aligned with the particular valorization of both the effects of Jamesian style this book traces and the queer potential it attributes to these effects. It would also include many critics who might not be dismayed but who have not, for whatever reason, aligned their writing with the "queer." One thinks, for instance, of Hugh Kenner's emphasis in *The Pound Era* (Berkeley: University of California Press, 1971) on "spacing," "enigmas," and "silence" in James's writing and of his characterizations of Jamesian style. The emphasis in Kenner's narrative of modernism is different, as is the logic underlying his stress on the impalpable, but the stylistic effects he notes are those that could be called queer. Although she tends to understand them in psychological terms of repression or evasion, Ruth Bernard Yeazell in *Language and Knowledge in the Late Novels of Henry James* (Chicago: University of Chicago Press, 1976) finds similar stylistic effects and links them to questions of sexuality. I would depart from the psychological model of repression, but her characterizations of metaphor in James remain, to my mind, crucial characterizations of his writing. The power of metaphor to become an object of perception and to

affect the action of the plot, for instance, points to the (self-consciously) linguistic character of reality in James. "Indeed at their most characteristic," Yeazell writes, "James's metaphors provoke a feeling of arbitrariness and extravagance, a sense of an uncomfortable break in the organic connection of things, that can be deeply disturbing,"—in part because they are governed by conceptual logics rather than by sense perception (40, 41). The discomfort she registers here—a "disturbing" effect she later calls "epistemological vertigo" (71)—points to the potential for linking the implicit characterization of a form of representation driven by considerations other than mimetic ones with the disruptive possibilities of queerness. Later critics might also be placed in this tradition. One thinks of Shelia Teahan's study of the "rhetorical logic" of the "center of consciousness" in James and the elegant readings of the novels she presents there (Teahan, *The Rhetorical Logic of Henry James* [Baton Rouge: Louisiana State University Press, 1995]). Also relevant is Julie Rivkin's claim that the "displaced agency and intermediaries," the "deputies, delegates, and substitutes" of James's novelistic method require "a different understanding of representation" (Rivkin, *False Positions: The Representational Logics of Henry James's Fictions* [Stanford: Stanford University Press, 1996], 2). While I would question Rivkin's choice (at times) to read in terms of anxiety James's relation to the different logics she admirably traces, her argument, like Teahan's, adumbrates a way of reading James that makes possible the queer reading I present here. Finally, my sense of the queer possibilities of James's style also follows from what might be called an "antipsychological" strand in James studies. The consequences for the representation of consciousness implicit in observations made, for instance, by Kenner and Yeazell are further pursued in the writings of Leo Bersani and Sharon Cameron, among others.

5. "The Art of Fiction," in *Henry James: Literary Criticism*, vol. 1, *Essays on Literature, American Writers, English Writers*, ed. Leon Edel and Mark Wilson (New York: Library of America, 1984), 49 (hereafter cited parenthetically as *AF*).

6. "The form, it seems to me, is to be appreciated after the fact: then the author's choice has been made, his standard has been indicated; then we can follow lines and directions and compare tones and resemblances" (*AF* 50).

7. His remarks echo those in his 1883 *Century Magazine* essay on Trollope (reprinted in *Partial Portraits* in 1888). See "Anthony Trollope," in *Henry James: Literary Criticism*, vol. 1, 1330–54. For a discussion of James's ostensible claim that the novel must ground itself in external reality in relation to *Roderick Hudson*, Hawthorne, and allegory, see Teahan, *Rhetorical Logic of Henry James*, 68–69, 80–81.

8. The logic implied by the framing of this assertion further emphasizes mediation: James's analogy appears in the argument as a way to lay to rest a curious atavistic suspicion of the novel that lingers, clandestinely, from its association with the image: "The Mahometans," James writes, "think a picture an unholy

thing, but it has been a long time since any Christian did." It is odd, he remarks, that this "suspicion of the sister art" should "linger," and "the only effectual way to lay it to rest is to emphasise the analogy to which I have just alluded—to insist on the fact that as the picture is reality, so the novel is history" (46). Painting, the argument seems to suggest, has escaped iconoclastic reprobation by insisting on its transparent relation to reality; the novel should make an analogous claim to history by making explicit the "dissimulated" link to its "sister" art. The proliferation of genetic relations—sororal arts and clandestine atavisms, the various invoked religious traditions—and the labyrinthine series of analogies (to say nothing of the curiously recursive structure of the proposal, which refutes an association by claiming it) trouble the analogy before it can be emphasized to lay to rest a dissimulated, lingering suspicion.

9. See Walter Besant, "The Art of Fiction: A Lecture: Delivered at the Royal Institution, April 25th, 1884," Chadwyck-Healey Literary Theory Full-Text Database, 1999; Thomas P. O'Neill, Jr., Library, Boston College, http://collections. chadwyck.com.proxy.bc.edu (original publication, London: Chatto and Windus, 1884), 15. Although his terms are different, John Carlos Rowe's characterization of "The Art of Fiction" resonates with the argument I present here about the essay's reformulation of "experience": the "vital difference between work and world . . . makes discovery and revelation possible in the very form of the critical perspective. . . . James's realism . . . achieves its authority in 'The Art of Fiction' by identifying the difference of life and art, then using that difference as part of its own energy" (Rowe, *The Theoretical Dimensions of Henry James* [Madison: University of Wisconsin Press, 1984], 232). On "experience," see also Deborah Esch, "The Senses of the Past: On Reading and Experience in James," *Henry James Review* 10, no. 2 (Spring 1989): 142–45.

10. "The power to guess the unseen from the seen, to trace the implication of things, to judge the whole piece by the pattern, the condition of feeling life in general so completely that you are well on your way to knowing any particular corner of it—this cluster of gifts may almost be said to constitute experience, and they occur in country and in town, and in the most differing stages of education. If experience consists of impressions, it may be said that impressions *are* experience, just as (have we not seen it?) they are the very air we breathe" (53).

11. As thematic renderings of fiction, subject to parody would, of course, likewise be readings emphasizing the representation of particular sexualities. Thus, a queer reading of James is not the same as what might be called a "gay studies" reading of his work—however much the felt urgency of the former might derive from the impetus given the study of sexuality by the antihomophobic imperatives of identity-centered gay work.

12. James also mocks Besant's assertion that fiction must not be without "adventure": "Why without adventure, more than without matrimony, or celibacy,

or parturition, or cholera, or hydropathy, or Jansenism?" (61). He then redefines *adventure* as he has *experience*: "And what *is* adventure, when it comes to that, and by what sign is the listening pupil to recognise it? It is an adventure—an immense one—for me to write this little article; and for a Bostonian nymph to reject an English duke is an adventure only less stirring, I should say, than for an English duke to be rejected by a Bostonian nymph" (61). The same assertion seems to animate James's later arguments against thinking of fiction in terms of the "parts" that make it up (54); elements such as "dialogue," "description," "incident," and "narrative" cannot be separated and objectified individually. James's turn to an image of organic unity—"the novel is a living thing, all one and continuous, like any other organism, and in proportion as it lives will it be found I think, that in each of the parts there is something of each of the other parts"—is also a turn away from an understanding of the novel in terms of discrete "contents" that could be rendered in an inventory.

13. This is also the effect, we might note, of James's use of Besant's title for his own essay. "The Art of Fiction," in James's gesture of appropriation, no longer coincides with itself.

14. "Literature should be either instructive or amusing, and there is in many minds an impression that these artistic preoccupations, the search for form, contribute to neither end, interfere indeed with both. They are too frivolous to be edifying, and too serious to be diverting; and they are moreover priggish and paradoxical and superfluous. That, I think, represents the manner in which the latent thought of many people who read novels as an exercise in skipping would explain itself if it were to become articulate. They would argue, of course, that a novel ought to be 'good,' but they would interpret this term in a fashion of their own, which indeed would vary considerably from one critic to another. One would say that being good means representing virtuous and aspiring characters, placed in prominent positions; another would say that it depends on a 'happy ending,' on a distribution at the last of prizes, pensions, husbands, wives, babies, millions, appended paragraphs, and cheerful remarks" (48). James's wry rendition of the "latent thought" of moralizers links an understanding of the novel in terms of content to a mode of objectification, to representation as a distribution of things.

15. I elaborate this argument in "Narcissists Anonymous: Reading and *Dorian Gray*'s New Worlds," chapter 2 of *Innocence and Rapture*, 61–121. See also Lee Edelman, *No Future: Queer Theory and the Death Drive* (Durham, N.C.: Duke University Press, 2004), which I discuss later.

16. "The Future of the Novel," in *Henry James: Literary Criticism*, vol. 1, 100–110.

17. "Germ" is, of course, the multivalent metaphor—whose organicism sometimes belies the evasiveness of the narratives it marks—through which James

names the equivocal relation between compositional conception and development or actualization in the New York Edition prefaces.

18. Not least important to understanding the historical context out of which
both "The Future of the Novel" and "The Art of Fiction" (and their discussions
of "the young") emerged are the debates about the corruptibility of the (in particular, female) child. According to Ruth Bernard Yeazell, female "modesty" had
been a crucial topos of the English novel from its inception; "The Future of the
Novel," she argues, emerges at a moment when social changes for various reasons
make the young girl's modesty (in the particular form it takes from Richardson
through James) impossible to sustain as a topic for novelistic representation.
Bringing out the internal incoherence of "modesty" (it cannot be aware of itself
and remain modesty, and the female blush, modesty's privileged signifier, bears
witness to a compromising knowledge—a structure Yeazell links to the imbrica-
tion of "silence" with regulating discourse in a Foucauldian history of sexuality),
"novels like *The Awkward Age* and *What Maisie Knew* bring the century-and-a-half
of the modest young person to a close by exaggerating a doubleness that can be
felt in her narrative at least as early as *Clarissa*" ("Podsnappery, Sexuality, and the
English Novel," *Critical Inquiry* 9 [December 1982]: 356). Of more interest, to my
mind, than the sociohistorical determinants of this English difference is the way
Yeazell links the paradox of modesty to the conditions of possibility of novelistic
representation. The "interval" between innocence and initiation—in other words,
the period of courtship, the topic par excellence of the English novel—and, in particular, the tension produced when the representation of its bridging is forbidden
by conventions or social strictures, is not only sexually enticing, but also makes
narrative possible: "Extended into narrative, the moment of the blush becomes
the time of the courtship novel, that period between innocence and erotic experience that marks the modest heroine's entrance into the world" (Yeazell, *Fictions
of Modesty: Women and Courtship in the English Novel* [Chicago: University of
Chicago Press, 1991], 76–77). In this sense, what adultery does for the continental
novel in the accounts of Tony Tanner and others, "modesty," Yeazell argues, does
for the English novel. The particular "continental system" (as James discusses it in
the preface to *The Awkward Age*) of excluding girls from the drawing room until
after they are married means, Yeazell suggests, that the narrative-founding transition is, in the continental tradition Tanner focuses on, adultery. "But in the tradition of the English novel, the initial border crossing is not the married woman's
transgression but the innocent young girl's awakening; and though the end is
marriage, the whole 'dilatory area' of the plotting, to borrow Roland Barthes's formula, is a function of her internalized capacity for erotic restraint and delay" (*Fictions of Modesty*, 79; she quotes from Barthes, *S/Z: An Essay*, trans. Richard Miller
[New York: Hill & Wang, 1974], 75). On the blush, see also Mary Ann O'Farrell,
Telling Complexions: the Nineteenth-Century English Novel and the Blush (Durham,

N.C.: Duke University Press, 1997). In *Innocence and Rapture*, I pursue some of the consequences of the internal incoherence of the category of "innocence"—for aestheticist writers a source of pleasure as it is for our moralizing contemporaries an endless resource for instigating panic. For an exploration of innocence—particularly as it appears in paradoxes of narrative temporality—as a way of coming to terms with James's equivocal relation to English aestheticism, see Kevin Ohi, "'The Author of 'Beltraffio': The Exquisite Boy and Henry James's Equivocal Aestheticism," *ELH* 72, no. 3 (2005): 747–67. I am grateful to Susan Griffin for pointing out the relevance of Yeazell's arguments here.

19. James's parenthetical remark, "indirectly as well as directly, and by what it does not touch as well as by what it does," further refines the understanding of reflection here: the "exact[] reflection" can be constituted by what the novel does not reflect.

20. I take the distinction between appositional and partitive from Otto Jespersen. See *Essentials of English Grammar* (Tuscaloosa: University of Alabama Press, 1964), 145–46. An instance of a partitive *of* is "some of us"; Jespersen gives as an example of the use of the appositional *of* "that clever little wretch of a Rebecca" (146).

21. I am grateful to Mary Ann O'Farrell for urging me to clarify the relation between the "future" in James's essay and "futurism" in Edelman's seminal book.

22. Colm Tóibín, *The Master* (New York: Scribner, 2004), 291–92.

23. Leo Bersani, "The It in the I," in *Intimacies,* ed. Leo Bersani and Adam Phillips (Chicago: University of Chicago Press, 2008), 23. "Marcher's fate," he writes, "is temporalized as both prior to and subsequent to its happening, as if it were a kind of being, or a form of law, inherently incompatible with the very category of happening" (20).

24. Bersani only glancingly refers to potentiality. See Giorgio Agamben, "Bartleby, or On Contingency," in *Potentialities: Collected Essays in Philosophy,* ed., trans. Daniel Heller-Roazen (Stanford: Stanford University Press, 1999), 243–71; and Daniel Heller-Roazen, "Editor's Introduction: 'To Read What Was Never Written,'" *Potentialities,* 1–23. Chapter 4 returns to potentiality in relation to the belated life. For a fascinating account of the "virtual" in relation to James (among others), see Katherine Biers, *The Promise of the Virtual: Writing and Media in the Progressive Era* (Minneapolis: University of Minnesota Press, forthcoming).

25. Edward Said, *On Late Style: Music and Literature against the Grain* (New York: Vintage Books, 2006), 9.

26. On this intuition about the time of languages, see Daniel Heller-Roazen, *Echolalias: On the Forgetting of Language* (Brooklyn, N.Y.: Zone Books, 2005).

27. Catherine Gallagher, "Formalism and Time," *Modern Language Quarterly* 61, no. 1 (March 2000): 229–51. This tendency, she suggests, is linked to an implicitly ahistorical bias toward the synchronic in formalist criticism: "Formalist analyses

seem bent on showing that, although a novel represents temporal sequence by means of temporal sequence, it nevertheless has, or should have, a form that can be made apprehensible all at once, in a picture or a fractal" (230).

28. Frances Ferguson, "Jane Austen, *Emma*, and the Impact of Form," *Modern Language Quarterly* 61, no. 1 (March 2000): 157–80. Ferguson's point at this moment in the essay is that *style indirect libre* ought to be considered a *formal* attribute of the novel—the novel's only formal contribution to literature, she suggests.

29. "F comme Fidelité," *L'abécédaire de Gilles Deleuze*, with Claire Parnet, produced and directed by Pierre-André Boutang (Editions Montparnasse [DVD], 2004; film copyright held by Sodaperanga). My sense that there is something impersonal in the charming person's hold on us comes partly from Deleuze's striking suggestion that the gesture excites in us a desire to make it our own. An urge neither to imitate nor to possess, this desire is, I think, more like a desire to memorize a beloved poem than it is like a desire to possess or to be recognized by another person, and it points to the ways that the gesture does not exactly "belong" to, or even "express," the charming person.

30. Roland Barthes, *Writing Degree Zero*, trans. Annette Lavers and Colin Smith (New York: Hill and Wang, 1967), 10–11.

31. Gilles Deleuze, *Proust and Signs: The Complete Text*, trans. Richard Howard (Minneapolis: University of Minnesota Press, 2000), 40.

32. See also 119–20: "The content is so completely lost, having never been possessed, that its reconquest is a creation. And it is precisely because Essence as individuating viewpoint surmounts the entire chain of individual association with which it breaks that it has a power not simply to remind us, however intensely, of the self that has experienced the entire chain, but to make that self relive, by re-individuating it, a pure existence that it has never experienced."

33. "Quite the contrary is a work whose object, or rather whose subject, is Time. It concerns, it brings with it fragments that can no longer be restored, pieces that do not fit into the same puzzle, that do not belong to a preceding totality, that do not emanate from the same lost unity. Perhaps this is what time is: the ultimate existence of parts of different sizes and shapes, which cannot be adapted, which do not develop at the same rhythm, and which the stream of style does not sweep along at the same speed" (Deleuze, *Proust and Signs*, 113).

34. Gilles Deleuze, "He Stuttered," in *Essays Critical and Clinical*, trans. Daniel W. Smith and Michael A. Greco (Minneapolis: University of Minnesota Press, 1997), 113, 109. On a minor literature, see Deleuze and Felix Guattari, *Kafka: Toward a Minor Literature* (Minneapolis: University of Minnesota Press, 1986).

35. Gilles Deleuze, "Literature and Life," in *Essays Critical and Clinical*, 5.

36. Gilles Deleuze, "Immanence: A Life," in *Pure Immanence: Essays on A Life*, trans. Anne Boyman (Brooklyn, N.Y.: Zone Books, 2001), 25–33. See also Giorgio Agamben, "Absolute Immanence," in *Potentialities*, 220–39.

37. "It is unclean to think such things," he remarks in the *Abécédaire*, on the idea that literature transcribes, or is inspired by, a more primary experience the reader might unearth; "It is not just mediocre. It's unclean [C'est immonde]." "E comme Enfance," in *L'abécédaire de Gilles Deleuze*.

38. Gilles Deleuze, "What Children Say," in *Essays Critical and Clinical*, 65. See also "Bartleby; or, The Formula," in *Essays Critical and Clinical*, 78.

39. "E comme Enfance," in *L'abécédaire de Gilles Deleuze*. "He becomes (a) child, yes, but it is not his childhood. It is no longer the childhood of anyone, but the childhood of a world. No one is interested, no one, no one worthy of anything is interested in his own childhood. It is another task to become-[a]-child through writing, to reach a childhood of the world, to restore the childhood of the world: that is a task for literature. All writers know this." ["Il devient enfant, oui, mais ce n'est pas son enfance. Ce n'est plus l'enfance de personne. C'est l'enfance d'un monde.... Personne ne s'interesse, personne, personne de digne, de digne de quoi de ce soit, ne s'interesse à son enfance. C'est une autre tâche de devenir-enfant par l'écriture, arriver à un enfance du monde, restaurer un enfance du monde, ça c'est une tâche de la littérature.... Tous les écrivains le savent."] (My translation.)

40. Roland Barthes, *Roland Barthes by Roland Barthes*, trans. Richard Howard (Berkeley: University of California Press, 1994), n.p. (front matter).

41. See *Intimacies*, especially "The Power of Evil and the Power of Love," 57–87. For an earlier formulation of related questions, see the discussion of André Gide in "The Gay Outlaw," in *Homos* (Cambridge, Mass.: Harvard University Press, 1995), 113–81.

42. Giorgio Agamben, "Genius," in *Profanations*, trans. Jeff Fort (Brooklyn, N.Y.: Zone Books, 2007), 13.

43. Wendy Graham, *Henry James's Thwarted Love* (Stanford: Stanford University Press, 1999), 49–50. ("Like John Marcher and Spencer Brydon, [James] had grown old without ever having really lived. If the late stories may be taken into evidence, in his late sixties James faced the 'sounded void of his life' and prepared to jump at any chance of love. But it was too late; he was too old; he was not wanted. And he could not bear to drain this bitter cup to the lees, to acknowledge the futility of his passional sacrifice as a means of enabling art and deferring the nervous crisis that had afflicted his family members. In a sense, James's nervous breakdown saved him from the unbearable self-knowledge that John Marcher acquired, for it confirmed James's whole cautious plan of existence. The beast had jumped after all.") Graham's larger argument, I should hasten to point out, is that James was in fact more knowing about homosexual possibility than is often registered in accounts of his life and work.

44. Sedgwick, *Epistemology of the Closet*, 1, 2 (emphasis added).

45. Lee Edelman, *Homographesis: Essays in Gay Literary and Cultural Criticism* (New York: Routledge, 1994).

46. James, *The Middle Years* (New York: Charles Scribner's Sons, 1917), 1–2.

47. For a (characteristically austere) consideration of gay transmission, see Bersani's reading of barebacking in "Shame on You," in *Intimacies*, 31–56.

48. Lee Edelman, *No Future*; Gilles Deleuze, "What Children Say," 61–67. See also Leo Bersani, "Psychoanalysis and the Aesthetic Subject," *Critical Inquiry* 32 (Winter 2006): 161–74 (especially 169).

49. Kathryn Bond Stockton, "Feeling Like Killing? Queer Temporalities of Murderous Motives among Queer Children," *GLQ: A Journal of Lesbian and Gay Studies* 13, nos. 2–3 (2007): 303. See also Stockton, *The Queer Child, Or Growing Sideways in the Twentieth Century* (Durham: Duke University Press, 2009); and "Eve's Queer Child," in *Regarding Sedgwick: Essays in Queer Culture and Critical Theory*, ed. Steven M. Barber and David L. Clarke (New York: Routledge, 2002), 181–200. My own work has also focused on the queer child in James. See Kevin Ohi, "Narrating the Child's Queerness"; Ohi, *Innocence and Rapture*; Ohi, "Forms of Initiation: 'The Tree of Knowledge,'" *Henry James Review* 29, no. 2 (Spring 2008): 118–31; Ohi, "'The Author of "Beltraffio"'"; Ohi, "Queer Maud-Evelyn," in *Henry James and the Supernatural*, ed. Kimberly Reed (Palgrave Macmillan, forthcoming); Ohi, "Children," in *Henry James in Context*, ed. David McWhirter (Cambridge University Press, 2010), 115-25. See also Ellis Hanson, "Screwing with Children in Henry James," *GLQ: A Journal of Lesbian and Gay Studies* 9, no. 3 (2003): 367–91.

50. Michael Moon, *A Small Boy and Others: Imitation and Initiation in American Culture from Henry James to Andy Warhol* (Durham, N.C.: Duke University Press, 1998), 6.

51. "The 'legend of the Master' continues to pervade many aspects of our understanding of Henry James and his writing. According to the legend, the 'Master' was as a writer a fascinated, voyeuristic chronicler of the powerful effects of intimacy—and especially of the betrayal of intimacy—on the lives of others. James's voyeuristic fiction, the story goes, was a displacement of his own lifelong unease with intimate relations" (Moon, *A Small Boy and Others,* 31). On the queer temporality of Walter Pater's writing, see Kevin Ohi, "The Queer Atavisms of Hippolytus," *Pater Newsletter* 58 (Spring 2008): 13–22.

52. Gilles Deleuze, "Re-presentation of Masoch," in *Essays Critical and Clinical,* 55.

1. Writing Queerness

1. Representative of this argument is Allon White, "'The Deterrent Fact': Vulgarity and Obscurity in James," in *The Uses of Obscurity: The Fiction of Early Modernism* (London: Routledge & Kegan Paul, 1981), 130–62.

2. Henry James, *The Golden Bowl* (Oxford: Oxford University Press [World's Classics], 1991 [text of the New York Edition]), 500. Parenthetical page citations apply to this edition.

3. On this image, see J. Hillis Miller, "Re-reading Re-vision: James and Benjamin," in *The Ethics of Reading: Kant, de Man, Eliot, Trollope, James, and Benjamin* (New York: Columbia University Press, 1987), 101–27.

4. On these personifications, see Cameron, *Thinking in Henry James* (Chicago: University of Chicago Press, 1989). I discuss this paradoxically nonpsychological affect in relation to free indirect narration in chapter 2 and, implicitly, in relation to the claims of the biographical in chapters 3 and 4.

5. See Leo Bersani, "The It in the I," in Leo Bersani and Adam Phillips, *Intimacies* (Chicago: University of Chicago Press, 2008), 20, 23. (I cite the relevant passage in the introduction.)

6. One is reminded of a similar literalization in "The Beast in the Jungle" as the tale turns to its eponymous figure to describe the intimacy of John Marcher and May Bartram: "The real form it should have taken on the basis that stood out large was the form of their marrying. But the devil in this was that the very basis itself put marrying out of the question. His conviction, his apprehension, his obsession, in short, wasn't a privilege he could invite a woman to share; and that consequence of it was precisely what was the matter with him. Something or other lay in wait for him, amid the twists and the turns of the months and the years, like a crouching beast in the jungle. It signified little whether the crouching beast were destined to slay him or to be slain. The definite point was the inevitable spring of the creature; and the definite lesson from that was that a man of feeling didn't cause himself to be accompanied by a lady on a tiger-hunt. Such was the image under which he had ended by figuring his life." *The Beast in the Jungle and Other Stories* (New York: Dover Thrift, 1993 [text of the New York Edition (1909)]), 43–44. See also Kevin Ohi, "The Beast's Storied End," *Henry James Review* (forthcoming).

7. "And how," asks the novel on behalf of the Prince, "when you came to that, *could* you know that a horse wouldn't shy at a brass band, in a country road, because it didn't shy at a traction-engine? It might have been brought up to traction-engines without having been brought up to brass bands" (117).

8. *Henry James and the Art of Power* (Ithaca, N.Y.: Cornell University Press, 1984), 14.

9. The reference is to Book IV of *Paradise Regained*, where Satan tempts Christ: "All these which in a moment thou behold'st/The Kingdoms of the world to thee I give," which inspires Christ's famous response, "Get thee behind me; plain thou now appear'st/That Evil one, Satan for ever damn'd." Milton, *Paradise Lost and Paradise Regained*, ed. Christopher Ricks (New York: Signet Classic, 1968), IV:162–63, 193–94. See also Matthew 4:5–11. On this book in *Paradise*

Regained, see Gordon Teskey, *Delirious Milton: The Fate of the Poet in Modernity* (Cambridge, Mass.: Harvard University Press, 2006), 169–79. The same image occurs, of course, in *The Wings of the Dove,* where we read of Milly Theale, "She was looking down on the kingdoms of the earth, and though indeed that of itself might well go to the brain, it wouldn't be with a view of renouncing them. Was she choosing among them or did she want them all?" *The Wings of the Dove,* ed. J. Donald Crowley and Richard Hocks, (New York: Norton, 1978 [text of the New York Edition]), 87.

10. Another way to understand temporal lags in the novel is to note that they often point to an overlap between consciousness and its narration. Consciousness relates to itself as if it were narrating itself; it lags behind its "knowledge" just as narration lags behind what it narrates. When, for instance, we are told of Maggie, "[I]f she herself had now avoided any such sacrifice, and had made herself, during the time at her disposal, quite inordinately fresh and quite positively smart, this probably added, while she waited and waited, to that very tension of spirit in which she was afterwards to find the image of her having crouched" (306), the delay seems to describe both the temporality of realization and a mode of narration—if, that is, to "find to an image" it is both to understand and to narrate.

11. See, in particular, Bersani, "The Narrator as Center in *The Wings of the Dove,*" *Modern Fiction Studies* 6 (1960): 131–43; and Yeazell, *Language and Knowledge in the Late Novels of Henry James* (Chicago: University of Chicago Press, 1976).

12. Like Woolf's *Lighthouse,* the bowl with the crack is a thoroughly overdetermined symbol, traversing the text in ways not contained by any one character or any one symbolic context. The question of the bowl, as Maggie notes, is not of its "intrinsic value" (416) but of its odd portability as a symbol. Marking at one point "the outbreak of the definite" (423), at another appearing as "an obscured figure," said at another to have "turned witness" (419), and to be "so strangely— too strangely, almost, to believe at this time of day—the proof" (417), appearing to Fanny as "inscrutable in its rather stupid elegance" but "vivid and definite in its domination of the scene," taking on a "sturdy, conscious perversity" as an "ugly" "document" that is oddly riveting to Fanny's gaze (419–20), and remaining to Fanny "a recurrent wonder" and "a recurrent protest" (428), with the "little word representing it" expressing Maggie's "whole situation" (421), it also has the "value" of giving Maggie the "truth" (437). Symbolically, the golden bowl, as Maggie remarks, "has everything" to do with her predicament (416). It represents Maggie's marriage in its ideal form as well as the marriage's flaw; it symbolizes the adultery of Charlotte and the Prince—the "full cup" of possibility they discover at Matcham (261) as well as the doom of their relationship. Made by a "lost art" of a "lost time" (85), it represents an encrypted past and enacts the novel's obscured causalities; as a perfect surface with a hidden flaw, it stands in not only for the

relations in the novel but for the pressure of epistemological uncertainty (as the shopman says to Charlotte of the crack, "But if it's something you can't find out, isn't it as good as if it were nothing?" [86]); as an ornament with a perfect surface, it figures Mr. Verver's view of the Prince's impeccable social grace and his value as an "acquisition" (102); it appears as a figure to represent Adam Verver's economic method of "tasting" life (145); brimming over, it symbolizes the filling up of Maggie's senses when she begins to suspect that something has changed (310); Charlotte's and the Prince's differing relations to it mark her courage ("I risk the cracks" [264]) and his "superstition"; it represents (and presents) definite proof for Maggie of the adultery; after it is broken, as Maggie tries to hold together its three pieces and is able only to manage two, it symbolizes the change in the couples' situation made by Maggie's knowledge, the eventual "solution" of the crisis, and the packing off of poor "doomed" Charlotte to America (432–33); as material proof Maggie stumbles upon "by the most wonderful of chances" (419), it marks an extraordinary coincidence, "the kind of thing," as the Prince remarks, "that happens mainly in novels and plays" (442); reduced to "formless fragments," it stands in for the ugly havoc Maggie could wreak—"terrors and shames and ruins"—with a "single sentence" (but doesn't) as well as Maggie's lost innocence (471); as Adam tells Maggie of his plan to return to America, it figures (as the "cup of her conviction, full to the brim" that "overflowed at a touch") Maggie's certainty of her father's plan to spare her (496); again as a brimming cup that Maggie cannot spill, it symbolizes the precarious social balance and "equilibrium" that Maggie has to maintain at Fawns (516); and, of course, it represents the unspeakable in a novel overburdened with the weight of silences.

13. See also Bersani, "The Narrator as Center."

14. See, in this regard, David Kurnick's reading of what he calls the "house style" that absorbs narrative voice and characters alike in late James: the striking—and, as far as I know, never before remarked upon—fact that the characters in late James all talk alike, and talk, moreover, strikingly like a Jamesian narrator. Kurnick, "What Does Jamesian Style Want?" *Henry James Review* 28, no. 3 (2007): 213–22.

15. For an inspired reading of "embarrassments," which was the title of one of James's collections of stories, see Eric Savoy, "Embarrassments: Figure in the Closet," *Henry James Review* 20, no. 3 (Fall 1999): 227–36.

16. Arlene Young, "Hypothetical Discourse as Ficelle in *The Golden Bowl*," *American Literature* 61, no. 3 (October 1989): 382–97. See also Karen Leibowitz, "Legible Reticence: Unspoken Dialogues in Henry James, *Henry James Review* 29, no. 1 (2008): 16–35.

17. One of my favorite lines from *The Portrait of a Lady*: "Madame Merle failed to burst into speech." *The Portrait of a Lady* (New York: Penguin Classics, 1986 [text of the New York Edition]), 412.

18. I return to Ann Banfield's "unspeakable sentences" in relation to free indirect style in chapter 2. These sentences in *The Golden Bowl* are not unspeakable in the sense that grammatical aspects of free indirect sentences (in particular, the coordination of tenses) eschew the possibility of assigning them to a singular voice, but they have a similar function insofar as they are marked as both quoted and unuttered speech, and insofar as their (non-)utterance has a corrosive effect on character, on the particular voice that doesn't utter them. Banfield, *Unspeakable Sentences* (London: Routledge, 1982).

19. This formulation brings to mind Williams James's discussion of "as if" in *The Varieties of Religious Experience* (New York: Penguin, 1985), where he suggests that the "life of religion" might be characterized "in the broadest and most generalized terms possible" as consisting "in the belief that there is an unseen order, and that our supreme good lies in harmoniously adjusting ourselves thereto" (53). He continues: "I wish to draw your attention . . . to some of the psychological peculiarities of such an attitude as this, of belief in an object which we cannot see." James then turns to the psychic efficacy of unseen "objects" and the mind's capacity to treat abstractions as if they were concrete, "sensible presences" (53). The "instrumentality of pure ideas" leads him to Kant (and "a particularly uncouth part of his philosophy" [55]), who, he argues, suggested that "objects of belief such as God, the design of creation, the soul, its freedom, and the life hereafter . . . are not properly objects of knowledge at all. Our conceptions always require a sense-content to work with, and as the words 'soul,' 'God,' 'immortality,' cover no distinctive sense-content whatever, it follows that theoretically speaking they are words devoid of any significance. Yet strangely enough they have a definite meaning *for our practice.* We act *as if* there were a God; feel *as if* we were free; consider Nature *as if* she were full of special designs; lay plans *as if* we were to be immortal; and we find then that these words do make a genuine difference in our moral life." These ungrounded concepts provide, in James's summary of Kant, "the full equivalent . . . from the point of view of our action, for a knowledge of *what* they might be, in case we were permitted positively to conceive them. So we have a strange phenomenon, as Kant assures us, of a mind believing with all its strength in the real presence of a set of things of no one of which it can form any notion whatsoever" (54–55). James uses the phrase to talk about the possibility of abstract concepts taking on the power of concrete objects, and of conceptualizing belief as functioning independently of sense perception. "It is as if there were in the human consciousness a *sense of reality, a feeling of objective presence, a perception* of what we may call *'something there,'* more deep and more general than any of the special and particular 'senses' by which the current psychology supposes existent realities to be originally revealed. If this were so we might suppose the senses to waken our attitudes and conduct as they so habitually do, by first exciting this sense of reality; but anything else, any idea,

for example, that might similarly excite it, would have that same prerogative of appearing real which objects of sense normally possess" (58). The phrase reappears throughout the text (for instance, 119, 189, 205) to describe, among other things, the "object" and workings of religious belief, (at moments) the operations of his own logical progression in the text, and the workings of what he comes to call the "unconscious." As is apparent in the passages quoted here, he also—somewhat disorientingly—uses the phrase to describe the conceptualization of "as if" in mental processes of belief, and in this sense to describe the philosopher's description of cognition. In any event, like William's, Henry James's use of "as if" conceptualizes, among other things, the psychic efficacy of objects (and persons) not present to perception. The relevance of William James was pointed out to me by Jonathan Warren. On "as if," see also Lee Clark Mitchell, "The Sustaining Duplicities of *The Wings of the Dove*," *Texas Studies in Language and Literature* 29, no. 2 (Summer 1987): 197; Bersani, who remarks on "the way what presumably takes place in a Jamesian fiction is reduced to mere hypotheses about it in all those sentences beginning with 'It was as if . . . .'" ("The It in the I," 20); Katherine Biers, "Realizing Trilby," in *The Promise of the Virtual: Writing and Media in the Progressive Age* (Minneapolis: University of Minnesota Press, forthcoming); and Barbara Johnson, "Bad Writing," in *Just Being Difficult?: Academic Writing in the Public Arena*, ed. Jonathan Culler and Kevin Lamb (Stanford, CA: Stanford University Press, 2003): 157–68. Finally, see David Kurnick, "'Horrible Impossible': Henry James's Awkward Stage," *Henry James Review* 26 (2005): 109–29, on James's "constant invocation of subjunctive spectatorship" (113) in *The Awkward Age*.

20. For a (potentially related) account of zeugma in James, see Andrzej Warminski, "Reading Over Endless Histories: Henry James's Altar of the Dead," *Yale French Studies* 74 (1988): 261–84. Very briefly, for Warminski, the "non-figure of zeugma" names a form of "asymmetrical difference" (276), "a precisely non-figural (or 'a-figural'), non-tropological, non-semantic alignment or juxtaposition of or passage between words" (271)—and, by extension, between metaphor and metonymy; grammar and semantics; the dialectical recovery of meaning and a stuttering, mechanical aspect to language; allegory and trope; the two altars (Stransom's and the woman's) in "The Altar of the Dead"; and so on—the confrontation with which he calls "reading." My account shares with Warminski's a stress on, as Jöttkandt puts it, "the asymmetry" in zeugma "between the grammatical coordination and its semantic opposition, a difference, that is, that is not reducible to either grammar or syntax but lies somewhere in between" (110). See her discussion of Warminski and of "The Altar of the Dead" in *Acting Beautifully: Henry James and the Ethical Aesthetic* (Albany: State University of New York Press, 2005), especially pp. 110–14. I am grateful to her for pointing me to Warminski's text and to her own reading of James's story.

21. "A figure in which a word—or a particular form or inflection—is made to refer to two or more other words in the same sentence, while properly applying to or agreeing with only one of them" (*Oxford English Dictionary*).

22. Another useful definition of zeugma: "The grammatical coordination of two words that possess opposed semantic features—for example, abstract and concrete." Oswald Ducrot and Tzvetan Todorov, *Encyclopedic Dictionary of the Sciences of Language*, trans. Catherine Porter (Baltimore: The Johns Hopkins Press, 1979), cited in Warminski, 271. See also Richard A. Lanham, *A Handlist of Rhetorical Terms*, 2nd ed. (Berkeley: University of California Press, 1991), 159–61.

23. Alexander Pope, *The Rape of the Lock*, canto II, 1.107; Alanis Morrisette, "Head over Feet," *Jagged Little Pill* (Maverick 1995).

24. Leo Bersani writes that the "dramatic pressure" in the novel is displaced "from novelistic events to the verbal surfaces of narrative." "The Jamesian Lie," in *A Future for Astyanax: Character and Desire in Literature* (Boston: Little, Brown, 1976), 128–55, 143.

25. As the Prince and Charlotte contemplate adultery at Matcham, Charlotte's sense of the Prince's face of "temporising kindness" is compared to a precious medal, "not exactly blessed by the Pope" (220); the narrator refers to the "series of sofas" where Adam Verver's "theory of contentment" had "sat" beside Maggie's (356); and, after Maggie has discovered the golden bowl and Fanny senses the crisis she knew she would recognize "by a consciousness akin to that of the blowing open of a window on some night of the highest wind and the lowest thermometer," the narrator remarks, "If the air in Maggie's room then, on her going up, was not, as yet, quite the polar blast she had expected, it was distinctly, none the less, such an atmosphere as they had not hitherto breathed together" (410). Likewise, after the Prince compares the day at Matcham to an exquisite flower he need only gather (260), Charlotte tosses him a rose from her window (262).

26. Freud, "Psychoanalytic Notes upon an Autobiographical Account of a Case of Paranoia (Dementia and Paranoides)," in *Three Case Histories*, ed. Philip Reiff (New York: Collier Books, 1963), 83–160; "A Case of Paranoia Running Counter to the Psychoanalytical Theory of the Disease," in *Sexuality and the Psychology of Love*, ed. Philip Reiff (New York: Collier Books, 1963), 87–96.

27. Leavis, *The Great Tradition* (New York: New York University Press, 1964), 167; quoted in Eileen Watts, "*The Golden Bowl*: A Theory of Metaphor," *Modern Language Studies* 13, no. 4 (Autumn 1983): 169–76, 171.

28. Later in the novel, as Charlotte sits alone in the garden at Fawns (before Maggie brings out the first volume of the book she is reading), Charlotte is said to have burned "the ships of disguise" (526).

29. Henry James, "Preface to *The Portrait of a Lady*," in *The Art of the Novel: Critical Prefaces by Henry James*, ed. Richard Blackmur (New York: Charles Scribner's Sons, 1962), 46. Further references are given parenthetically in the text.

30. Puttenham, *The Arte of English Poesie* (1589), vol. III, in *Arber's English Reprints* (1869), vol. xix, 208 (citation from *Oxford English Dictionary*).

31. For this I am indebted to Sheila Teahan, who in a paper presented at a symposium celebrating the publication of *Palgrave Advances: Henry James Studies* in Salem, Massachusetts, pointed out the very strange phrasing here: "a figure with a pair of eyes, or at least with a field-glass." It's hard to imagine, she pointed out, what good the field-glass would do a figure without eyes.

32. Gilles Deleuze, *Proust and Signs: The Complete Text*, trans. Richard Howard (Minneapolis: University Of Minnesota Press, 2000), 110.

33. The redoubled perspective that has a character view herself as if from the perspective of a narrator also marks, I suggest in the following chapter, *The Wings of the Dove*, although perhaps without the same effects of paranoia.

34. Letter of September 25, 1906, in *Henry James Letters, Volume IV: 1895–1916*, ed. Leon Edel (Cambridge, Mass.: Belknap Press of Harvard University Press, 1984), 415. Emphasis in original.

35. Letter of November 19, 1911, in Edel, *Letters*, Vol. IV, 591.

36. Letter of October 23, 1902, in Edel, *Letters*, Vol. IV, 247.

2. The Burden of Residuary Comment

1. D. A. Miller, *Jane Austen, or The Secret of Style* (Princeton, N.J.: Princeton University Press, 2003), 60.

2. Perhaps the best readers of moral questions in the novel (who, no moralizers, are also far from "blind") are Michael Wood, in "What Henry Knew," *London Review of Books* 25, no. 24 (December 18, 2003): 21–22, and David Kurnick, in "What Does Jamesian Style Want?" *Henry James Review* 28, no. 3 (2007): 213–22. See also Wood, "What Henry Knew," *Literature and the Taste of Knowledge* (Cambridge: Cambridge University Press, 2005), 13–36. Another exemplary account of the complexities of the novel's moral questions is Lee Clark Mitchell, "The Sustaining Duplicities of *The Wings of the Dove*," *Texas Studies in Language and Literature* 29, no. 2 (Summer 1987): 187–214. As an account less about moral questions than about ethics in the novel—and in James more generally—also illuminating is Sigi Jöttkandt's "'A Poor Girl with Rent to Pay': *The Wings of the Dove*" in *Acting Beautifully: Henry James and the Ethical Aesthetic* (Albany: State University of New York Press, 2005), 43–97.

3. It thus enacts a reversal like that marked by zeugma. Leo Bersani writes, "One has the impression in reading the novel that the course the action takes is being determined by the demands of the point of view James wishes to develop. There is a curious reversal of the relationship one would expect between point of view and situation. One does not have the illusion that the latter is the given basis of human experience toward which a human perspective must be created,

developed. Rather, the subject of the novel is so entirely the growth of a certain point of view, an inner choice, that the plot of the novel seems to be created step by step by the stage of inner recognition and choice to which James wants his center to proceed" (142). Leo Bersani, "The Narrator as Center in *The Wings of the Dove*," *Modern Fiction Studies* 6 (1960): 131–44.

4. Similarly, by way of Densher: "Little Miss Theale's individual history was not stuff for his newspaper; besides which, moreover, he was seeing but too many little Miss Theales" (191). Or, from Kate: "She regards me as already—in these few weeks—her dearest friend" (200). Henry James, *The Wings of the Dove*, ed. J. Donald Crowley and Richard Hocks (New York: Norton, 1978 [text of The New York Edition]). Parenthetical page citations apply to this edition.

5. Ann Banfield, *Unspeakable Sentences: Narration and the Representation in the Language of Fiction* (Boston: Routledge & Kegan Paul, 1982).

6. Deleuze, *Proust and Signs: The Complete Text*, trans. Richard Howard (Minneapolis: University of Minnesota Press, 2000), 110. Emphasis added.

7. Seminar April 15, 1980. *Les cours de Gilles Deleuze*, http://www.webdeleuze.com. My translation. As in Bersani's remarks in "Narrator as Center," this reversal could be conceptualized through syllepsis or zeugma. On James's perspectivism, see David Lapoujade, "Henry James: perspective et géométrie," *Études anglaises* 59, no. 3 (2006): 319–28 and *Fictions du Pragmatisme: William et Henry James* (Paris: Les Éditions de Minuit, 2008).

8. Otto Jespersen, *Analytic Syntax* (New York: Holt, Rinehart and Winston, 1969), 35. Some of his examples: "Zionism—what is that to me?"; "The rain it raineth every day"; "The man who is coming there, do you know his name?" (35). "Extraposition" offers a way to classify elements of a sentence whose syntactical function would otherwise be ambiguous; as will become clear, the term is attractive for *The Wings of the Dove* for resonances probably quite extraneous to Jespersen's use of the term.

9. I was inspired by Georgia Warnke to think about the oddity of this structure.

10. On the subject of waiting, see Diane Elam, "Waiting in the Wings," in Carol Jacobs and Henry Sussman, eds., *Acts of Narrative* (Stanford: Stanford University Press, 2003), 31–46. See also Jonathan Warren, "'A Sort of Meaning': Handling the Name and Figuring Genealogy in *The Wings of the Dove*," *Henry James Review* 23 (2002): 105–35. For another reading of Kate's externalized gaze, see Mitchell, "Sustaining Duplicities," 189.

11. See Wood, "What Henry Knew."

12. See my "Narrating the Child's Queerness in *What Maisie Knew*," in Steven Bruhm and Natasha Hurley, eds., *Curiouser: On the Queerness of Children* (Minneapolis: University of Minnesota Press, 2004), 81–106, and "Children," in

Henry James in Context, ed. David McWhirter (Cambridge: Cambridge University Press, 2010), 115–25.

13. See the preface to *The Spoils of Poynton.* Henry James, *The Spoils of Poynton* (New York, Penguin, 1987), 29. Of Fleda Vetch, in contrast, it is said that "she had character" (29).

14. On Lionel Croy, see Eve Kosofsky Sedgwick, "Is the Rectum Straight?: Identification and Identity in *The Wings of the Dove,*" in *Tendencies* (Durham, N.C.: Duke University Press, 1993), 73–103.

15. On this sticky furniture, and, more generally, for a reading of late James that, challenging readings of James's late style as dematerializing, might at first glance seem more incompatible with mine than, in the end, I believe it is, see Victoria Coulson, "Sticky Realism: Armchair Hermeneutics in Late James," *Henry James Review* 25 (2004): 115–26.

16. For an account of vision in the novel in relation to (primarily, occluded) homoerotic thematics and power relations around gender, see Michael Moon, "Sexuality and Visual Terrorism in *The Wings of the Dove,*" *Criticism* 28 (Fall 1986): 427–43), which also situates the novel (and its Venice) in relation to historical (and historico-geographical) determinations of male homoerotic possibilities.

17. See the preface to *The Awkward Age,* in James, *Literary Criticism,* Vol. II (New York: Library of America, 1984), 1120–37.

18. For a very different account of groundlessness in the novel, see Michael Trask, "The Romance of Choice in *The Wings of the Dove,*" *Novel: A Forum on Fiction* 32, no. 3 (Summer 1999): 355–83. "James's late fiction," he writes, "responds to a cultural context imagined on every level to be in danger of groundlessness" (358). For his reading of the novel's opening, see page 357.

19. On the names—and naming—in the novel, see Warren, "A Sort of Meaning." On the name Croy, see Warren, "A Sort of Meaning," 113–14 and 129; see also Trask, "Romance of Choice," 370.

20. On "apotheosis," and, more generally, for an exemplary reading of this scene, see Jöttkandt, "A Poor Girl."

21. On this moment and Kate's gaze into the mirror in relation to prosopopoeia, see Shelia Teahan, *The Rhetorical Logic of Henry James* (Baton Rouge: Louisiana State University, 1995), 117.

22. The indeterminate identificatory commerce between Milly and the painting is, of course, what is explicitly at stake in the scene—an exchange also picked up in Milly's famous turning of her face to the wall. The reference, I think, is to *Isaiah* 38:2, where Hezekiah, told by Isaiah to set his house in order because he was soon to die, "turned his face toward the wall, and prayed unto the Lord." (Hezekiah's prayer is answered, and he is given fifteen more years to live.) The reprieve often disappears in later echoes—as it does in James, where it seems to signal the end of a reprieve—which thus turns the prayer to despair.

See, for example, the anonymous ballad "Bonny Barbara Allen." Rebuked by the callous Barbara Allen, Sir John Graeme "turned his face unto the wall, / And death was with him dealing." *The Norton Anthology of English Poetry*, 5th ed., ed. Margaret Ferguson, Mary Jo Salter, and Jon Stallworthy (New York: W.W. Norton, 2005), 107. James, by suggesting (visually) a painting (framed, hung, and subsequently turned to the wall), articulates that turn toward death with an aestheticization, an assumption into art. In "The Beldonald Holbein," we read the following description of the death of Mrs. Brash: "[W]hat had occurred was that the poor old picture, banished from its museum and refreshed by the rise of no new movement to hang it, was capable of the miracle of a silent revolution, of itself turning, in its dire dishonour, its face to the wall. So it stood, without the intervention of the ghost of a critic, till they happened to pull it round again and find it mere dead paint," James, *Complete Stories, 1898–1910* (New York: Library of America, 1996), 402. The phrase appears—differently, but again with the sense of "dire dishonour"—to describe the disarray of the Moreens in the final smash in "The Pupil": "Mrs. Moreen had lost her recokoning of the famous 'days'; her social calendar was blurred—it had turned its face to the wall," *Complete Stories, 1884–1891* (New York: Library of America, 1999), 754. Jöttkandt points out that the phrase also appears in Pater's "A Prince of Court Painters" in *Imaginary Portraits* (London: Macmillan, 1910), 43; cited in Jöttkandt, 151 (note 11). The turning of her face to the wall might thus represent in any number of ways the arrival—lagging behind itself—of the Matcham "apotheosis" that occurs "too soon."

23. Sharon Cameron writes of this moment: "It is difficult to understand the process represented in the passage, even at the grammatical level. The 'this' in 'I shall never be better than this' seems as if it would signify either 'better than I am now' or 'better than this lady in the portrait.' In fact neither is implied. For Milly looks at the portrait and has thoughts not of her present self, and not of the woman as painted, but rather of the representation of the woman epitomized by its lifelessness, of an image of death, which Milly analogizes to her own image and which she sees in the woman's place." Sharon Cameron, *Thinking in Henry James* (Chicago: University of Chicago Press, 1989), 127.

24. The externalization is, of course, one of the emphases of Cameron's reading of the scene.

25. Other moments come to mind that are likewise structured by chiasmus. For instance:

"She looked at him a minute as if he were the fact itself that he expressed." 'Then you know?'

"'Is she dying?' he asked for all answer."

"[Later on the page]: It was a tone that, for the minute, imposed itself in its dry despair; it represented, in the bleak place, which had no life of its own, none but the life Kate had left—the sense of which, for that matter, by mystic channels, might fairly be reaching the visitor—the very impotence of their extinction. And Densher had nothing to oppose it withal, nothing but again: 'Is she dying?'"

"It made her, however, as if these were crudities, almost material pangs, only say as before: 'Then you know?'" (332)

On chiasmus (especially in relation to "reversal" and the thought of death, and on Milly's "It was perhaps superficially more striking that one could live if one would; but it was more appealing, insinuating, irresistible in short, that one would live if one could" [157]), see Cameron, *Thinking in Henry James* (esp. 143–45).

26. Such might be one effect of the blurring of character and narrator that Bersani traces in the text. See "The Narrator as Center."

27. Frances Ferguson, *Pornography, The Theory: What Utilitarianism Did to Action* (Chicago: University of Chicago Press, 2004), 96.

28. She quotes from Flaubert, *Madame Bovary*, trans. Paul de Man (New York: W.W. Norton, 1965), 117.

29. Thanks to Ti Bodenheimer and David Kurnick for helping me to see the idiosyncrasy and to formulate it.

30. David Kurnick, "What Does Jamesian Style Want?" See also Bersani, "Narrator as Center."

31. Ann Banfield, "Describing the Unobserved: Events Grouped around an Empty Centre," in *The Linguistics of Writing: Arguments between Language and Literature*, ed. Nigel Fabb, Derek Attridge, Alan Durant, and Colin MacCabe (New York: Methuen, 1987), 265–85; and *Unspeakable Sentences*.

32. One thinks, for instance, of the novels of E. F. Benson (also, if later, of Lamb House), where the exquisite acidity of the narrative voice is, in large part, an effect of its power to mimic not simply the self-deluding or self-aggrandizing thoughts of characters but also their highly individualized quirks of expression. See, for example, *Mapp and Lucia* (Wakefield, R.I.: Moyer Bell, 2000).

33. Notably, for Kurnick and Ferguson, questions of free indirect style lead to questions of sociality and community. (This would be one way to phrase what Kurnick sees as the ethics of the text.) Free indirect style in Austen, Ferguson asserts, "recognizes what we might want to think of as a communal contribution to individuals" (164). Her retelling of the history of free indirect style as developing out of drama and the epistolary novel (where the former presents an "individuality" socialized, as it were, to the point of complete externalization, and, the latter, a completely hermetic, asocial individuality—of relentless self-examination) through a retelling of the marriage plot in Austen suggests that free indirect style is the novel's way of thinking about the communication between the psychic and the social—without reducing either one to a mere reflex of the other. Frances Ferguson, "Jane Austen, *Emma*, and the Impact of Form," *Modern Language Quarterly* 61, no. 1 (March 2000): 157–80.

34. This dynamic of exposure internal to Austen and redounding upon a reader is a central mechanism of Miller's reading. See, for instance, his account of the mention of Austen in Leo Bersani's "Is the Rectum a Grave?" (Miller, *Jane Austen*, 4–9). See also Andrew H. Miller, "Perfectly Helpless," *Modern Language Quarterly* 63, no. 1 (2002): 65–88.

35. Jane Austen, *Emma* in *The Novels of Jane Austen*, vol. IV, ed. R. W. Chapman (Oxford: Oxford University Press, 1988), 283 (emphasis in original).

36. For a reading of one such vacillation—in the assertion about the Croys' broken sentence that it "*would* end with a sort of meaning" (*Wings*, 22) see Warren, "A Sort of Meaning," 111–12.

37. As with many other such scenes, this one is doubled by another one, in this case when a comparison of Kate's past with Milly's leaves Kate feeling comparatively grey: "[S]uch a picture quite threw in the shade the brief biography, however sketchily amplified, of a mere middle-class nobody in Bayswater" (113). Of more interest (to my mind) than the parallel forms of desire (which don't, after all, lead to any complementary relation) is the fact of parallel characterization, as if characterization itself produced parallel forms and formal symmetries quite extraneous to character psychology. Reflection and extraposition might extend, this also suggests, to the structure of the novel, at whatever macro- or micro-level of coherence.

38. On the "broken sentence," see also Warren, "A Sort of Meaning," 106. The broken sentence, writes Teahan, "names the trope of anacolouthon, whose grammatical or syntactical displacement points to a larger failure of narrative continuity or casual sequence" (*Rhetorical Logic*, 125).

39. The most elaborate of such series tend to appear around Milly: "She might leave her conscientious companion as freely alone with it as possible and never ask a question, scarce even tolerate a reference; but it was in the fine folds of the helplessly expensive little black frock that she drew over the grass as she now strolled vaguely off; it was in the curios and splendid coils of hair, 'done' with no eye whatever to the *mode du jour*, that peeped from under the corresponding indifference of her hat, the merely personal tradition that suggested a sort of noble inelegance; it lurked between the leaves of the uncut but antiquated Tauchnitz volume of which, before going out, she had mechanically possessed herself. She couldn't dress it away, nor walk it away, nor read it away, nor think it away; she could neither smile it away in any dreamy absence nor blow it away in any softened sigh. She couldn't have lost it if she had tried—that was what it was to be really rich. It had to be *the* thing you were" (86). Or: "Her welcome, her frankness, sweetness, sadness, brightness, her disconcerting poetry, as [Densher] made shift at moments to call it, helped as it was by the beauty of her whole setting and by the perception at the same time, on the observer's part, that this element gained from her, in a manner, for effect and harmony, as much as it gave—her whole

attitude had, to his imagination, meanings that hung about it, waiting upon her, hovering, dropping and quavering forth again, like vague faint snatches, mere ghosts of sound, of old-fashioned melancholy music" (286).

40. Beyond serving, as a repeated element, to structure the sentence, "as it were" further complicates things by introducing another layer of (indeterminately located) mediation: signaling the figural status of the assertion (denying, perhaps, that Milly is to be literally smelled or tasted while thereby raising that exact possibility), Kate's formulation also raises the question of what it would mean to smell "as if" of drugs.

41. For another explanation of Britannia, see Jottkändt, "A Poor Girl."

42. See Trask, "Romance of Choice," on the aleatory aspects of Kate and Merton's relation—and, more broadly, the depicted effort to make chance a "choice."

43. Teahan notes that much of the action of the novel—Densher's turn to Milly at the end, for instance—is unmotivated if read in narrative or psychological (or even logical) terms. Causality, she suggests, follows a "rhetorical logic." (In different terms, Bersani notes that "there is very little development of character in *The Wings of the Dove*" ["Narrator as Center," 138]). On chance and contingency in the novel, see also Trask, "Romance of Choice." Mitchell also notes the inversion of cause and effect in the novel ("Sustaining Duplicities," 210), and notes that "possession" in the text marks "a persistent disjunction between having and owning, identity and control" ("Sustaining Duplicities," 191). On the seeming lack of any cause for Kate and Densher's sudden pledge to each other, see Warren, "A Sort of Meaning," 113.

44. There are many such effects in the novel. One thinks, for instance, of Sir Luke Strett's curious mode of diagnosis, which seems to take place in the interval between Milly's two office visits. Lionel Croy, writes Jonathan Warren, "serves . . . as the prosopopoeia of a notion of history that departs from a linear cause-and-effect scheme" ("A Sort of Meaning," 114; on such moments, see also 120–21).

45. See Teahan's reading of the "congenital disproportion or incommensurability in the novel" (*Rhetorical Logic,* 129).

46. See the "Conclusion" in *The Renaissance: Studies in Art and Poetry,* ed. Donald L. Hill (Berkeley: University of California Press, 1980). On this logic in Pater, see my "Doomed Creatures of Immature Radiance: Renaissance, Death, and Rapture in Walter Pater," in *Innocence and Rapture: The Erotic Child in Pater, Wilde, James, and Nabokov* (New York: Palgrave Macmillan, 2005), 13–60.

47. As I suggest in more detail of *The Golden Bowl,* the temporality seems to dictate that the action not coincide with itself in time—a noncoincidence that can move forward and backward. As Diane Elam notes, *The Wings of the Dove* "begins not with Kate waiting but with Kate having already waited" (33).

48. As elsewhere, this structure extends outward beyond the central plot of the novel. Moving to Aunt Maud's, Kate finds in her appreciation of material goods

a "feeling of a wasted past" (35). Traveling with Milly, Susan finds an "embalmed 'Europe' of her younger time" (84): "The irrecoverable days had come back to her from far off; they were part of the sense of the cool upper air and of everything else that hung like an indestructible scent to the torn garment of youth—the taste of honey and the luxury of milk, the sound of cattle-bells and the rush of streams, the fragrance of trodden balms and the dizziness of deep gorges" (85). The destruction of Milly's letter at the end might be read in relation to these structures: "Then he took to himself at such hours, in other words, that he should never, never know what had been in Milly's letter. The intention announced in it he should but too probably know, only that would have been, but for the depths of his spirit, the least part of it. The part of it missed forever was the turn she would have given her act" (398).

49. On this passage, see Teahan, *Rhetorical Logic*, 128–30. More generally, my reading here is indebted to Teahan's argument about "abysmal consciousness" in the novel and its "representational strategy . . . of 'gaps' and 'lapses'" (*Rhetorical Logic*, 108, 109).

50. In context, the gap is, of course, between Milly's death and the bequest that will have made Densher's action (and Milly's love) not "for nothing"; the ambiguity (as with Kate's "you won't have loved *me*," where the ellipsis that omits "for nothing" leaves open a more generalized negation) also seems, however, to comprise Milly's love, to leave it stranded between what she "has had" and what she "will have had."

51. This is perhaps the flip side of Bersani's observation about the novel: the "centers" of reflection (Kate, Densher, Milly) "live their experience as if they were writing about it" ("Narrator as Center," 134).

3. Hover, Torment, Waste

1. Pierre A. Walker, ed., *Henry James on Culture: Collected Essays on Politics and the American Social Scene* (Lincoln: University of Nebraska Press, 1999).

2. Leon Edel, *The Life of Henry James: The Master (1901–1916)* (Philadelphia: J. B. Lippincott, 1972), 513. On his wartime activity, see page 511 and the following.

3. See Edel, *Life of Henry James*; see also David Kirby, "The Sex Lives of the James Family," *Virginia Quarterly Review* 64, no. 1 (Winter 1988): 56–73. As Pierre Walker writes, "James's biographers have generally concluded that when World War I began, James threw himself into a frenzy of war-related activity as an act of redemption of sorts for his evasion of military service in the Civil War" ("Introduction," *Henry James on Culture*, xviii). James explicitly addresses the apparent link, for him, between the two wars (in "Within the Rim"), only to write that "the moment anyhow came soon enough at which experience felt the ground give way and that one swung off into space, into history, into darkness, with every lamp extinguished

and every abyss gaping" (*Henry James on Culture,* 178). For an important reading of the biographical details of James's life—particularly of the infamous "obscure hurt" and the Civil War—in relation to the *textual* use James made of them ("an abuse of the past that has become an art of fiction" [67]), see Peter Rawlings, *Henry James and the Abuse of the Past* (Basingstoke: Palgrave Macmillan, 2005). "Whether James was either unable or unwilling to take up arms is less significant," he writes, "than the use to which he put his negative experience of the Civil War in terms of the discourse of fiction-compelling obscurity it enabled" (xi–xii).

4. Fred Kaplan, *Henry James: The Imagination of Genius* (New York: William Morrow, 1992), 555. To Kaplan, this recovery of the Civil War was also a merging with Walt Whitman: like Whitman, James "had become a nurse to the wounded flower of the nation. Having over the decades become a lover of Whitman, he now had a chance to do what Whitman had done" (555). (See also 554.)

5. Edel, *Life of Henry James,* 516.

6. To Charles Sayle, June 16, 1909. *Henry James Letters,* vol. IV: 1895–1916, ed. Leon Edel, 524. "Smitten" is Edel's gloss of "insidious" (525).

7. To Edward Marsh, March 28, 1915. Edel, *Letters,* vol. IV, 745. James asked Marsh to send the letter to Brooke, and a copy reached Brooke two days before his death. (Edel's note, 747.)

8. Edward Marsh, *Rupert Brooke: A Memoir* (New York: John Lane, 1918).

9. Henry James, "Preface to Rupert Brooke's *Letters from America,*" *Literary Criticism,* vol. 1 (New York: Library of America, 1997), 749–50. (Originally published by Charles Scribner's Sons, 1916.) Hereafter cited parenthetically.

10. To Edmund Gosse, 23 October 1914, in *Selected Letters of Henry James to Edmund Gosse, 1882–1915: A Literary Friendship,* ed. Rayburn S. Moore (Baton Rouge: Louisiana State University Press, 1988), 303.

11. From the *London Times,* April 26, 1915; quoted in Marsh, *Memoir,* 185–86. (The *Times* itself identifies the writer as "W. S. C.") http://infotrac.galegroup.com.

12. April 24, 1915. Edel, *Letters,* vol. IV, 752.

13. April 25, 1915. Moore, *Literary Friendship,* 307.

14. "Henry James's First Interview." *Henry James on Culture,* 144. "One finds it in the midst of all this as hard to apply one's words as to endure one's thoughts. The war has used up words; they have weakened, they have deteriorated like motor car tires; they have, like millions of other things, been more overstrained and knocked about and voided of the happy semblance during the last six months than in all the long ages before, and we are now confronted with a depreciation of all our terms, or, otherwise, with a loss of expression through increase of limpness, that may well make us wonder what ghosts will be left to walk" (144–45).

15. Virgil, *The Aeneid,* trans. Christopher Pitt (1753), Bk. I, ll. 574–79. From Chadwyck-Healy collections online. Boston College. http://gateway.proquest

.com/openurl?ctx_ver=Z39.88-2003&xri:pqil:res_ver=0.2&res_id=xri:ilcs-us&rft_id=xri:ilcs:ft:e_poetry:Z300462235:3.

16. Pope, "Winter: The Fourth Pastoral, or Daphne," l. 56. *The Works of Alexander Pope*, vol. 1 (London: John Murray, 1871), 296. See also Keats, *Endymion*, Bk IV, ll. 421–24: "He blows a bugle—an ethereal band/Are visible above: the Seasons four,—/Green-kyrtled Spring, flush Summer, golden store/In Autumn's sickle, Winter frosty hoar/Join dance with shadowy Hours" (in *John Keats: Selected Poems and Letters*, ed. Douglas Bush [Boston: Houghton Mifflin Company (Riverside Edition), 1959]: 117); and Percy Shelley, *The Revolt of Islam*, canto X, l. 3946–54:

> There was no food, the corn was trampled down,
> The flocks and herds had perished; on the shore
> The dead and putrid fish were ever thrown;
> The deeps were foodless, and the winds no more
> Creaked with the weight of birds, but, as before
> Those wingèd things sprang forth, were void of shade;
> The vines and orchards, Autumn's golden store,
> Were burned; so that the meanest food was weighed
> With gold, and Avarice died before the god it made.

The Poetical Works of Percy Bysshe Shelley, ed. Mary Wollstonecraft Shelley (London: Edward Bloxham, 1839), 120. Dryden, in his translation of Book 13 of Ovid's *Metamorphoses*, uses the phrase to mean simply hidden treasure (Ovid's *Metamorphoses*: translated by eminent persons. [In each volume: 'Ovid's *Metamorphoses*: translated by Dryden, Addison, Garth, Congreve, Pope, Gay, and other eminent persons.'] Published by Sir Samuel Garth. . . . Vol. 4. London, 1794, p. 8. 4 vols. Based on information from the English Short Title Catalogue. Eighteenth Century Collections Online. Gale Group. http://galenet.galegroup .com.proxy.bc.edu/servlet/ECCO), and Wordsworth refers to a "golden store of books." (*Prelude* [1850], Book V, l. 479.)

17. *The Holy Bible* (King James translation) (New York: American Bible Society, 1816), 582.

18. "It takes our great Ally, and her only, to be as vivid for concentration, for reflection, for intelligent, inspired contraction of life toward an end all but smothered in sacrifice, as she has ever been for the most splendidly wasteful diffusion and communication," he writes, of "our incalculable, immortal France" ("France," in *Henry James on Culture*, 149–50).

19. *A Small Boy and Others: A Memoir* (Chappaqua, N.Y.: Turtle Point Press & Gibson Square Books, 2001), 5.

20. Waste also figures, of course, in James's discussion of the relation of art to life in the preface to *The Spoils of Poynton*: "Life," he famously writes, "being all inclusion and confusion, and art being all discrimination and selection, the

latter, in search of the hard latent *value* with which alone it is concerned, sniffs round the mass as instinctively and unerringly as a dog suspicious of some buried bone." (*Henry James, Literary Criticism*, vol. 2 [New York: Library of America, 1984]: 1138.) Life is all but defined as waste, and that waste makes "art" possible: "life has no direct sense whatever for the subject and is capable, luckily for us, of nothing but splendid waste. Hence the opportunity for the sublime economy of art, which rescues, which saves, and hoards and 'banks,' investing and reinvesting these fruits of toil in wondrous useful 'works' and thus making up for us, desperate spendthrifts that we all naturally are, the most princely of incomes" (1139). Among the many difficulties of the passage is that of tracking the relation between "waste" and "economy"; if it is unclear whether "sublime economy" describes a particular mechanism (one that would, for instance, represent to the mind what exceeds its capacities for representation—"waste" as the sublime, for instance) or whether the operation of that economy presents a spectacle that is itself sublime, the result of the rescuing, saving, and hoarding presents a potentially wasteful economy, or an economy that is productive *because* it is wasteful. Reinvested in "works," these "fruits of toil" (thus, in a sense, already works of art?), the germs that would be wasted by life, are stored up in art in order to give us spendthrifts "the most princely of incomes"—saved up, it seems, in order to be spent, they also suggest that we can both spend and save at the same time, that we can spend our capital and collect a return on it. The "sublime economy" is perhaps in contrast to the "exquisite economy" later in the preface, through which he was led to present the novel's events by way of "a mere little flurried bundle of petticoats"— "where a light lamp will carry all the flame I incline to look askance at a heavy" (1146). (One doesn't need Hamlet or Milton's Satan when Fleda Vetch will do.) But Fleda herself, in contrast to the mule-like Mona Brigstock, is valorized for something like her capacity for waste: "The will that rides the crisis quite most triumphantly is that of the awful Mona Brigstock, who is *all* will, without the smallest leak of force into taste or tenderness or vision, into any sense of shades or relations or proportions. She loses no minute in that perception of incongruities in which half of Fleda's passion is wasted and misled, and into which Mrs. Gereth, to her practical loss, that is by the fatal grace of a sense of comedy, occasionally and disinterestedly strays. Everyone, every thing, in the story is accordingly sterile *but* the so thriftily constructed Mona, able at any moment to bear the whole of her dead weight at once on any given inch of a resisting surface. Fleda, obliged to neglect inches, sees and feels but in acres and expanses and blue perspectives; Mrs. Gereth too, in comparison, while her imagination broods, drops half the stitches of the web she seeks to weave" (1149).

Sterility and waste—valorized terms, in contrast to "will" or "force"—are linked to observation as opposed to action; they leave little mark on the world, have comparatively little to show for themselves. (Fleda's is a power of "appreciation," the preface asserts, a term that also appears, for instance, in the preface to *The Princess Cassimassima:* "the affair of the painter is not the immediate, it is the reflected field of life, the realm not of application, but of *appreciation*" [1091].) Another relevant context for "waste" in James (and for his valorizing of it) is the anal erotic thematics Sedgwick traces, particularly in the New York Edition prefaces. See Sedgwick, "The Beast in the Closet," 208 (note 33) and "Shame, Theatricality, and Queer Performativity: Henry James's *The Art of the Novel*," in *Touching Feeling: Affect, Pedagogy, Performativity* (Durham, N.C.: Duke University Press, 2003): 28–65. I discuss the notion of a "wasted life" in relation to *The Ambassadors* (and Sedgwick's text) in chapter 4.

21. The use of "economy" in the discussion of education that leads up to the untraceability of grounds here is in contrast to the "sublime economy of art" in the preface to *Spoils*. A "sublime economy," it seems, from the perspective of this contrast, would mark an exorbitant form of exchange, one in which causes and effects, for instance, could not be tallied, where a life's form would be untraceable to the experience that formed it. From this angle, *The Spoils of Poynton*, by positing things that are as if endowed with consciousness, might be said thereby to push to its limit—and thus to render inoperative—an understanding of consciousness as a container-like "thing" that contains other "things."

22. "Our consensus, on all this ground, was amazing—it brooked no exception; the word had been passed, all round, that we didn't, that we couldn't and shouldn't, understand these things, questions of arithmetic and of fond calculation, questions of the counting-house and the market; and we appear to have held to our agreement as loyally and to have accepted our doom as serenely as if our faith had been mutually pledged. The rupture with my grandfather's tradition and attitude was complete; we were never in a single case, I think, for two generations, guilty of a stroke of business" (99).

23. Similarly: "I think with compassion, altogether, of the comparative obscurity to which our eventual success in gathering the fruits, few and scant though they might be, thus relegates those to whom it was given but to toy so briefly with the flowers. They make collectively their tragic trio. J. J. the elder, most loved, most beautiful, most sacrificed of the Albany uncles; J. J. the younger—they were young together, they were luckless together, and the combination was as strange as the disaster was sweeping; and the daughter and sister, amplest of the 'natural,' easiest of the idle, who lived on to dress their memory with every thread and patch of her own perfect temper and then confirm the tradition, after all, by too early and woeful an end" (*Small Boy,* 101).

24. Similar language appears in *The Wings of the Dove* to describe Densher's view of Milly: "her whole attitude had, to his imagination, meanings that hung about it, waiting upon her, hovering, dropping and quavering forth again, like

vague faint snatches, mere ghosts of sound, of old-fashioned melancholy music" (286). I discuss this passage in greater detail in chapter 3.

25. *Thinking in Henry James* (Chicago: University of Chicago Press, 1989). On James's "initiation" by style, see Michael Moon, *A Small Boy and Others: Imitation and Initiation in American Culture from Henry James to Andy Warhol* (Durham: Duke University Press, 1998).

26. My reference is to Cynthia Chase's reading of prosopopoeia in "Giving a Face to a Name: De Man's Figures," *Decomposing Figures: Rhetorical Readings in the Romantic Tradition* (Baltimore: The Johns Hopkins University Press, 1986), 82–112.

27. To this group of concerns (as *prefigurement* here suggests) could be added the text's tendency to blur temporal boundaries, to unsettle the line between narrating consciousness and the small boy whose experiences it narrates. The blurring of the lines between narrating and narrated time further unsettles the establishing of a narrative voice in the text (and unsettles, too, the establishing of a past consciousness whose development is to be narrated).

28. "I find that at such a rate I remember too much, and yet this mild apparitionalism is only part of it. To look back at all is to meet the apparitional and to find in its ghostly face the silent stare of an appeal. When I fix it, the hovering shade, whether of person or place, it fixes me back and seems the less lost—not to my consciousness, for that is nothing, but to its own—by my stopping however idly for it" (49).

29. We can see this possibility in another syntactical overlap: the "thrill" here evokes James's phrasing, in *Small Boy and Others,* of the vanishing of youthful cousins (their turn to unfathomed silences and significant headshakes): "I feel how one's impression of so much foredoomed youthful levity received constant and quite *thrilling* increase" (23, emphasis added).

30. Brooke died on a hospital ship, not in battle; later, James describes fate's gentle treatment of him as part of the luck that marks his life: "the event came indeed not in the manner prefigured by him in the repeatedly perfect line, that of the received death-stroke, the fall in action, discounted as such; which might have seemed very much because even the harsh logic and pressure of history were tender of him at the last and declined to go through more than the form of their function, discharging it with the least violence and surrounding it as with a legendary light" (768).

31. Immediately before this passage, we read: "we simply see him arrested by so vivid a picture of the youth of the world at its blandest as to make all his culture seem a waste and all his questions a vanity. That is apparently the very effect of the Pacific life as those who dip into it seek, or feel that they are expected to seek, to report it; but it reports itself somehow through these pages, smilingly cools itself off in them, with the lightest play of the fan ever placed at its service" (764–65).

32. J. L. Austin, *How to Do Things with Words*. 2nd ed., ed. J. O. Urmson and Marina Sbisà (Cambridge, Mass.: Harvard University Press, 1975). *Felicitous* describes a performative that works. (The word most often appears in negative form—performatives that go awry are termed "infelicities," in contrast to the "smooth or 'happy' functioning of the performative" [14].)

33. "Rupert Brooke, at any rate, the charmed commentator may well keep before him, simply did all the usual English things—under the happy prevision of course that he found them in his way at their best; and it was exactly most delightful in him that no inordinate expenditure, no anxious extension of the common plan, as 'liberally' applied to all about him, had been incurred or contrived to predetermine his distinction. It is difficult to express on the contrary how peculiar a value attached to his having simply 'come in' for the general luck awaiting any English youth who may not be markedly inapt for the traditional chances" (751).

34. At moments in the essay, Brooke is made to sound like no one so much as Milly Theale: "heir of all the ages" (756), as James calls him (like Milly), "he was going to have the life ... was going to have it under no more formal guarantee than that of his appetite and genius for it; and this was to help us all to the complete appreciation of him" (754).

35. "The repetitive erasures by which language performs the erasure of its own positions can be called disfiguration." "Shelley Disfigured," *The Rhetoric of Romanticism* (New York: Columbia University Press, 1984), 119. For the "starting, catachretic decree," see De Man, "Hypogram and Inscription," in *The Resistance to Theory* (Minneapolis: University of Minnesota Press, 1993), 48.

36. "Face is not the natural given of the human person. It is given in a mode of discourse, given by an act of language. What is given by this act is figure. Figure is no less than our very face. ... The face given by an act of language is the only face in de Man's reading: this usage bars retreat to a word for an independently existing phenomenon, the face we think we always have. Prosopopoeia, or the giving of face, is *de*-facement, then, insofar as if face is given by an act of language it is 'only' a figure." (Chase, "Giving a Face to a Name," 84–85.) For a reading of Chase and de Man in relation to homophobia and the constitution of gender, see Lee Edelman, "Imagining the Homosexual: *Laura* and the Other Face of Gender," in *Homographesis: Essays in Gay Literary and Cultural Theory* (New York: Routledge, 1994), 192–241. I dwell in greater detail on Chase's and de Man's readings of prosopopoeia (in relation to apostrophe, faces in "The Beast in the Jungle," and readings of that tale by Eve Kosofsky Sedgwick and Leo Bersani) in "The Beast's Storied End," *Henry James Review* (forthcoming).

37. On the stakes of de Man's argument against aesthetic formalization, see Cynthia Chase, "Literary Theory as the Criticism of Aesthetics: De Man, Blanchot, and Romantic 'Allegories of Cognition,'" in *Critical Encounters: Reference and Responsibility in Deconstructive Writing*, ed. Cathy Caruth and Deborah

Esch (New Brunswick, N.J.: Rutgers University Press, 1995), 42–91; and "Trappings of an Education toward What We Do Not Yet Have" in *Responses: On Paul de Man's Wartime Journalism,* ed. Werner Hamacher, Neil Hertz, and Thomas Keenan (Lincoln: University of Nebraska Press, 1989), 44–79. For Neil Hertz, the appearance of "lurid figures"—Shelley's corpse, figures of "suspending" or "hanging," and effects of what Hertz calls "the pathos of uncertain agency" ("Lurid Figures," 86)—mark, among other things, the resurgence of an identificatory logic in de Man's linguistic system. Or, in other terms, perhaps, the traces of the difficulty of sustaining any recognition of "face" as "figure," without, that is, giving figure the contours of a human form. See "Lurid Figures," in *Reading de Man Reading,* ed. Wlad Godzich and Linsday Waters (Minneapolis: University of Minnesota Press, 1989), 82–104; and "More Lurid Figures," *Diacritics* 20, no. 3 (Autumn 1990): 2–27.

38. "Is There a Life after Death?" *Henry James on Culture,* 127.

39. "This mere fact that so small a part of one's visionary and speculative and emotional activity has even a traceably indirect bearing on one's doings or purposes or particular desires contributes strangely to the luxury—which is the magnificent waste—of thought, and strongly reminds one that even should one cease to be in love with life it would be difficult, on such terms, not to be in love with living" (123).

40. Also striking is the dependence of the assertion on negation: "who shall say over what fields of experience . . . it shall *not* spread the protection of its wings? No, no, no."

41. "Letter to the Hon. Robert S. Rantoul," *Henry James: Literary Criticism,* Vol. 1, *Essays on Literature, American Writers, English Writers* (New York: Library of America, 1984), 470, 469 (letter: 468–74). [From *The Proceedings in Commemoration of the One Hundredth Anniversary of the Birth of Nathaniel Hawthorne* (Salem, Mass.: Essex Institute, 1904).]

42. Eliot, "Tradition and the Individual Talent," in *Selected Essays of T. S. Eliot* (New York: Harcourt Brace, 1950), 3–11. See also "What Is a Classic?" in *On Poetry and Poets* (London: Faber, 1956), 53–71.

43. *Sustaining*—in its etymological roots of support (material or otherwise) from below—also links the "question" to the "mere hovering spectator." The sense of endurance further allows the word to mark affliction or hardship (to sustain an injury is to endure but also to undergo it).

44. "Introduction to *The Tempest,*" in *Henry James: Literary Criticism,* Vol. 1, *Essays on Literature, American Writers, English Writers* (New York: Library of America, 1984), 1205. Originally published in Sidney Lee, ed., *The Complete Works of William Shakespeare,* Vol. XVI (New York: George D. Sproul, 1907).

45. For "magnificent waste," see "Is There a Life after Death?" 123. The fact that torment is a common term in, for instance, the prefaces to The New York

Edition (to name just one late Jamesian context) argues a little against Stanley Cavell's claim that "torment" is a lexical sign of Emerson in James's essay. (His assertion that "expression" is such a marker is, to my mind, more convincing.) "Henry James Reading Emerson Reading Shakespeare," in *Emerson's Transcendental Etudes,* ed. David Justin Hodge (Stanford: Stanford University Press, 2003), 238. ("Wonder," which also appears in Cavell's list, presents similar problems for me. In the Rupert Brooke essay, the "hushed watch" of the "unrelieved" spectator "consists at once of so much wonder for why . . ." [766]; later, his "chance" is said to have "required, in the wondrous way, the consecration of the event" [768]. The term appears at crucial junctures elsewhere. I think, for instance, of Maisie's "active, contributive, close-circling wonder" in the preface to James's *What Maisie Knew:* "the case being with Maisie to the end that she treats her friends to the rich little spectacle of objects embalmed in her wonder. She wonders, in other words, to the end, to the death—the death of her childhood, properly speaking . . ." [Oxford: Oxford University Press World's Classics Edition, 1992], 10, 7. On this wonder, see Neil Hertz, "Dora's Secrets, Freud's Techniques," in *The End of the Line: Essays on Psychoanalysis and the Sublime* [New York: Columbia University Press, 1985]: 122–43. On the death of her childhood, see also Ohi, "Narrating the Child's Queerness in *What Maisie Knew,"* in *Curiouser: On the Queerness of Children,* ed. Steven Bruhm and Natasha Hurley (Minneapolis: University of Minnesota Press, 2004), 81–106.)

46. "The face that beyond any other, however, I seem to see The Tempest turn to us is the side on which it so superlatively speaks of that endowment for Expression, expression as a primary force, a consuming, an independent passion, which was the greatest ever laid upon man" (1211).

47. Emerson, "Shakespeare, or The Poet," (in *Representative Men* [1850]). *Works of Ralph Waldo Emerson* (London: George Routledge and Sons, 1883), 148.

48. Cavell: "The search for the utterer, or maker (not necessarily a single one, nor among them anyone inhumanly transparent to herself or to himself), has a double function, one expansive and one restrictive: to mark that a text is written unsurveyably beyond itself (not merely so that it is preserved in another age or a foreign place, but that it continues to find meaning there); and yet that not every expansion of a text can be pertinent to a given response, so that to say and to hear something is to allow something else not to be said and not to be heard, is not to say and to hear something else, until the present needs it, namely, the present of another age or another place, for example, your present" (247–48).

49. *Torment* is also a crucial word in the preface to *The Princess Cassimassima*— where Hyacinth Robinson is (repeatedly) "my tormented young man" (*Henry James: Literary Criticism,* vol. 2, *European Writers, Prefaces to the New York Edition* (New York: Library of America, 1984), 1088, 1089. There, too, the term indexes a relation of idea to world circuited through James's relation to a character. That

torment is—like the Jamesian observer left unrelieved by any action of his own to take—initially a sense of exclusion: Hyacinth's exclusion, for example, from society, hospitality, even comfort, by virtue of his social position. Walking through London suggests the torment of one excluded—as James repeatedly insists that *he* was not—from its beauty and gregarious social scene. The torment of exclusion, however, becomes more complicated as the preface turns to the "center of consciousness." In the first place, the breaking down of the distinction between "doing" and "feeling" (1091) makes it difficult to sustain any opposition between an (ostensibly passive) observer and an (ostensibly active) participant. Exclusion thus comes to seem a function of perspective—of the "bewilderment" that comes from inhabiting one, "our own precious liability to fall into traps and be bewildered." That bewilderment is fundamental to narrative: "It seems probable that if we were never bewildered there would never be a story to tell about us; we should partake of the superior nature of the all-knowing immortals whose annals are so dreadfully dull so long as flurried humans are not, for the positive relief of bored Olympians, mixed up with them" (1090). (One thinks in this regard of the "bewildered and brooding years" of artistic latency when the young gaping pilgrim has nothing to show for his gift [*Small Boy*, 5].) "Torment," then, becomes a description of a compositional problem—that of striking a balance between the intelligence of a center of consciousness (necessary for the interest of the story) and the verisimilitude (its staying true to our own precious propensity for bewilderment): "Extreme and attaching always the difficulty of fixing at a hundred points the place where one's impelled *bonhomme* may feel enough and 'know' enough—or be in the way of learning enough—for his maximum dramatic value without feeling and knowing too much for his minimum verisimilitude, his proper fusion with the fable. This is the charming, the tormenting, the eternal little matter *to be made right*, in all the weaving of silver threads and tapping on golden nails" (1094–95). One can't help but link, then, this (productive) compositional torment to Hyacinth's "torment" when James returns to it a couple of pages later: "The complication most interesting then would be that he should fall in love with the beauty of the world, actual order and all, at the moment of his most feeling and most hating the famous 'iniquity of its social arrangements'; so that his position as an irreconcileable pledged enemy to it, thus rendered false by something more personal than his opinions and his vows, becomes the sharpest of his torments" (1097). James's refiguring of his own exclusion at the end of the preface—at this moment, from any first-hand knowledge of revolutionary underworlds—further underlines an implicit identification with Hyacinth, particularly as the writer is contrasted with a "fool" lacking "the sense of life and the penetrating imagination" (1102). Hyacinth's "sharpest" torment is to be divided, to be put in a "false" position by something "more personal than his opinions and his vows." In a sense, his torment is an irreconcilable tension between aesthetic pleasure and intellectual conviction, and it might therefore be read to figure a tension between form and matter and, by extension, between text and world. The "tormenting" problems of the novel's composition, then, are perhaps not unrelated to the observer's torment in the Rupert Brooke essay.

50. *The Riverside Shakespeare,* 2nd ed. (Boston: Houghton Mifflin, 1997).

51. Agamben, "The Author as Gesture," *Profanations,* trans. Jeff Fort (Brooklyn, N.Y.: Zone Books, 2007), 61–72.

52. The quotation is from Foucault, "What Is an Author?" in *Aesthetics, Method, and Epistemology,* ed. James D. Faubion, trans. Robert Hurley (New York: New Press, 1998), 205–22.

53. Deleuze, *Proust and Signs: The Complete Text,* trans. Richard Howard (Minneapolis: University of Minnesota Press, 2000), 111.

54. See Deleuze, "What Children Say," *Essays Critical and Clinical,* trans. Daniel W. Smith and Michael A. Greco (Minneapolis: University of Minnesota Press, 1997), 61–67.

4. Lambert Strether's Belatedness

1. Richard P. Blackmur, *The Lion and the Honeycomb: Essays in Solicitude and Critique* (New York: Harcourt, Brace, and World, 1955). Quoted in Albert E. Stone, Jr., *Twentieth-Century Interpretations of* The Ambassadors (Englewood Cliffs, N.J.: Prentice Hall, 1969), 49, 50.

2. F. W. Dupee, *Henry James: His Life and Writings* (Garden City, N.Y.: William Morrow, 1956). Quoted in Stone, *Twentieth-Century Interpretations of* The Ambassadors, 33; F. O. Matthiessen, *Henry James: The Major Phase* (London: Oxford University Press, 1944), 27.

3. Bennett, *The Savour of Life* (New York: Doubleday, 1928). Quoted in Stone, *Twentieth-Century Interpretations of* The Ambassadors, 28–29. He continues: "He was a man without a country. He never married. He never, so far as is commonly known, had a love-affair worthy of the name. And I would bet a fiver that he never went into a public-house and had a pint of beer—or even a half a pint. He was naïve, innocent, and ignorant of fundamental things to the last" (28–29).

4. Maxwell Geismar, *Henry James and the Jacobites* (Boston: Houghton Mifflin, 1963); Allon White, *The Uses of Obscurity: The Fiction of Early Modernism* (London: Routledge & Kegan Paul, 1981). Noting that Strether is unable "to play the man's part in the scene of sexuality" (whatever that might mean), Elizabeth Dalton reads Strether's suggestion that he had "dressed" the possibility of sex "in vagueness, as a little girl might have dressed her doll" (396) as an image for James's style: "The image of the girl with her doll may even reveal something about the impulse behind the style of the novel, that difficult late style that also dresses

possibility in vagueness" (467). Dalton, "Recognition and Renunciation in *The Ambassadors*," *Partisan Review* 59, no. 3 (Summer 1992): 457–68.

5. On virtuality, see Leo Bersani, "The It in the I," in Bersani and Adam Phillips, *Intimacies* (Chicago: University of Chicago Press, 2008), 26.

6. It is worth noting that—in readings of James, as in readings of Pater, Dickinson, Hopkins, Woolf, and others—this assumption is, more often than not, homophobic, or shares with homophobia the inability to register the possibility of happy modes of being outside procreative heterosexuality. One instance among many is Arnold Bennett's use of "he never married" to mean "he never lived." (Such an assumption would be reductive even were a universalized possibility of gay marriage to make it cease to be homophobic.)

7. For earlier considerations of James's style, see Seymour Chatman, *The Later Style of Henry James* (Oxford: Basil Blackwell, 1972); Ian Watt, "The First Paragraph of *The Ambassadors*," *Essays in Criticism* 10 (1960): 250–74.

8. Julie Rivkin, "The Logic of Delegation in *The Ambassadors*," *PMLA* 101 (October 1986): 819–31; Shelia Teahan, *The Rhetorical Logic of Henry James* (Baton Rouge: Louisiana State University Press, 1995); Mary Cross, *Henry James: The Contingencies of Style* (New York: St. Martin's Press, 1993). More crucial than renunciation, Rivkin suggests, is the logic of "ambassadorship" and delegation, which she links to Derrida's concept of the supplement. Teahan, suggesting that the novel "both thematizes and exemplifies the problematic of deviation, . . . a problematic that must be understood not as the result of artistic failure or unrealized intention, but as a phenomenon internal to narrative itself" (98), explores a deviation internal to Strether's function as "center of consciousness." Cross suggests that the novel is a "story of signifiers," that the text itself shows Strether's search for names in a way that parallels the typical sentence structure in the text (100). The emphasis falls in different ways in these readings. To my mind, Teahan's emphasis on "deviation" is more compelling than Cross's on "unity." While Cross offers insightful descriptions of the syntax of *The Ambassadors*, I depart from the conclusions to which her analyses lead her. She writes, for example, of James's efforts "to totalise the discourse and bring about . . . unity": "In the face of a language that works always already against his quest, James devised a hermetic system of signs which could speak only of themselves, 'motivated' to serve the text and to erect the arbitrary fictional orders that would stem the tide of contingency and trace threatening to dissolve them in difference. . . . James mobilised a style that could accommodate and exploit the oppositions words mount against determinancy, a play of difference whose infinite movement he yet struggled to contain" (194).

9. See Bersani, "The It in the I"; Bersani, "The Jamesian Lie," in *A Future for Astyanax: Character and Desire in Literature* (Boston: Little, Brown, 1976), 128–55;

Bersani, "The Narrator as Center in *The Wings of the Dove*," *Modern Fiction Studies* 6 (1960): 131–43; Sharon Cameron, *Thinking in Henry James* (Chicago: University of Chicago Press, 1989).

10. Sheldon Novick, *Henry James: The Young Master* (New York: Random House, 1996); Fred Kaplan, *Henry James: The Imagination of Genius* (New York: Morrow, 1992); Lyndall Gordon, *A Private Life of Henry James: Two Women and His Art* (New York: Norton, 1999); Colm Tóibín, *The Master* (New York: Scribner, 2004); David Lodge, *Author, Author* (New York: Penguin, 2005). These books, along with recent collections of James's letters (Susan Gunter and Steven Jobe, *Dearly Beloved Friends* [Ann Arbor: University of Michigan Press, 1991]; Rosella Zorzi, *Beloved Boy: Letters to Hendrik C. Andersen, 1899–1915* [Charlottesville: University Press of Virginia, 2004]) and the ongoing project of editors Pierre Walker and Gregory Zacharias to issue his complete letters, all suggest a resurgence of interest, for vastly different critical projects, in James's life. On the controversy surrounding Novick's speculations about James's sex life, see the *Slate* articles by Edel, Kaplan, and Novick cited in the Introduction.

11. See Giorgio Agamben, *The End of the Poem: Studies in Poetics*, trans. Daniel Heller-Roazen (Stanford: Stanford University Press, 1999), 93.

12. "Project for a Novel by Henry James," in *The Notebooks of Henry James*, ed. F. O. Mattheissen and Kenneth B. Murdock (New York: Oxford University Press, 1947), 375.

13. Henry James, *The Ambassadors* (Oxford: Oxford University Press [World's Classics], 1985). Text of the New York Edition.

14. Beyond critics' preoccupation with it in accounts of *The Ambassadors* in particular, the thematics of missed experience articulated at this moment might simply define a major mode of James criticism *tout court*, biographical and otherwise, homophobic and antihomophobic alike.

15. Here is Lord Henry to Dorian Gray: "Ah! Realize your youth while you have it. Don't squander the gold of your days. . . . Live! Live the wonderful life that is in you! Let nothing be lost on you. Be always searching for new sensations." Oscar Wilde, *The Picture of Dorian Gray* (Oxford: Oxford University Press [World's Classics], 1981), 22. I am grateful to Rob Odom, who—years ago—pointed me to the passage in James's *Notebooks* about Whistler, Sturges, and Howells.

16. Rivkin also notes that the promised freedom is explicitly an illusion ("Logic of Delegation," 822).

17. The change is thus also an interpretive one that the novel connects to a form of sexual normativity. Europe demands finer distinctions—and thus accommodates a wider array of "types." The difference between "Europe" and Woollett in the novel lies in, among other things, the variety of types they present: "Those before him and around him were not as the types of Woollett, where, for that

matter, it had begun to seem to him that there must only have been the male and the female" (36).

18. My reading of the discovery of lack and deceit in this scene is indebted to Maud Ellmann, "'The Intimate Difference': Power and Representation in *The Ambassadors*," in *Henry James: Fiction as History*, ed. Ian Bell (Totowa, N.J.: Barnes & Noble, 1984), 98–113.

19. U. C. Knoepflmacher points out the echoes of *Antony and Cleopatra* in this scene with Madame de Vionnet and draws some implications of the novel's use of Cleopatra. Knoepflmacher, "'O Rare for Strether!' *Antony and Cleopatra* and *The Ambassadors*," *Nineteenth-Century Fiction* 19 (1964–65): 333–44.

20. The possibility of eroticism does not emerge for him *here*. David McWhirter has persuasively argued (in several recent conference presentations) that *flirtation* (which is sometimes erotic, but sometimes not) is a compelling term for describing Strether's mode of relation to nearly everyone in the novel (except the elder Pococks [all but Maimie]). More generally, his writing on friendship and flirtation in late James offers a very persuasive account of attachment in his texts, one that, among other things, allows us to think about a movement away from the erotic couple without thinking of it in terms of lack, repression, or even protest or resistance.

21. For a beautiful exploration of this experience (in terms not particularly related—though not unrelated—to those of this chapter) and for a consideration of *The Ambassadors*, among other texts, see Andrew H. Miller, "On Lives Unled," in *The Burdens of Perfection: On Ethics and Reading in Nineteenth-Century British Literature* (Ithaca, N.Y.: Cornell University Press, 2008), 191–217.

22. *The Riverside Shakespeare*, 2nd ed. (Boston: Houghton Mifflin, 1997).

23. This language returns in the preface, where he writes of the "advertised vulgarity" of setting a novel about aesthetic awakenings in Paris (xxxviii).

24. On "homosexual panic," see Eve Kosofsky Sedgwick, "The Beast in the Closet: James and the Writing of Homosexual Panic," in *Epistemology of the Closet* (Berkeley: University of California Press, 1990), 182–212; see also *Between Men: English Literature and Male Homosocial Desire* (New York: Columbia University Press, 1985), 83–96. My reading does not, of course, contradict Sedgwick's; from a certain angle, this reading of Strether's belatedness pursues some of the implications of her theorization of knowingness—John Marcher's knowingness, for instance, about what *his* loss entails—and its importance as the central mechanism of homosexual panic.

25. F. R. Leavis, *The Common Pursuit* (London: Chatto & Windus, 1952); quoted in Stone, *Twentieth-Century Interpretations of* The Ambassadors, 34–35.

26. Eve Kosofsky Sedgwick, "Shame, Theatricality, and Queer Performativity: Henry James's *The Art of the Novel*," in *Touching Feeling: Affect, Pedagogy, Performativity* (Durham, N.C.: Duke University Press, 2003), 35–65. On "reparative

reading," see Sedgwick, "Paranoid Reading and Reparative Reading: or, You're So Paranoid, You Probably Think This Essay Is about You," in *Touching Feeling*, 123–51.

27. See Silvan Tomkins, *Shame and Its Sisters: A Silvan Tomkins Reader*, ed. Eve Kosofsky Sedgwick and Adam Frank (Durham, N.C.: Duke University Press, 1995), 135; see also Michael Franz Basch, "The Concept of Affect: A Re-examination," *Journal of the American Psychoanalytic Association* 24 (1976): 759–77. Both cited in Sedgwick, *Touching Feeling*, 35–36.

28. See Dimitris Papanikolaou, "'Words That Tell and Hide': Revisiting C. P. Cavafy's Closets," *Journal of Modern Greek Studies* 23, no. 2 (2005): 235–60.

29. On this argument about *Dorian Gray*, see my "Narcissists Anonymous: Reading and Dorian Gray's New Worlds," in *Innocence and Rapture: The Erotic Child in Pater, Wilde, James, and Nabokov* (New York: Palgrave Macmillan, 2005), 61–122.

30. My earlier point about Dorian Gray was challenged by Andrew Miller, who pointed out to me how young Yeats, for example, was when he wrote "Down by the Salley Gardens." It has taken me several years to grasp the importance of what (I think) he meant.

31. Giorgio Agamben, "Bartleby, or On Contingency," in *Potentialities: Collected Essays in Philosophy*, ed., trans. Daniel Heller-Roazen (Stanford: Stanford University Press, 1999), 243–71. See also Heller-Roazen, "Editor's Introduction: 'To Read What Was Never Written,'" in *Potentialities*, 1–23, which traces the concept of potentiality through the history of philosophy and allows one to see why the "actualizing" of writing also entails its potentialization. I discuss potentiality in greater detail, and spell out its relation to what I see as the queer erotics of Pater's historiography in "The Queer Atavisms of Hippolytus," *Pater Newsletter* 58 (Spring 2008): 13–22.

32. Ross Posnock, *The Trial of Curiosity: Henry James, William James, and the Challenge of Modernity* (Oxford: Oxford University Press, 1991), 173.

Index

Please note: The last name "James" appearing in subentries always refers to the author Henry James unless otherwise specified.

KEVIN OHI is associate professor of English at Boston College and the author of *Innocence and Rapture: The Erotic Child in Pater, Wilde, James, and Nabokov.*